LEADERSHIP, TYPE
AND CULTURE

Perspectives

From

Across the Globe

CAPT

Published by the Center for Applications of Psychological Type, Inc.

2815 NW 13th Street

Suite 401

Gainesville, Florida

CAPT, the CAPT logo, Center for Applications of Psychological Type and Looking at Type are trademarks of the Center for Applications of Psychological Type, Inc., Gainesville, Florida. Myers-Briggs Type indicator, MBTI and Introduction to Type are registered trademarks of Consulting Psychologists Press, Inc., Palo Alto, California.

ISBN 0-935652-60-4

Library of Congress

Cataloging-in-Publication Data

Leadership, culture, and psychological type: perspectives from across the globe / Charles W. Ginn, editor.

p. cm.

"The First joint publication by members of the Central and Eastern European Center for Applied Psychology (CEECAP)" --P.

Includes bibliographical references.

ISBN 0-935652-60-4

1. Leadership. 2. National characteristics. 3. Typology (Psychology)

I. Ginn, Charles W., 1949–   . II. Center for Applications of Psychological Type.

III. Central and Eastern European Center for Applied Psychology.

HD57.7.L4324 2000

658.4'092--dc21

                                00-047453

CONTENTS

ACKNOWLEDGEMENTS

The reader will find a special dedication to Dr. Mary McCaulley, the founder of the Center for the Applications of Psychological Type and colleague of Isabel Briggs-Myers. Dr. McCaulley has played a key role in the development of CEECAP and our efforts to apply Jungian type theory and the MBTI to build bridges across political borders and ethnic lines.

I would like to recognize the contributions of our various authors who worked diligently to ensure that their efforts reflected leadership models and adaptations within their respective countries. I also want to recognize CAPT's CEO, Betsy Styron, for her encouragement and support, Jamelyn Johnson, Dr. Charles Martin and others from the CAPT staff for their contributions to this work. Special thanks to Heather Curry of the CAPT staff for her assistance in preparing the manuscript for publication.

Finally, I would like to recognize the support of my Australian colleague, and dear personal friend, Dr. Peter Geyer who was to serve as my co-editor. Unfortunately, Peter experienced a series of personal crises over a two-year period that pre-empted his ability to dedicate the level of time and energy he felt this project warranted. During this most difficult period in his life, Peter has repeatedly demonstrated courage, wisdom and insight that have inspired many in the type community. I look forward to a future collaboration with Peter as we pursue our mutual goal of promoting Jungian type theory and the ethical use of the MBTI across the globe.

PRELUDE

Dr. Charles Ginn
Editor
University of Cincinnati, Clermont College

Leadership, Personality Type and Culture: Perspectives from Across the Globe brings together experts from a broad cross-section of countries to explore leadership from their unique cultural perspectives.

Each chapter includes profiles of one or more highly successful leaders from that country. Some of the profiled leaders hail from private sectors, some are political leaders, while others excelled in the field of education. The one commonality among the contributors is their desire to explore leadership from the perspective of typology, and readers can observe the different stages of typologyís development in each country.

Leadership refers to altering, often in a fundamental manner, the way a business, university, government agency or other institution pursues its goals.

Personality Type refers to Jungian personality type theories as expanded upon by the American mother-daughter team of Katherine Briggs and Isabel Briggs-Myers. These theories are operationalized through the use of the Myers Briggs Type Indicator.

▼▼▼▼▼▼▼▼▼▼▼▼▼▼▼▼▼▼▼▼▼▼

Culture refers to the influence of cultural factors on leadership models. A cursory review of materials available on the topic of leadership suggests a bias towards leadership models appropriate for first world countries with free economies. Perhaps leadership models appropriate in Syracuse may not be as useful in Skopje or Sofia. What works in Buffalo may, or may not, prove useful in Budapest.

The reader will find that each chapter in Leadership, Personality Type and Culture includes the profile of a leader(s), a socio/economic/historical perspective on the country, theory and models of leadership, and information on the study and applications of Jungian type theory and the MBTI in that country. However, the degree of coverage of each of these topics is not of equal depth across the book. In some chapters, such as Australia, a great deal of information and research on the use of personality type theories and the MBTI within the country is available and well covered by the author. In other chapters, originating from countries such as Albania, the introduction of personality type theories and the MBTI is much more recent and the exploration of type theory is just getting underway. In such chapters, potential research and applications are emphasized.

Leadership, Personailty Type and Culture is the first joint publication by members of the Central and Eastern European Center for Applied Psychology (CEECAP). Dr. Cvetko Smilevski of the St. Cyril and Methodius University in Skopje, Macedonia and I formed CEECAP in November 1994 during the First Conference on Psychology and the Transition, which was held in Kruchevo, Macedonia. Colleagues from Bulgaria, Macedonia, Slovenia, the USA and Yugoslavia were founding members.

CEECAP links professors, students and trainers (both university and NGOs) to conduct joint research projects and to plan and implement applications of social science models in its membersí respective countries. Since its inception, CEECAP has grown to include colleagues from Finland, Hungary, Latvia, Northern Cyprus, Poland and Turkey.

Bringing together colleagues from across the globe brings with it certain challenges. For example, each chapter incorporates the authorís preference for American English, English-English or Australian English. This editorial decision was adopted so that the flavor, or flavour, of a culture can be reflected through the subtle variations in spelling of common terms. In a similar fashion, the citation formats reflect the protocols for each country rather than enforcing the APA guidelines popular in the United States.

Events beyond one's control can impair the best attempts to bring together colleagues from across the globe. In this instance, the conflict in Kosovo led to our colleagues from the University of Belgrade being unable to compete their efforts on a chapter that profiled successful leaders within Yugoslavia. Indeed, the father of one of the authors was unable to secure heart medicine and died shortly after the beginning of a NATO air raid on Belgrade. Despite such tragedies, our colleagues in Yugoslavia remain optimistic that conditions will normalize and that their efforts with type and the MBTI will lead to an enhanced understanding across ethnic lines in Central Europe.

The reader will find a special dedication to Dr. Mary McCaulley, the founder of the Center for the Applications of Psychological Type and colleague of Isabel Briggs-Myers. Dr. McCaulley has played a key role in the development of CEECAP and our efforts to apply Jungian type theory and the MBTI to build bridges across political borders and ethnic lines.

The authors of this book have given their time and their knowledge to what we hope is an ongoing look into leadership across the globe. I thank them for their immense contributions, not only to this book, but also to the effort toward a global understanding and appreciation of other cultures.

DEDICATION TO MARY MCCAULLY

Charles W. Ginn, Ph.D.
Co-Founder
Central and Eastern European Center
for Applied Psychology

INTRODUCING TYPE TO THE GLOBAL VILLAGE

A great deal of social commentary focuses on the desire for instant gratification by the internet generation. To many, the ideal life involves instant wealth and fame. It seems difficult to comprehend that Isabel Briggs-Myers labored on the first version of the Myers-Briggs Type Indicator from the early years of World War II until it's commercial introduction in 1975. Like so many pioneers, her efforts were rewarded not in her lifetime, but rather, by those generations that followed.

As we enter the new millennium, the MBTI has become well known across English speaking and other first world countries. This success can be traced to the tireless efforts of Mary McCaulley. Isabel Myers and Dr. McCaulley joined together in 1975 to introduce the world to the constructive use of differences that is the basis of Jungian personality type theory and the MBTI.

At a point in her life where her contemporaries were enjoying their retirement years, Dr. McCaulley was not content to set back and bask in the success of the MBTI in first world countries. When presented with the possibility of introducing the MBTI in Central Europe, with the express goal of using type to celebrate the constructive use of differences among cultures with long histories of conflict and mistrust, Mary embraced the role of dedicated mentor and tireless supporter. She brushed aside the inevitable skepticism of introducing the MBTI in the Balkans by embracing our focus on one dyad at a time.

Because of Mary McCaulley the MBTI is now present and quickly developing in countries as diverse as Turkey and Yugoslavia. Bulgarians are collaborating with Macedonians who are collaborating with Albanians. Hungarians are teaming with their neighbors in Central Europe while the Latvians work on their MBTI validation efforts to simultaneously introduce the MBTI across the Baltics. MBTI translations in Greek and Turkish may serve as a tool for building bridges across Northern Cyprus. Colleagues in Finland are providing valuable advice to their colleagues across Europe. Indeed, colleagues from around the world are embracing the MBTI.

Those who will benefit from the MBTI in the next millennium by better understanding and communicating with their brothers and sisters in the global village thank Dr. McCaulley for her vision and tireless resolve.

ALBANIA

Aleksander Hoxha
University Hospital Center, Tirana

EDITOR'S NOTES. In this chapter Dr. Hoxha introduces us to leadership through a profile of George Castriot Scanderbeg, Albania's most important historical figure. Dr. Hoxha then provides a history of Albania up to and including recent developments in Kosovo. Aleksander suggests that one must know the Albanian history to understand the Albanian psyche in order to be an effective leader within Albania.

Dr. Hoxha gives us insight into Albania's emergence from decades of isolation under Evner Hoxha and the resulting absence of alternative leadership models in Albania. We learn about recent efforts with psychological type and the MBTI and the potential for type to enhance emerging paradigms of leadership within Albania.

Relatively brief in comparison to other chapters, Dr. Hoxha imparts valuable understanding and sheds light on Albanian culture, the historic importance of the clan and the role of leadership in a culture only recently emerging from near total isolation from the global community.

▼▼▼▼▼▼▼▼▼▼▼▼▼▼▼▼▼▼▼▼▼▼▼

SCANDERBEG GJERGJ KASTRIOTI (1405–1468)

Our history shows the figure of the distinguished national hero George Castriot Scanderbeg (1405–1468) as an excellent leader who demonstrated a keen ability to understand his people. This understanding of interpersonal dynamics helped him unite the Albanian lords, opening the way to the organization of the resistance to Turkish invasion. During his twenty-five year reign, Albanians won every battle with their foes.

A strong point of Scanderbeg's leadership style was the way he had selected his closest collaborators and high officers every time by considering first their personal gifts and preferences. His mature use of power ensured a continuous growth of the commanding staff expertise and capabilities. Relying on his intuition Scanderbeg had excellent skills in team building and change management. He was prone to support those who make mistakes or failed at a task, giving them the opportunity to correct themselves. The way he managed leadership problems ensured the success of his governing team and provided wide popular support. Scanderbeg's experience, and the experience of other great Albanians, clearly shows that when personal gifts and preferences are considered, capable and efficient teams are created.

With Scanderbeg's management style as a model, Albania is in the process of introducing new methods of psychological assessment. Ideally, every Albanian will learn his or her preferences and strong points at the beginning of their first job. Yet, centuries of occupation and communist methods of administration didn't permit the development of any positive tradition in leadership style or team formation. Let's now explore that history and the subsequent impediments to effective leadership that resulted from an iron fist and isolation from the rest of the global community.

ALBANIA

Albania is a European country approximately 28,000 square kilometers in area and has a population of 3.5 million people. About 95 percent of our population is ethnic Albanian; the remaining population includes ethnic Greeks, Aroumans and Slavs. It is a mountainous country, with narrow valleys and plains along its long coastline on the Adriatic Sea opposite Italy. The country is bordered by Yugoslavia, Macedonia and Greece. Albanian is the native language, the only representative of its branch of the family tree of Indo-European languages.

Albania's geographic position and its characteristics have played an important role in its history. It is a Mediterranean country with an ancient history of European civilization. Archaeological findings have dated the Pelasgian civilization, the autochthonous inhabitants of the Western Balkans, to the late Paleolithic period (4000–3000 B.C.E.).

Invasions of Indo-European peoples to these areas brought the Illyrian tribes, the progenitors of Albanians today. They ruled over the Pelasgs, gradually assimilating the original inhabitants, but also assimilated from them many traditions, their pantheon of gods, and several linguistic patterns. The Illyrians reached the acme of their development around 300 B.C.E. when the Romans invaded the blooming Illyrian kingdoms. During that period, Illyria was a prospering province of the empire through which the most important land routes passed from Rome to the eastern provinces of the Empire. The cities were at the acme of their cultural and economic development. City life was strongly influenced by ancient Roman and Greek cultures so there was a great difference between them and the country.

Illyrians won Roman citizenship quite early and took active part in the political life of the late Roman Empire. There were five consecutive Emperors of Illyrian origin who ruled in Rome during its decline and prolonged considerably the life of the Roman Empire with their reforms. Constantine, the last of them, moved the capital of the empire from Rome to Constantinople (Byzantium, now Istanbul). The Christian religion began its spread in the Illyric provinces during the first century C.E. City population was the first to embrace Christianity for the strong influences of Roman and Greek cultures and psychology. In the highlands, the penetration of Christianity was much slower, so for a long period of time their population remained pagan. That phenomenon increased even more the contrast in the way of life between cities and highlands.

At the end of the fourth century C.E., all the population appeared to be Christian. After the disintegration of the Roman Empire, Illyric provinces ruled by the Byzantine Empire became a remote periphery of the Byzantine Empire. That change was accompanied by the establishment of Christian Orthodox rite in the

▼▼▼▼▼▼▼▼▼▼▼▼▼▼▼▼▼▼▼▼▼▼

south of the country. The population of the north and middle areas remained loyal to the Roman Catholic Church. During the Byzantine rule, there were some waves of Slavic invasions. On the eve of Ottoman invasion (13th century C.E.), corresponding to the appearance of the name "Albania," there were some well-organized feudal domains of local landlords. It was the last blooming of Albanian cities before their slow renaissance on the eve of our century.

The resistance of the Albanian people, led by George Castriot Scanderbeg, against Ottoman invasion lasted for twenty-five years. Though they won all battles against military expeditions, they couldn't preserve their freedom. During the five centuries of occupation, the country remained a peripheral and oppressed province of the Ottoman Empire.

After the installation of the occupation regime, the population suffered massacres, forcing a massive exile to Italy and the highlands. The Muslim religion was obligatory, but a considerable part of Albanians remained Christians, suffering discrimination on the part of the official Muslim religion. The change of the religion being obligatory was accepted by the people as a relief from the oppression of the occupation regime. Thus, there has never been serious religious intolerance in Albania. It was not until 1912 at the time of decay of the Ottoman Empire that Albania won independence.

The Second Balkan War (1912–1914) seriously threatened the existence of the newly created Albanian independent state. Only the mediation of contemporary European Big Powers provided the acknowledgment of its sovereignty and integrity, as well as the definition of its present borders. That agreement was achieved in Berlin (1913) after difficult negotiations consigned vast territories populated by Albanians to neighbors. Austria-Hungary supported the young Albanian state and in opposition, Russia supported the expansion of the Christian Orthodox neighbors. The precedent is still very active, generating acute ethnic tensions in Kosovo and Macedonia.

The consolidation of the independent Albanian state passed through numerous social and political tumults, including the occupation of the country during the First World War by belligerent military forces. Violent conflicts between local landlords were common as were antagonisms between northern and southern clans. Landlords suppressed a short-lived democratic revolution in 1924, opening the way to the institution of the monarchy. Self-proclaimed monarch Zog presented himself as a very efficient politician. He put an end to tumults and opened the way to establishment and consolidation of legal institutions in Albania.

The approval of the first Albanian constitution with lots of progressive elements created a stimulating environment for the economic and cultural revival of the country, appeased the clans' conflicts and opened Albania to Western countries. A new class of intellectuals who had strongly influenced the spiritual unity of the nation was grown.

During World War II, Albania, as well as her neighbors, was occupied by Nazi-Fascist armies (1939–1944). Albanian people took active part in the war through support of the anti-Fascist Allies. Albania suffered great human loss and heavy economic damage during the war. Also during the war, fierce conflict took place among Albanian political forces. The Communists undertook an unmerciful war against those who supported the Axis powers. They also extended the conflict to other real nationalist anti-Fascist and non-Communist forces, most of whom were forced into exile after the installation of communism in Albania. Liberation from German invaders (1944) marked the beginning of the communist dictatorship.

Strong ties with other communist countries characterized the history of communist rule in Albania, managed with heavy hands by Enver Hoxha. However, every time international communist leaders threatened Hoxha's personal and absolute power in Albania, he would withdraw from collaboration with them. That brought to the end flirts with Yugoslavia (1949), USSR (1961) and China (1978). Relationships with western countries were very cold and superficial, characterized by ideological war and isolation.

Internally, every form of opposition was exterminated and human rights were suppressed. Private property and the most part of the pre-communist culture were eliminated. The religious activity was prohibited, and free movement of the people was restricted. A socialist-type constitution was instituted and the concentration of power in the dictator's hands was absolute.

▼▼▼▼▼▼▼▼▼▼▼▼▼▼▼▼▼▼▼▼▼▼▼

TRANSITIONAL LEADERSHIP IN ALBANIA:
FROM SOCIALISM TO DEMOCRACY

The class struggle based on Marxist-Leninist doctrine was the main mechanism of dictatorial power wielding. As a consequence, the "new socialist man" was "born" — a frightened individual, without great ideals, suspicious and groveling. The prohibition of private property was the economic base of the dictatorship and class struggle. The Albanian communist regime was one of the cruelest in Europe, and left Albania totally isolated.

Under communist rule, the Albanian people worked hard and the country made steps in the way of progress. Albanians made little personal profit due to the very low effectiveness of the national economy and a very restraining centralized salary system.

The end of the Cold War shook up Albanians from the communist dullness. At the end of 1990, after massive student protests, democratic changes opened to Albania a way to join the western democratic societies. During the next years up to today, Albanians desired and believed in rapid establishment of democracy, but the events 1996–1998 showed the difficulties of such a transition. Inherited from pre-communist or communist times, there remain certain mentalities, concepts, living ways, methods of management, attitudes to private and state property, and residual perceptions of personal positions in social life, which may be counter productive to personal and cultural growth.

A worse phenomenon is the reality that politicians are rejecting very slowly the negative heredity of communist rule. The dramatic events of 1997 showed that they trampled every democratic and civil concept in their way to power or to retain it. There were frequent attempts to install dictatorship with a democratic facade, and the failure to institute a new democratic constitution, polling frauds, pyramidal companies which swallowed the most part of Albanians' savings and the economic collapse after their bankruptcy, widespread smuggling and corruption, the civil war of 1997, massive armament of the people after the looting of military arsenals, and violent attempts to overthrow the political rivals in power have had disastrous repercussions on institutional, social and democratic reforms initiated in early 1990 and strongly supported by the United States and the European Union.

As a result, Albania lags behind other East European countries on the road to democratic changes.

History and geographic environment, mainly mountainous, have determined the spiritual and economic life of Albanians. On the eve of the Ottoman invasion, there were some well-organized feudal domains in Albania. The cities were important trade and manufacturing centers with close ties to contemporary European trade centers such as Venice and Raguza (now Dubrovnik). The regime installed by the Turks after the occupation of the country during the 15th century was preceded by ravages and massacres, destroying the cities and the life in the plains. Many Albanians preferred the way of exile, and the remainder had to seek refuge in the highlands. Those phenomena, along with the interruption of contacts with Italian trade republics and the inferior position in the structure of the Ottoman Empire, conditioned the late revival of Albanian cities. In such a way, the Albanian population remained isolated for all the period of the European Renaissance and Industrial Revolution.

In such conditions, especially in the highlands, the structures of patriarchal (multi-couple) family organization reinforced relationships inside the clan and between the clans. All social relationships were based on a special unwritten code inherited from the Pelasgic epoch known as the "Canon Code of Lek Dukagjin," which provided stability to the patriarchal family, helping to ensure its unity and survival in difficult conditions. This was achieved through the institution of very rigid rules, which determined the position of each member with his precise rights and obligations, reserving severe punishments to the breakers. So a pyramidal structure of interfamily power was created, enhancing the competition between couples in the family, between families in the clan or between clans.

The key mechanism that ensured the functioning of the clan was "besa" — the given word that had the weight of a signed declaration. The clan elites conducted lots of traditional meetings, and the code had reserved very few rights to women, leaving them out of the social life. Times showed the effectiveness of such a type of social organization, in that it was one which conditioned a very conservative approach to any change.

Blood feud was a sacrosanct obligation for the members of the family and the clan. That obligation was so strong that it remains active up to today. Betrothals in childhood had been usual and were an effective tool in formation of ties between clans. Few possibilities remained to the simple members of the patriarchal family or clan to express their opinions, constraining them to obedience and the heavy burden of physical work. Very little time was spared for the numerous children growing in a family.

The influence and power of a clan's elite were nearly unlimited. Personal life had little value in front of clan's interests. "The disobedient" faced two rude alternatives: leave his country and face the difficulties of accommodation on their own in a new place, or lose the support of the patriarchal family and the clan. From their childhood, Albanians were educated to consider the Code as sacrosanct, so they had little opportunity to express personal preferences, natural gifts or opinions. This limited the intellectual and cultural progress of the country.

In contrast, many Albanians abroad, far from the Code's influence showed excellent intelligence and abilities. There were lots of Albanians who gave great contributions to the history of other countries. Apart from the five Roman emperors mentioned previously, there is a pope of the Roman Church, many Byzantine and Ottoman officials of the highest rank and Mother Theresa of Calcutta.

The process of decomposition of the patriarchal family began in the southern part of the country in the middle of the 19th century, earlier than in the North, where the Code was widely used until the liberation of the country from the Nazis/Fascists. The laws promulgated during the monarchy's rule had very little influence in the traditional areas of the Code's application in the North.

About 85 percent of the population was in the villages, especially in the highlands, at the advent of Communism in Albania. The communist reforms destroyed the economic base of the Albanian patriarchal family but they didn't support the economic consolidation of the single couple families, which had the absolute predominance over old structured families in socialist years. The decrease in power and influence of clan leaders was substituted by continuous threatening of communist dictatorship. Communist initiative for the creating of the "new socialist man" conjointly with the partial crushing of old Albanian customs and the insufficient family incomes created a psychology of a frightened but wary person to profit what he could. The abolition of private ownership gave an end to personal profit and progress, so Albanians lived without racking their minds because they were hopeless for a future of their own.

On the eve of democratic changes, only a few people, mainly the progeny of traditionally intellectual families, had real democratic visions. Albanians were "drunk" with freedom at the beginning of the democratic reforms. These reforms were never totally realized, and had changed really only the part of their psychology linked with fear. The newly created private property was too weak to really support the family economic progress. Weakness of the legal state and the psychology cultivated in socialist times were the main causes of the very slow consolidation of democratic state structures and plundering of ex-socialist state property. Massive economic corruption, smuggling of stolen goods, illegal arm trade and an immense waste of precious commodities during the years 1997–98 were contributing factors to the state of chaos within Albania.

Massive population migration from the highlands to the cities enlarged city population two to three times during the last seven years. Albanian cities were incapable of absorbing such a number of new inhabitants. In the last years of the communist regime, the unemployment level was high and there were lots of other social-economic problems. Many of the newly arrived were without any capital and immediately began the occupation of lands around cities for housing, creating a very tense social conflict with legal owners who did not possess their lands. The problem of squatters was aggravated by governmental delays in returning the properties grabbed by the communist regime to their legal owners. The issue of the newly arrived people has been the most explosive contingent utilized for tumults and revolts by rival political leaderships.

Fierce political war out of every democratic rule is another major factor holding back the process of democracy in Albania. The intensity of that political war reflects the mentalities of present Albanian political leaders inherited from the customary Code and socialist political concepts. But in the thick midst of Albanian post-communist history, characterized by fierce rivalry between two major political groups, new factors are emerging, signaling optimistic prospects for the future.

Actually, the most important factor is the continuous attention and support of the western democracies, mainly the USA and the EU. International factors have played the determinant role in avoidance of national catastrophes in the years 1997–98. That support will determine Albanian stability in the future for a long time.

Technical aid offered by international partners for the institutional consolidation is another important contribution to the weak Albanian democracy. The assistance in the fields of culture and education are another major contribution to enhance the contacts with other democratic cultures and to hasten the separation from the communist mentalities.

Due to the authority of these countries, the ethnic problem in Kosovo, a vast area in Yugoslavia populated mainly by Albanians, has taken up the attention of the whole world, giving us hope for the peaceful resolution of the conflict in the near future. That will provide the necessary stability to the region and will incite the democratic and economic progress of the region.

Drastic demographic changes are another major progressive factor. Rapid growth of city populations is a big potential factor for economic progress. The integration of the newly settled in the city life will give a new stimulus to social and economic progress of the country. The closer contact with citizen life and psychology will eradicate the influence of the Code and other pre-democratic epoch notions. It's the first time since the Ottoman invasion that so wide contact has taken place between two mentalities.

As a consequence of the population drift, an intensive mixing of people occurs. The most part of migrants are settled in central Albanian areas, and mixing up of the people coming from Northern and Southern areas occurs. So in the future, central areas will increase their role in the political life of the country, diminishing the role of others. This will put a definite end to north-south clan antagonisms that are still active today. Rapid growth of the private businesses in the near future will provide a strong economic base to the Albanian economy. It is the only effective way to resolve the acute unemployment problem, to recover the state budget deficit and ensure the stability for the normal functioning of the institutions.

Our history shows that Albanians have lots to do and to improve. Today the old patriarchal clan organization is essentially crashed and communist methods are generally defeated. But in the absence of a new widely accepted outlook about the future of Albania, old concepts often create serious problems. Today when the life intensity is growing and people's contacts are increasing every day, it is vital for everybody to know his strong points. This knowledge will be a great help for better choice of work environment and the ways of communicating with others.

The Albanian people have suffered a lot from their political leaders who have neglected the former statement. Today when businesses and state administration are claiming for competent leaders and efficient teams, the knowledge of personal preferences and of others working with them is a pressing challenge.

THE MBTI IN ALBANIA

Among alternative methods for such assessments, the Myers-Briggs Type Indicator (MBTI), which makes known personal preferences, has a special position for its simplicity and abundance of information provided.

The use of the MBTI in Albania was started by Janet G. Boyles, M.M., R.N. in 1997 with groups of health workers during seminars about healthcare management organized by AUPHA/AIHA in the framework of USA-Albania cooperation. In 1998, Charles W. Ginn, Ph.D., of the University of Cincinnati, and Janet Boyles, organized other seminars and lectures on MBTI in Tirana.

Boyles' initiative with the MBTI may be considered a landmark. Over the past forty years Albania has been isolated from progressive developments in many fields, including advances in the understanding of leadership and management of organizations. The uniqueness of the Albanian language, especially in comparison to neighboring countries, has been a contributing factor to Albania's isolation. However, the uniqueness of the Albanian language has also served to preserve the Albanian national identity over the centuries. Thus, the MBTI serves to both enhance understanding across the region while preserving our native language.

Our country's transition from authoritarian rule to a fledging democracy, from public ownership of the means of production to a private economy, and from almost pre-industrial methods to the age of cyberspace is just now beginning. Boyles has combined the use of the Internet with the enhanced understanding possible with the MBTI to help us move forward into the new millennium.

▼▼▼▼▼▼▼▼▼▼▼▼▼▼▼▼▼▼▼▼▼

REFERENCES

Noli, F.S. (1947). *George Castrioti Scanderbeg.* New York: International University Press.

Inst. i Historise dhe Gjuhesise. (1959). *Historia e Shqirperise,* Vol. I [The History of Albania, Vol. I]. Tirana: Author.

Zavalani, T. (1998). *Historia e Shqipnis* (Bot. II) [The History of Albania (2nd ed.)]. Tirana: Phoenix.

AUSTRALIA

Greg Latemore
Latemore & Associates Pty Ltd

EDITOR'S NOTES. Dr. Latemore begins his exploration of leadership in Australia with the fascinating story of Moira Scollay, a successful Australian entrepreneur. He then provides an historical and demographic profile of Australia.

We next learn about the evolution of type and the MBTI in Australia. This segment is of particular interest to those in countries where the exploration of type and the MBTI is just getting underway. The Australians have achieved an extensive network of type enthusiasts. They conduct numerous conferences and publish an excellent journal on psychological type. In short, the Australian experience can serve as a model for how to develop a type community for those in countries where type is just being introduced.

▼▼▼▼▼▼▼▼▼▼▼▼▼▼▼▼▼▼▼▼▼▼

I love a sunburnt country,
A land of sweeping plains,
Of ragged mountain ranges,
Of droughts and flooding rains,
I love her far horizons,
I love her jewel-sea,
Her beauty and her terror,
The wide, brown land for me!

From "My Country" by Dorothea Mackellar
(cited Hansen 1962: 128)

The world knows Australia. Australians have long been admired for our survival in a harsh land, our courage on the sporting and battlefield and for our rugged individualism.

This chapter addresses leadership within the Australian context. We first showcase a remarkable leader, Moira Scollay, Chief Executive Officer of the Australian National Training Authority. Moira is exceptional in her personal qualities and yet typical of a new breed of Australian leaders.

We then survey Australia itself — the land, its people and its history. We also set the context for leadership within current social and political issues. We also consider the search for a national identity and our tendency to cut down our "tall poppies."

Leadership research and practice in the past and in the present is considered within Australian corporate and community life. We conclude with some suggestions about the nature of "Aussie" leadership.

MOIRA SCOLLAY

Moira Scollay was born in Canberra, the capital of Australia, on 6th May 1950. Her family focussed on the development of her brothers because the expectation was that girls "just got married."

Moira began her professional career in 1972 in history research at the Australian National University in Canberra. In the mid-1980s, Moira headed a team that redesigned the office classification structures and the "factory-like" environment in the Australian Public Service (APS).

In 1987, she joined the Australian Taxation Office (ATO) as Assistant Commissioner (People and Structures) and was promoted to First Assistant Commissioner (Corporate Services) in 1990. In both positions, she was responsible for driving massive organisational change in a large, traditional bureaucracy.

In 1994, Moira was appointed Second Commissioner of Taxation and for two years headed the Child Support Agency (which was part of the ATO). In February 1997, she was appointed as Privacy Commissioner of the Australian Human Rights and Equal Opportunity Commission. In 1999, she was appointed the CEO of the Australian National Training Authority. She is now based in Melbourne and travels extensively.

ON STYLE

Moira believes that if Australians are to reach our full potential as a successful and innovative country, we cannot rely simply on "grey men in grey suits with grey minds and grey faces, carrying grey files and driving grey cars." We need a much more diverse, colourful and textured workforce. David Karpin ("The Karpin Report"), chairman of Enterprising Australia (1995), agrees when he argues for a leadership which is less directing and more coaching; less male-dominated and more gender and ethnically diverse.

Moira was introduced and impressed with the Myers-Briggs Type Indicator (MBTI) while attending an executive program with the author through the Centre for Strategic Leaders in Brisbane in 1988 and later, when attending an accreditation program in Canberra. Her own MBTI type is ENFP. She presents as a person who is enthusiastic, innovative, people-oriented and she demonstrates a genuineness that is most appealing. Moira has a quick mind, a dry humour and an earthy naturalness that is both warm and engaging. She is tenacious, hard working and strives to be honest and sincere in her dealings with people.

Moira is content to "be herself" as a woman in a world dominated by men. She is a role model and mentor to many younger women in the Australian public and private sectors. She has worked for prominent and influential leaders in the Australian scene. At executive presentations, she states that her career has consciously followed great leaders:

I have had the chance to work with many who were giants in their field, such as Robin Gollan, Professor of Australian History at the ANU [Australian National University, Canberra]; Phillip Hughes, Head of the School of Education at the University of Canberra; Eric Willmot, the first Aboriginal principal of the Australian Institute of Aboriginal and Torres Strait Islander Studies; Peter Wilenski, Chairman of the Public Service Board, and Trevor Boucher, Australian Tax Commissioner — take your pick.

Moira states that she has always given herself the freedom to do what she believes in. Her advice to younger leaders is to come to work always prepared to be sacked or to resign if you have to go against your conscience.

Moira consistently wins the hearts and minds of her people. She is transparent in her expectations of others, in her trust and in her enthusiasm.

ON LEADERSHIP

Moira's current position is Chief Executive Officer of the Australian National Training Authority (ANTA). ANTA has responsibility for advising all Australian Governments at both state and federal levels about how to achieve a national focus for the vocational education and training system. The challenge Moira now faces is to work with many stakeholders to achieve the vision for vocational education and training in Australia. That vision is to inspire a passion in people to learn throughout their lives and to create a system that is responsive to the individual needs of all Australians in this rapidly changing world. She reports that her role is satisfying, stimulating and of course, exhausting.

Her views on the nature and importance of leadership are that whatever you read in the books about the importance of leadership, you should multiply that at least ten times. For Moira, there is no static leadership model, or no one model that works. However, all the great leaders she has known have had the following characteristics: they know themselves and they have guts, broad vision, heart, a strategic eye for detail (that is, "the things that will jump up and hit you"), good people skills, sound judgment, passion, drive and perseverance.

For Moira, leadership also requires a team at the top who speak with one voice. This point was strongly reiterated by the Kakabadse report (1996), which criticised SES (senior executive service) officers in the Federal public service for their poor quality dialogue and for their lack of "cabinet solidarity" (see also Barratt et al 1996).

Moira gives leadership lectures in which she describes "the leadership challenge" as:

- to build and communicate shared vision,
- to build a senior team that models the behaviour you want from your people,
- to analyse the total system of external expectations and internal culture,
- to know your clients,
- to provide an environment that promotes self esteem,
- to pay attention to tangibles and intangibles,
- to develop an ability to think and feel.

She regards her own leadership strengths as energy, commitment, enthusiasm and the ability to relate to lots of different kinds of people. She has a big picture focus and an intuition that can be relied upon, although this can lead some of her peers to view her as a little illogical on occasion. However, she is widely perceived to demonstrate a high level of integrity.

Nonetheless, Moira sees Australia as a beautiful country with a future that offers lots of potential. She is nonetheless concerned because of the increasing division between the rich and the poor, racial tension, levels of violence and a lack of trust within the community. She reflects, "Perhaps these are global problems, too."

THE FACE OF THE WORLD

Moira tells a story about herself, a story that signals her approach as a leader. Some years ago when her daughter was five, Moira came home and her daughter wanted to tell Moira all about her day. At that particular moment in time, all Moira wanted was a cold beer! So she gave her daughter a task to keep her occupied for a while until she could pay attention to her.

On the telephone table inside the front door, Moira found a magazine that was open to a map of the world. Moira tore the map out of the magazine, ripped it into little pieces and said, "Now, that's a jigsaw, Dan. Just put that map of the world back together and we'll talk after that." Some minutes later, her daughter was back with the completed map of the world. Surprised, Moira wondered how she could have finished the map of the world so quickly.

It turned out that on the other side of the map of the world was a face. Dan had simply put the eyes and the nose and the mouth together and the jigsaw was done. The moral of the story for Moira is, "If you get the people side right, the rest of the world falls into place."

AUSTRALIA

Australia is the oldest, flattest and driest continent on earth. Her harsh beauty is admired by poets, painters and travellers alike, even though some English inhabitants might have earlier dismissed Australia as "bare, bald and prosaic" (Wannan 1977: 224).

We have some of the most unusual flora and fauna on the planet: eucalyptus ("gum") trees, kangaroos, echidnas, emus, koalas, kookaburras, wombats, quolls and platypus. So outrageous did the platypus seem that early British naturalists refused to consider that stuffed specimens were real.

The land is ravaged in turn by droughts, fires, cyclones and floods. It is a harsh and unforgiving environment, and yet possesses a haunting beauty: the sheer fragility of the land seems to make her treasures much more poignant. Australia's "weird melancholy" is still "worthy to be loved" (Marcus Clarke [1856–1881] as cited in Wannan 1977: 225–227).

Nomadic indigenous Australians lived here for some 60 thousand years in the "Dreamtime" until Captain James Cook sailed the *Endeavour* into Botany Bay and took possession of the land for Britain in 1770. Captain Arthur Phillip and the First Fleet of convicts arrived at Port Jackson on 26th January 1788. In 1988, white Australia celebrated their bicentenary. For indigenous Australians however, this anniversary marked "invasion day." As Willmot (1987: 55) soberly reminded us:

> Unfortunately this date recalls two other less joyous beginnings: 1788 was the beginning of the brutal destruction of the first Australian social order and also marks the founding of the first prison in Australia.

Our folklore is rich with stories "yarns" about explorers, Aboriginal trackers, pioneer women, gold miners, bullock drivers, shearers, squatters, swagman and soldiers.

It is always difficult to highlight key events in the history of a nation. Several examples can be cited. On the Ballarat goldfields in 1854 at Eureka, the miners rebelled against the British soldiers the "traps" for enforcing an exorbitant "diggings" licence. When Peter Lalor hoisted the "Southern Cross" flag at Bakery Hill, the miners pledged, "We swear by the Southern Cross to stand truly by each other, and fight to defend our rights and liberties" (Carboni Raffaello, *The Eureka Stockade*).

This event is often cited as marking the beginnings of our independence. As Mark Twain commented (Wannan 1977: 171):

> ... I think it may be called the finest thing in Australian history. It was a revolution; it was a strike for liberty, a struggle for a principle, a stand against injustice and oppression ...It is another instance of a victory won by a lost battle. (*More Tramps Abroad*)

Australia became a Federation on the 1st January 1901 as the Commonwealth of Australia. This was finally agreed to standardise a variety of State taxes, defence forces, currencies and postal systems as well as to present a united face to the world. Surprisingly, with federal, state and local governments, we are now some of the most governed people on earth — which is especially curious, given our widespread disregard for authority as a nation.

During World War I, on 26th April 1915 at Gallipoli Peninsula in Turkey, the AIF (Australian Infantry Forces) combined with the New Zealanders as the Australian and New Zealand Army Corps (ANZAC). Their Turkish opponents, under what is generally regarded as incompetent British generalship, killed thousands of Australian soldiers. ANZAC day is a national holiday. Since the "Australia Remembers" campaign of 1995, which commemorated the 50th anniversary of the end of World War II, and coincided with the 80th anniversary of Gallipoli, record numbers now participate in ANZAC parades throughout the country. It is a fascinating comment on our nation's story: a military disaster and the loss of so many young lives marked a defining moment in our nationhood. Mark Twain was right: "a victory won by a lost battle." Or as the poet David Campbell reflects, "the tragic grandeur in the story of Australia."

In September 1999, Australia headed a United National peacekeeping force into East Timor. In the aftermath of the UN poll, which confirmed the desire of the East Timorese for independence, the militia and Indonesian army systematically murdered the East Timorese and drove the survivors from their homeland. Under intense international pressure, Indonesia finally agreed to allow a peace-keeping force into East Timor. Australia's involvement as "INTERFET" has again tested and demonstrated our prowess under arms and our leadership within the Asia Pacific region.

Finally, the Sydney 2000 Olympic games will be a new occasion to celebrate our identity and our sporting prowess. Australia and Greece are the only two nations who have attended every summer Olympiad in the modern era. Our athletes from many disciplines continue to win gold medals and to set world records. Australians typically do not exhibit much patriotism. But few events, including Grand Finals for our various football codes, elicit such fierce national pride as our Olympic victories every four years.

Australia is a polygeneric society (Willmot 1987: 15). That is, like the United States, Canada and New Zealand, among others, Australia is made up of human groups from different origins and with different racial memories. Nevertheless, our record on how we have treated our own indigenous peoples is shameful: the report, *Bringing Them Home* (Wilson 1997), chronicles a policy of virtual genocide that was inflicted upon our first Australians. Still, some early white settlers questioned the morality of the dispossession of Aboriginal people from their own land (Reynolds 1998).

Once the White Australia Policy ended in 1972, we began to attract people from all over the world. We Australians usually pride ourselves on our tolerance of others. As Professor W. K. Hancock wrote (Wannan 1977: 141):

"Intolerance of oppression and sympathy with the underdog are among the most attractive features of the Australian character"

Prime Minister Bob Hawke said of his fellow Australians (Hansen 1996: 24):

They're very friendly people, people not prone to, as we say, 'dip your lid' to others in a sense of recognizing a superiority in one class of people. There is a phrase we have in Australia the 'fair go'. The fair go means that all people are created with the right to develop and express themselves.

However, there were worrying signs that Australia's famous tolerance for the "underdog" and for letting everyone have a "fair go" was being threatened by Pauline Hanson's One Nation party. In its first electoral test in the Queensland State election on June 13, 1998, the crude and simplistic policies of One Nation gained eleven seats in parliament. One Nation gave a voice to those alienated by economic rationalism as well as being a magnet for the ravings of the ultra right. Fear and disillusionment put a party into parliament that based its appeal, in part, on prejudice against Aboriginal Australians and against Asian immigration.

> One Nation's success [has] reverberated around the world and sent a
> very different message from that of the model multiracial society which
> Australia has projected with increasing confidence in recent decades.
> (Steketee 1998)

Since then, Pauline Hansen failed to be re-elected in the 1998 Federal Election and One Nation has imploded due to internal bickering and a paucity of credible policy.

The image persists that Australians:

- are all "bronzed Aussies" (despite the fact that we are now careful of the sun as we have the highest levels of skin cancer in the world),
- drink beer by the litre (despite the fact that per capita we are now as much a wine-drinking nation),
- come from the "Land of the Long Weekend" (despite the fact that record levels of workaholism and stress are now reported).

A persistent phrase in Australia is that we are "The Lucky Country." This is what we tend to say of ourselves. This evokes a vision of a nation with great natural resources and easily accomplished influence. Further, as Willmot says (1987: 36):

> ...It suggests that the vast majority of its people live 'the good
> life' free from political, economic and social problems that appear to
> continually disturb virtually every nation on earth. Yet the only real
> protection we had against such problems, was isolation, distance and
> unimportance.

The originator of this phrase, Donald Horne (1976), meant something quite different. Horne stated, "Australia is a lucky country run by second rate people who share its luck." That Australians view themselves in this way and in a manner opposite from the original criticism says a lot. Ruth Richardson (1998), a previous Treasurer from New Zealand, was quoted as saying that "The Lucky Country" is not a blessing for Australia but a curse. We are not "The Lucky Country" but a country now "desperately seeking competitiveness."

Most Australians have a love affair with "the bush." Henry Lawson (1867–1922), probably our greatest poet, is remembered as a bush balladist. He is less remembered for his harsh criticism of the country and how an unforgiving land broke many pioneers. The fantasy of the bush and the outback continues: our verandas bring the outside into our living space and, per capita, Australians purchase more four-wheel drive vehicles than any other developed nation. However, less than 10 percent of these ever go "off road." We remain a nation of urban dwellers, clinging to the coastal rim for survival and for a sense of community.

Australians combine a laconic humour with deep cynicism and a profound suspicion of authority:

> We have become the world's cynics, a nation of sceptics. There are
> few of us who are passionate and committed. Some are moved for a
> time by popes and rainbow serpents, and some by yacht races and foot-
> ball matches, but most of us by nothing. We are a people waiting, and
> trying things, looking for a new way. (Willmot 1987: 55)

There is also a profound distrust of government. For example, in a provocative book, *Future Tense*, Paul Kelly and the national affairs team of *The Australian* assert:

> Governments are not the effective problem-solvers they were once.
> Yet the public is equivocal about governments. It holds them in con-
> tempt but expects them to solve too many of its problems and politi-
> cians often pretend that they can. (Murray 1999: 23–24)

We are waiting for leadership, especially at a national level. We hear cries for better leadership and better quality debates about major issues, instead of shallow explanations. As Xavier Clarke, one participant at the May 1999 "Australia Unlimited" conference, lamented:

> Where is the leadership here, where is the dynamism, the inspiration and the excitement? I think the challenge in Australia is to get people excited. (Rintoul 1999)

To give a sense of the quality and character of Australians, it might be helpful to scope some of our most famous and infamous identities. We also present some of our icons and symbols, which are recognised internationally.

Well known Australians include:

- Caroline Chisholm
  (protector of young women)

- Henry Lawson
  (bush poet and social critic)

- Mother Mary MacKillop
  (Australia's first Christian saint)

- Sir Charles Kingsford Smith
  (pioneer aviator)

- Sir Edward "Weary" Dunlop
  (doctor and prisoner of war hero)

- Sir Donald Bradman
  (cricketer)

- Dame Joan Sutherland
  (opera soprano, *La Stupenda*)

- Cathy Freeman
  (Olympic athlete-track and field)

- Kieren Perkins
  (Olympic athlete-swimming)

- Suzie Maroney
  (world record endurance swimmer)

▼▼▼▼▼▼▼▼▼▼▼▼▼▼▼▼▼▼▼▼▼

- Victor Chiang
  (heart surgeon)

- "Mum Shirl"
  (foster mother to Sydney Aboriginal children)

- Andy Thomas
  (Australian astronaut)

A list of more infamous Australians would include:

- Ned Kelly
  (bushranger)

- Alan Bond
  (failed entrepreneur from Western Australia)

- Christopher Skase
  (failed entrepreneur from Queensland)

- Martin Bryant
  (deranged murderer at Port Arthur in 1996)

Recognised Australian icons/symbols include:

- Uluru ["Ayres Rock"]
  (largest rock in the world at the "Red Centre")

- The Great Barrier Reef
  (largest living structure on the planet)

- Vegemite
  (dark, yeasty spread)

- The Sydney Opera House
  (most recognised building in Australia)

- The "slouch hat"
  (distinctive broad-brimmed hat)

- QANTAS
  (world's safest airline)

- The Melbourne Cup
  (horse race on the first Tuesday in November)

- R.M. Williams
  (stockman and creator of bush apparel)

- Ken Done
  (popular artist)

Traditionally Australia's wealth rode "on the sheep's back": our pastoral and mining industries contributed much to our GDP. These days, tourism also enjoys a central place. We are striving to develop a knowledge economy: we have produced a number of internationally recognised scientists, to say nothing of the quality of our artists, scholars and writers. Australian universities are well respected in the Southeast Asian region.

There is a curious mixture of prosperity and record share prices in the private sector combined with a penchant for "downsizing" within the public sector. At the Federal election in 1996 and the restoration of conservative government, the public sector was severely slashed: an estimated fifty thousand public servants lost their jobs, largely as a result of the "yellow pages" test. In other words, if a public service is in the Yellow Pages (telephone book), then it should be delivered by the private sector. The jury is still out on whether downsizing has been an effective strategy for productivity improvement (see Littler et al 1997). Australian Governments at all levels seem to court the notion of smaller government while at the same time lamenting the loss of essential services to remote areas.

So, too, the quality of leadership in Australia varies greatly from the sublime to the ridiculous, as we say "down under."

THE SEARCH FOR A NATIONAL IDENTITY

With the forthcoming centenary of Federation (on 1st January 2001), we seem to be a nation now struggling to find our own identity. There are republican whisperings and not just by people of a left-wing political persuasion. As we increasingly recognise our place in the Asia Pacific, and as we witness increasing levels of Asian immigration, any traditional ties to "Mother England" become meaningless for an increasing majority of Australians.

▼▼▼▼▼▼▼▼▼▼▼▼▼▼▼▼▼▼▼▼▼▼

Australia is a constitutional monarchy with Queen Elizabeth as the monarch. On 6th November 1999, Australians voted in a referendum about whether Australia should become a republic. The vote for a republic failed, by a slim margin.

Australians also decided at this referendum whether a preamble should be included in the Constitution. While also unsuccessful, this preamble was intended to provide a statement of our values as Australian people. It read:

> With hope in God, the Commonwealth of Australia is constituted as a democracy witha federal system of government to serve the common good. We, the Australian people commit ourselves to this Constitution:

proud that our national unity has been forged by Australians from many ancestries;
never forgetting the sacrifices of all who defended our country and our liberty in time of war;
upholding freedom, tolerance, individual dignity and the rule of law;
honouring Aborigines and Torres Strait Islanders, the nation's first people, for their deep kinship with their lands and for their ancient and continuing cultures which enrich the life of our country;
recognising the nation-building contribution of generations of immigrants;
mindful of our responsibility to protect our unique natural environment;
supportive of achievement as well as equality of opportunity for all;
and, valuing independence as dearly as the national spirit which binds us together in both adversity and success.

Some scholars lament the "spiritual poverty" among white Australians (McBride 1979). In his thesis submitted to the C.G. Jung Institute in Zurich, McBride highlights the "soullessness" in white Australia — the heavy consumption of alcohol, undervaluing the feminine, the neglect of Spirit and materialism.

> In the Aboriginal society, I found an alienation from their own racial unconsciousness, a rootless and spiritual disorientation. In the white

society, I feel there is a soullessness, a split between the rational, adapted, conscious life on the one hand and the ancient land, the earth, nature and the instincts on the other. (McBride 1979: 136)

Yet others have recognised our increasing connectedness with each other, nature and the universe. Low levels of Church attendance across all religious denominations, is juxtaposed with widespread spiritual commitment especially among the young to racial tolerance, world peace and genuine respect for the natural environment. David Tacey (1995) recognises a rediscovering of the sacred in Australia which springs from the very landscape. Tacey quotes Les Murray (1983) who says, "We have gills for dream-life in our head: we must keep them wet."

In the midst of all this, there are high levels of youth unemployment, drug dependency, violent crime and teenage suicide. Any wonder Hugh Mackay (1993: 6), our best-known social scientist, calls this the "Age of Redefinition":

We have been plunged into a period of unprecedented social, cultural, political, economic and technological change in which the Australian way of life is being radically redefined.

Australia has reached a psychological and cultural crossroad. We are perhaps the "last experiment" for a polygeneric society.

Of the major polygeneric nations, such as Canada, the United States, Mexico, New Zealand, South Africa and Australia, we remain the only one that has not officially recognised the ancient sovereignty of the original inhabitants. (Willmot 1987: 48)

The Mabo ruling by the High Court of Australia overturned the English view upon occupation in 1788 that Australia was "terra nullius" that is an empty land. Despite this reversal in law, under the subsequent "Wik" legislation, the balance shifted away from indigenous Australians in favour of pastoral leases.

The Australian Council for Aboriginal Reconciliation attempts to foster reconciliation between indigenous and non-indigenous Australians. Indigenous Australians also seek a formal apology on behalf of the nation. That the current conservative government refuses to say "sorry" causes wide debate and controversy in this country.

▼▼▼▼▼▼▼▼▼▼▼▼▼▼▼▼▼▼▼▼▼▼

Until the mid 1970s, Australian managers generally replicated the traditional British approach to "labour." The approach was scientific management with decision making purely in the hands of owners and management. Relations were somewhat adversarial: the rise of unionism marked the need to protect the rights of workers. Our experience at Eureka and Gallipoli perhaps reinforces a general distrust of management and authority in the workplace.

We still tended to suffer from a "cultural cringe," best exemplified by Prime Minister Robert Menzies sycophantic tribute to Queen Elizabeth II in 1956 at the opening of parliament when he said, "I did but see her passing gently by, and I will love her dearly till I die."

When Japan attacked Darwin in February 1942, Australia looked to America for military support as England was preoccupied with the war against the Axis powers in Europe. We are still somewhat dependent upon America for lessons about leadership — the *Harvard Business Review* would be better known than any Australian publication on management.

Everything American now tends to be imported here except among those aware of the dangers of "fad surfing" (Shappiro 1994). Bill Gates of Microsoft would be better known than most Australian CEOs, apart from James Strong, the Chairman of Qantas, our national airline. We have also experimented with most management trends from Japan — TQM, JIT, BPR — with little real success. We have yet to develop our own distinctive approach to leadership.

LEADERSHIP DEFINED AND THE MBTI IN AUSTRALIA

A simple definition of leadership would be appropriate here:

Leadership is the art of consistently influencing or directing people towards the achievement of a clear and common goal in such a way as to engender loyalty, respect and willing co-operation. (Stokes and James 1996: 222)

Before we examine current Australian thinking and practice on leadership, it is useful to consider the typology among Australians.

THE TYPOLOGY OF AUSTRALIANS

The Myers-Briggs Type Indicator (MBTI) has been known and respected in Australian organisations since the 1970s. The Australian Association for Psychological Type (AAPT) was re-established in 1991 and branches now exist in all States and Territories within Australia. A number of Australian organisations have also provided accreditation for MBTI practitioners, while Australia has two main distributors of type-related materials: Australian Psychologists' Press (APP), and the Australian Council for Educational Research (ACER), both based in Melbourne.

In a recently undertaken joint venture between AAPT and Deakin University in Victoria, a Psychological Type Research Unit has been established to collate and report on the use of type throughout Australia. Associate Professor Ian Ball is Head of the Unit and he recently reported the data shown in type tables 1 and 2 of Australian males and females (February 2000):

AUSTRALIAN MALES
compared with
AUSTRALIAN FEMALES
N=7569

Psychological Type
Research Unit
Australia

	N	%	I
E	3438	45.42	1.01***
I	4131	54.58	0.99
S	4233	55.93	1.05**
N	3336	44.07	0.95**
T	6036	79.75	1.86***
F	1533	20.25	0.35***
J	5083	67.16	1.13***
P	2486	32.84	0.81***
IJ	2860	37.79	1.09***
IP	1271	16.79	0.82***
EP	1215	16.05	0.80***
EJ	2223	29.37	1.19***
ST	3570	47.17	2.03***
SF	663	8.76	0.29***
NF	870	11.49	0.43***
NT	2466	32.58	1.66***
SJ	3317	43.82	1.12***
SP	916	12.10	0.85***
NP	1570	20.74	0.79***
NJ	1766	23.33	1.15***
TJ	4296	56.76	2.03***
TP	1740	22.99	1.55***
FP	746	9.86	0.38***
FJ	787	10.40	0.33***
IN	1724	22.78	0.95
EN	1612	21.30	0.94
IS	2407	31.80	1.02
ES	1826	24.12	1.09**
S dom	2333	30.82	1.04
N dom	1742	23.01	0.91***
T dom	2806	37.07	1.91***
F dom	688	9.09	0.35***

ISTJ	ISFJ	INFJ	INTJ
N = 1637	N = 275	N = 201	N = 747
% = 21.63	% = 3.63	% = 2.66	% = 9.87
I = 2.14***	I = 0.27***	I = 0.44***	I = 1.83***
ISTP	**ISFP**	**INFP**	**INTP**
N = 375	N = 120	N = 257	N = 519
% = 4.95	% = 1.59	% = 3.40	% = 6.86
I = 1.81***	I = 0.30***	I = 0.41***	I = 1.65***
ESTP	**ESFP**	**ENFP**	**ENTP**
N = 332	N = 89	N = 280	N = 514
% = 4.39	% = 1.18	% = 3.70	% = 6.79
I = 1.78***	I = 0.31***	I = 0.44***	I = 1.24***
ESTJ	**ESFJ**	**ENFJ**	**ENTJ**
N = 1226	N = 179	N = 132	N = 686
% = 16.20	% = 2.36	% = 1.74	% = 9.06
I = 2.04***	I = 0.30***	I = 0.41***	I = 1.99***

Note: ■ = 1% of sample   Print Date: 7/2/00
Base total N = 6507. Groups are independent.
Calculated values of Chi Square or Fisher's exact probability (underlined).

*<.05   **<.01   ***<.001

Type Table Significance			
340.02	434.52	98.40	97.43
45.64	145.70	158.29	48.48
38.54	104.91	136.42	10.26
219.63	233.75	77.55	109.03

E	0.50	IJ	13.82	SJ	29.90	IN	2.39
I	0.50	IP	30.40	SP	13.94	EN	3.59
S	8.34	EP	38.99	NP	60.02	IS	0.42
N	8.34	EJ	38.06	NJ	19.76	ES	7.21
T	2036.88	ST	867.33	TJ	1176.20	Sd	2.36
F	2036.88	SF	1062.75	TP	5.00	Nd	9.44
J	88.83	NF	548.70	FP	150.01	Td	532.14
P	88.83	NT	302.38	FJ	616.02	Fd	694.53
					966.32		

Table 1: Australian Data (Males)

Psychological Type
Research Unit
Australia

	N	%	I
E	2917	44.83	0.99***
I	3590	55.17	1.01
S	3481	53.50	0.96**
N	3026	46.50	1.06**
T	2788	42.85	0.54***
F	3719	57.15	2.82***
J	3871	59.49	0.89***
P	2636	40.51	1.23***
IJ	2262	34.76	0.92***
IP	1328	20.41	1.22***
EP	1308	20.10	1.25***
EJ	1609	24.73	0.84***
ST	1513	23.25	0.49***
SF	1968	30.24	3.45***
NF	1751	26.91	2.34***
NT	1275	19.59	0.60***
SJ	2555	39.27	0.90***
SP	926	14.23	1.18***
NP	1710	26.28	1.27***
NJ	1316	20.22	0.87***
TJ	1823	28.02	0.49***
TP	965	14.83	0.65***
FP	1671	25.68	2.61***
FJ	2048	31.47	3.03***
IN	1554	23.88	1.05
EN	1472	22.62	1.06
IS	2036	31.29	0.98
ES	1445	22.21	0.92**
S dom	1928	29.63	0.96
N dom	1642	25.23	1.10***
T dom	1262	19.39	0.52***
F dom	1675	25.74	2.83***

ISTJ	ISFJ	INFJ	INTJ
N = 638	N = 861	N = 392	N = 351
% = 10.11	% = 13.23	% = 6.02	% = 5.39
I = 0.47***	I = 3.64***	I = 2.27***	I = 0.55***
ISTP	**ISFP**	**INFP**	**INTP**
N = 178	N = 339	N = 541	N = 270
% = 2.74	% = 5.21	% = 8.31	% = 4.15
I = 0.55***	I = 3.29***	I = 2.45***	I = 0.61***
ESTP	**ESFP**	**ENFP**	**ENTP**
N = 160	N = 249	N = 542	N = 357
% = 2.46	% = 3.83	% = 8.33	% = 5.49
I = 0.56***	I = 3.25***	I = 2.25***	I = 0.81***
ESTJ	**ESFJ**	**ENFJ**	**ENTJ**
N = 517	N = 519	N = 276	N = 297
% = 7.95	% = 7.98	% = 4.24	% = 4.56
I = 0.49***	I = 3.37***	I = 2.43***	I = 0.50***

*<.05   **<.01   ***<.001

Note: ■ = 1% of sample.   Print Date: 7/2/00
Base total N = 7569. Groups are independent.
Calculated values of Chi Square or Fisher's exact probability (underlined).

Type Table Significance			
340.02	434.52	98.40	97.43
45.64	145.70	158.29	48.48
38.54	104.91	136.42	10.26
219.63	233.75	77.55	109.03

E	0.50	IJ	13.82	SJ	29.90	IN	2.39
I	0.50	IP	30.40	SP	13.94	EN	3.59
S	8.34	EP	38.99	NP	60.02	IS	0.42
N	8.34	EJ	38.06	NJ	19.76	ES	7.21
T	2036.88	ST	867.33	TJ	1176.20	Sd	2.36
F	2036.88	SF	1062.75	TP	5.00	Nd	9.44
J	88.83	NF	548.70	FP	150.01	Td	532.14
P	88.83	NT	302.38	FJ	616.02	Fd	694.53
					966.32		

Table 2: Australian Data (Females)

Based upon a reported population of 7,569, we observe that Australian males are more likely to present as Introverted (55 percent), Sensing (56 percent), Thinking (80 percent) and Judging (67 percent). The modal type for Australian males is ISTJ (22% of the reported population), followed by ESTJ (16 percent of the reported population). It is interesting that men are still as highly likely to present as Thinking types as they did some years ago (Moss 1991). For example, in 1996, the Psychological Type Research Unit reported a Thinking preference for males as high as 88 percent.

Based upon a reported population of 6,507, we observe that Australian females are more likely to present as Introverted (55 percent), Sensing (54 percent), Feeling (57 percent) and Judging (59 percent). The modal type for Australian females is ISFJ (13 percent of the reported population), closely followed by ISTJ (10 percent of the reported population). It is also fascinating that women are now slightly more likely to present as Feeling types (57 percent), whereas just a few years ago (1996), Australian women reported slightly more as Thinking types (64 percent).

While the trend among Australian women to present as Feeling types is highly unlikely to reflect a significant shift in "genetic predisposition" (Jung) from T to F, it might suggest that the socialisation of Australian women *in the workplace* is still fostering reported typologies that are more in tune with their dominant male cultures (see also Cox 1996). The implications for Australian women here are uncertain. Nevertheless this author and his senior consulting colleagues are aware of high levels of role ambiguity, role overload and occupational stress among professional women in the Australian workplace. The interaction between the authentic development of typology and its cultural context is indeed a complex one!

Moira Scollay, our showcased leader presented at the beginning of this chapter, is a conspicuous exception. While Moira has experienced high levels of work-related stress, she has remained true to her "ENFP-self." She has managed to preserve her feeling-oriented values within more thinking-oriented cultures.

TEMPERAMENT AS A PREDICTOR OF AUSTRALIAN ORGANISATIONAL CULTURE

While we should be cautious about equating the common temperament among senior managers with the organisation's culture (Latemore, 1997a), temperament is still a useful predictor of an organisation's culture. The author has for many years combined Harrison's model (1972) of organisational "characters" with Hickman and Silva's model (1984) of organisational excellence (see Latemore and Crawford, 1988). A full discussion of this application is beyond the scope of this chapter, but this general approach is now represented in the following diagram:

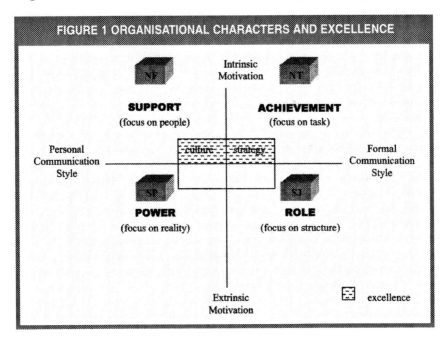

FIGURE 1 ORGANISATIONAL CHARACTERS AND EXCELLENCE

▼▼▼▼▼▼▼▼▼▼▼▼▼▼▼▼▼▼▼▼▼▼

The modal organisational character reported by Australian managers at workshops with the author for some years now is predominantly NT/SJ:

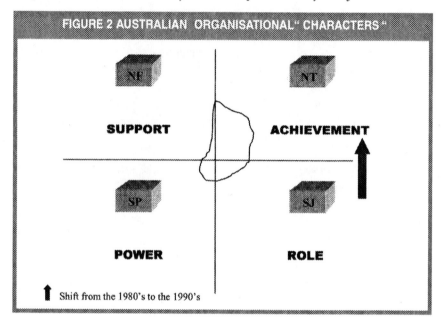

FIGURE 2 AUSTRALIAN ORGANISATIONAL "CHARACTERS"

In other words, the predominant organisational character currently reported among Australian organisations combines a predominant achievement orientation (NT) with a back-up role orientation (SJ). Ideologies that are somewhat under-represented are support orientation (NF) and power orientation (SP). Some ten years ago, the reported organisational character was more SJ/NT with similar low representations of NF and SP.

That is, the thrust of most organisational life now seems to be devoted to achieving client-related goals (NT) as well as system-related compliance (SJ). Of course, there are other configurations of culture depending upon the industry and sector (see also Chorn & Nurick 1997).

Therefore, the main organisational context for leaders in this country seems to be one of striving for client competitiveness (NT or "Achievement") while being somewhat constrained by traditional, bureaucratic systems (SJ or "Role"). This point is addressed by the "Karpin Report" (1995), which we now consider.

THE KARPIN REPORT

The Karpin Report highlighted the need for Australian managers to embrace the "Asia-Pacific Century" through workplace reform and internationally competitive enterprises. Addressing the need for better leaders and managers in particular, the Report identifies five key levers for improving management skills:

- Upgrade vocational education and training and business support.
- Capitalise on the talents of diversity.
- Achieve best practice in management development.
- Reform management education.
- Create a positive community attitude to enterprising behaviour.

This Report (x) distinguishes the old and new paradigms of management:

NEW PARADIGM	OLD PARADIGM
organisational learning	organisational discipline
virtuous circles	vicious circles
flexible	inflexible
leaders	administrators
open communication	distorted communication
markets	hierachies
product development through core competencies	product development through business units
strategic learning is widespread	strategic learning is at the apex
assumption that most employees are trustworthy	assumption that most employees are untrustworthy
most employees are empowered	most employees are disempowered
local knowledge of all employees is critical to success and creativity creates its own prerogative	local knowledge of all employees must be disciplined by managerial prerogative

Peter Sheldrake (1998), Executive Director of the Graduate School of Business at the Royal Melbourne Institute of Technology agrees. He sees different models of human cooperation emerging in Australia, models that transcend traditional, bureaucratic organisations.

In addition, the Karpin Report (xi) scopes the emerging senior manager profile:

1970	TODAY	2010
Male	Male	Male or Female
Anglo-Celt, British or Australian citizenship	Anglo-Celt, Australian citizenship	Wide range of ethnicities, citizenships
Started as message boy	Graduate	Graduate with MBA
Very local focus. Travelled once to England	Expanding focus. Travels to Asia, USA, Europe	Global focus, travels frequently. Lived in two or more countries
Established competitors, Cartels	Recently deregulated marketplace	Manages in both regulated and deregulated economies
Paternal view of the workforce	Sees workforce as stakeholders in business	Shares information and delegates heavily
Stable environment, low stress, home to see kids most nights, long term position	Turbulent environment high stress, long hours, fears burnout	Environment typified by rapid change. Limited term appointment, high stress, results driven

Likewise, Peter Goldrick of DDI Asia Pacific (1997) also argues for a shift from the traditional leadership roles of "controller, commander, ruler, judge and guard" to high-involvement leadership roles such as "catalyst, inspirer, coach, supporter/ champion and facilitator/partner."

OTHER AUSTRALIAN CONTRIBUTIONS ON LEADERSHIP

A number of Australian writers have explored critical themes in their views about leading others. These themes include: the importance of context, the feminisation of the workplace, being flexible change champions and transformational leadership. These themes are now considered.

UNDERSTANDING CONTEXT

It is perhaps useful to reflect here with Alistair Mant (1997: 22) that leadership is about *process* (what goes on between leaders and followers) and about *context* (the destination towards which the leader points). Mant reminds us that intelligent leadership is not an oxymoron. We need perceptive leaders who understand complexity, exercise judgment, are sane, virtuous, not afraid to exercise authority and who have the courage to pursue a useful purpose (1997: 14–15).

THE FEMINISATION OF THE WORKPLACE

Increasingly, feminine values are being sought in organisational life, where collaborative behaviour, exploratory decision-making and an open approach to learning are needed (Chorn 1995). Despite this, "pink ghettos" and "glass ceilings" still persist for women managers in both public and private sector Australian organisations. Eva Cox yearns for a more civil society based upon social capital and grows weary of "testosterone-driven, macho leadership" (1996). Cox argues for a collective view, with shared power and a whole life agenda for all, male *and* female. Women like Sara Henderson, who rebuilt a remote cattle station in northern Australia, embody courage and determination, but bring a real humanity to their efforts (Henderson 1991).

Male managers are also beginning to feel the need "to find a job with heart." Steve Biddulph in his best selling book *Manhood* urges:

> If you're a boss, realise that you are a father-figure. You are there
> to nourish and care for your people so they can do their jobs. Give
> more positive feedback. Share your vision. Ask people their opinions.
> Don't put people down ...Love, fun and idealism have as much place
> at work as in any other aspect of life. (1994: 167)

So, too, Margot Cairnes (1998) argues for organisations with a "corporate heart." She rightly distinguishes warriors from heroes. Warriors are people with strong, active energy who tend to have narrow, rationalistic visions, and an instrumental view of relationships. We witnessed this "warrior" style of workplace relations in 1998 on the Australian waterfront. Patrick Stevedores and the Maritime Union of Australia (MUA) were engaged in dismissals, picket lines and confrontational language.

Warriors, says Cairnes, have reached their use-by dates because:

> Unfettered warrior energy no longer fits the changing reality of the
> corporate marketplace; business is now being called on to be socially
> responsible; living life on the battlefield is killing the warrior on a per-
> sonal level; warriors tend to be young and male, and no one has much
> use for an aging warrior. (Cairnes 1998: 25–30)

Amanda Sinclair (1998) proclaims the need for a different kind of leadership. She argues that we need to foster and respond to new archetypes for leadership as the old paradigms of masculine and competitive behaviours are just not working.

LEADERS AS FLEXIBLE CHANGE AGENTS

Sally Rundle of Melbourne, has completed her doctorate at Monash University. Sally has discovered that the criteria for success among Australians who invest and work in Asia also reflect the emerging profile scoped by Karpin (above). To prosper in turbulent and highly competitive markets, managers must exhibit "*far*ness" — that is, flexibility, adaptability and responsiveness (Rundle 1997; see also Dunne 1998).

As a senior management consultant in Australia, the author is acutely aware of the need for us to embrace the next century and a globalised economy (Friedman 1999), and to do so with "emotional intelligence" (see Goleman 1995; Cooper and

Sawaf 1997). Many of his clients are striving to meet the challenges identified by Karpin, often against considerable odds. In co-conducting Executive Leadership Programs throughout the country, the author works with managers who are striving to enrich their personal and professional abilities. Capabilities in advanced communication, emotional capital (Thomson 1998) and other essential competencies are now being fostered.

Australians are pioneers in change management (Centre for Corporate Change at the Australian Graduate School of Management), in strategic alignment (Chorn and Nurich 1997), in team building strategies (Margerison and McCann 1990), in strategic alliances (Limerick & Cunnington 1993) and in values-based development (see Colins & Chippendale 1995).

Many Australian senior managers are quite sophisticated with current leadership trends. For example, many use the principles of John Kotter (1995 and 1996) on change management (see also Latemore 1997b) and are familiar with 360 degree leadership assessment, such as employed by James Kouzes and Barry Posner in their *Leadership Practices Inventory* (1993) and *Benchmarks* from the Center for Creative Leadership (Lombardo & McCauley 1998–1994).

While there is scrutiny about how the management development dollar is being spent, larger Australian organisations are, in the main, enhancing the capability, the learning potential and the employability of their people (see also Handy 1995). Professor Victor Callan, Head of School at the Graduate School of Management, The University of Queensland, also witnesses the genuine efforts by specialists to enrich their management qualifications to be more personally effective and internationally competitive (1992 & 1998).

Managers are generally open to change their ways except for a few "dinosaurs" who still endeavour to protect their turf, their parochialism and their patriarchal ways. Moira Scollay is a breath of fresh air among this "mob"!

Clancy and Webber (1997) distinguish the role of a manager from the role of a leader. They postulate that organisations are less about "great big meccano sets to manage" than about "gardens which need the care of leaders" — hence their title, *Roses and Rust*. They highlight the need to create vital connections where critical leaders "...provide organisations with the ability to define the meaning of

▼▼▼▼▼▼▼▼▼▼▼▼▼▼▼▼▼▼▼▼▼▼

work as: helping organisations to adapt and grow; and helping individuals to be the best they can be" (1997: xxiii).

In Moira Scollay, showcased above, we recognise these two leadership roles in action. She strives to foster both organisational and personal development.

Norman Chorn (1997), a prominent Australian strategist, presents some challenging assumptions about leadership:

- Leadership is elitist (in that a few exert influence over the many).
- Leadership is a multiple concept (in that leaders can be found at every level).
- "Followership" is an important counterpoint (in that empowerment must exist).
- Leadership assumes self-awareness (in that leadership is about "bringing yourself to the table").
- Leadership is not context free (in that knowledge of the strategic context must underpin any contribution).
- Leadership must foster relevance (in that leaders must ensure external alignment with clients and internal alignment with their culture).

Other recent and worthwhile Australian contributions to leadership theory include the work of Dunphy and Stace (1990), Avolio (1996), Sarros and Putchatsky (1996) and Ken Parry (1996). Their models of leadership are now briefly summarised.

Dexter Dunphy and Doug Stace from the Australian Graduate School of Management have long contributed to our understanding of the change process. In groundbreaking work (1990 and 1994), they present a typology that combines the pace of change with leadership style during change. The following model outlines their approach as well as summarising the conditions for their use.

FIGURE 3 TYPOLOGIES FOR CHANGE		
	INCREMENTAL CHANGE	**TRANSFORMATIVE CHANGE**
COLLABORATIVE/ CONSULTATIVE MODES	**1. Participative evolution** Use when organisation is in fit but needs minor adjustment, or is out of fit but time is available and key interest groups favour change.	**2. Charismatic transformation** Use when organisation is out of fit, there is little time for extensive participation but there is support for radical change within the organisation.
DIRECTIVE/ COERCIVE MODES	**3. Forced evolution** Use when organisation is in fit but needs minor adjustment, or is out of fit but time is available, but key interest groups oppose change.	**4. Dictatorial transformation** Use when organisation is out of fit, there is no time for extensive participation and no support within the organisation for radical change, but radical change is vital to organisational survival and fulfillment of basic mission.

TRANSFORMATIONAL LEADERSHIP

Considering the importance of leadership, Bruce Avolio (1996) focuses on what he calls the four Is of transformational leadership:

- Individualised consideration
  (gaining trust, respect and confidence)
- Intellectual stimulation
  (articulating the future and a plan)
- Inspirational motivation
  (questioning and innovating)
- Idealised influence
  (energizing people to their full potential)

James Sarros and Oleh Butchasky (1996) depict a breakthrough model of leadership and argue, that background variables like family and education contribute to the character of a CEO, but it is the *metanoia*, or breakthrough experience, alone that will produce the required outcomes of continuous learning, confidence, competence and commitment.

Many Australian managers tell stories about their growing through personal and organisational crises and how this has helped "make or break" them as leaders (see Kaye 1996; Mant 1997; Moodie 1998). Key breakthrough leadership behaviours include: respect for others, values clarification, a willingness to look, listen and learn and a systems approach. These themes consistently emerge among current Australian thinking and practice on leadership. Sarros and Butchasky also argue for "post heroic leadership":

> Virtual leadership is in vogue today. This type of leadership is where the leader works closely with all workers and managers to deliver the organisation's objectives. A virtual or post-heroic leader does not seek the adulation of his or her peers; in fact, this leader feels as comfortable out of the spotlight as on the stage. The post-heroic leader is committed to developing leaders at all levels of the [organisation] by modelling appropriate behaviour and willingly distributing the power to make decisions and be held accountable for the outcomes to all workers. (1996: 283)

A PROFILE FOR FUTURE AUSTRALIAN LEADERS

Beyond economics, in a world of diminishing "religiousness" and aberrant fundamentalism, the search for authenticity within Australian organisations is as strong as ever (Jones 1998). Corporations are striving for "sustainability" (Dunphy and Stace 1998), conferences are asking "heart at work or just hard at work?" (Banks and Latemore 1999), and we are all being encouraged to lead, learn and innovate for a "planetist future" (Ellyard 1998).

Ken Parry (1996) recognises that we are very hard on our leaders, we are quick to blame them, we are cynical about authority and we do not tolerate indiscretions. To be considered a good leader by Australians, he has found that leaders must:

- be positive role models,
- engage in individually considerate behaviour at all times,
- espouse positive visions about the future only when this is accompanied by credible action,
- keep monitoring and controlling behaviour to a minimum,
- be intellectually stimulating when the occasion arises.

In similar vein to Karpin (1995), Parry offers a profile for future leaders based upon an iterative process of interpreting a variety of research findings. He believes future leaders will:

- be developed rather than trained,
- be continuously learning,
- develop and train other leaders,
- have a desire to be changed as well as to change,
- possess ethical and socially responsible values,
- be part of a team as much as the 'head' of a team,
- possess feminised characteristics,
- communicate up, down and sideways,
- be transformational and transactional.

THE TALL POPPY SYNDROME

Australians often cut their "Tall Poppies." Robert Spillane from the Macquarie Graduate School of Management highlights this tendency:

> We love the thought of [Sir Donald] Bradman hitting the cricket ball against a wall for hours and hours and we love the idea of women grinding their way up and down the swimming pool. But once you've 'made it', you'll find Australians are waiting to see how you cope with it. If you utter a political statement, you're gone. The people who are tremendous successes and who have survived the Tall Poppy Syndrome are the ones who have learnt to keep their mouths shut. (Moodie 1998: 1-2)

Susan Mitchell admires those who refuse to be cut down, and points out:

> Australians have always liked to cut down their successful people, their 'tall poppies', especially when they consider they are getting too tall. It's often hard for successful men to avoid this fate — it's doubly hard for successful women. (1984: 1)

The "Tall Poppy Syndrome" is thought to have its roots in the earliest days of white settlement in Australia when convicts showed disrespect, and in many cases, hatred for authority. There is an argument that the Tall Poppy Syndrome originated and then persisted as a way of making sure successful Australians didn't get too big headed (Moodie 1998:2).

Australian reaction to Christopher Skase and Alan Bond is another good example: they were once seen as successful entrepreneurs, but eventually were judged by the courts as criminals. Their fall from grace makes us uneasy about admiring other leaders too much. Australians seem very cautious about admiring heroes and heroines lest they eventually disappoint us.

Other prominent Australians seem to have escaped such harsh judgment: we maintain a deep affection for people like "Weary" Dunlop, Mary MacKillop and "Mum Shirl." Perhaps we do need heroes and heroines after all to help connect us with our past and to co-create a living tradition that makes a difference (Latemore and Callan 1998). Dowling (1998) agrees: "Maybe our need for heroes and something larger to believe in just can't be met by politicians, movie stars and sporting celebrities."

You only have to see Paul Hogan in the film Anzacs: *The War Down Under* (1985) to catch a glimpse of our irreverence for authority. Indeed, the image of the "larrikan" runs deep within the Australian psyche (Wannan 1977). Australians are well known overseas for our dry and laconic sense of humour — maybe our unforgiving climate and the harsh environment foster such a perspective on life.

Above all, we seem to appreciate humility. As Sir Edward "Weary" Dunlop says, "The leader is the servant of all, able to show a disarming humility without the loss of authority" (as quoted in Cole 1998: 454).

The visible self-confidence of many American leaders does not sit well with us; Frank Blount, the previous CEO of Telstra, Bob Joss of Westpac and others of American origin do not enjoy an automatic following among Australians (Blount and Joss, 1999). And yet, we do not treat our "home-grown" leaders any less cynically. It was interesting to see for example, how briefly we allowed Poppy King, of lipstick fame, to enjoy her success in America before her star fell from the heroic heavens.

This humility and the "Tall Poppy Syndrome" will perhaps be our Achilles heel. It is precisely confident and decisive leadership that is needed as we face the next Asia-Pacific century (Karpin 1995). We cannot afford the resigned approach, "she'll be right mate," in the face of a falling dollar, domestic disquiet, regional unrest (especially in Papua New Guinea and Indonesia) and the loss of international competitiveness.

TOWARDS A MODEL OF AUSTRALIAN LEADERSHIP

A single Australian model of leadership remains elusive. Nevertheless, glimpses can be seen. The Commandant of the Royal Military College of Australia, Brigadier Peter Cosgrove, is well versed on this subject. Cosgrove initially lead the UN peace-keeping "INTERFET" force into East Timor. Leadership, says Cosgrove, is being able to express what he calls "four qualities plus one": integrity, courage, compassion, humility — and communication. As he elaborates:

▼▼▼▼▼▼▼▼▼▼▼▼▼▼▼▼▼▼▼▼▼▼▼▼

'First of all a leader must have integrity. [If you're flawed or corrupt], you might be able to push through with authority, but you won't enjoy natural loyalty ...The second quality is courage, both the physical, but more importantly, the moral kind ...Compassion is the third quality of leadership. You need to balance courage with compassion, otherwise you will wear people down and lose their respect, and because you won't have taken into account the frailties of human nature...

The fourth quality is humility. A leader must be self-analytical and acknowledge his or her weaknesses and failures. The 'big head' syndrome will get you nowhere, and once megalomania sets in, it's downhill from there ...The 'plus one' quality is communication. If you have integrity, moral courage, compassion and humility but you sit there like a pet rock, forget it.' (as quoted in Moodie 1998: 4-5)

Based on the acronym AUSTRALIA, a cautious model of the Aussie leadership style is suggested:

A Authentic
We do not respect tradition for its own sake. Australians seem to be born with well-tuned "Bullshit Detectors" — we recognise dishonesty and inauthenticity in an instant. Genuine and natural relationships seem to be valued over veiled and guarded communications. We might be "quirky" and "mavericks" as leaders (Mant 1997), but our authenticity is obvious.

U Understated
While our type profile exhibits an increasing balance between introverted and extroverted preferences (Ball 1998), we still don't like obviously extroverted behaviour.

S Survivors
We tend to bounce back from adversity, which is just as well since the climate, the environment and our remoteness from the rest of the world are quite demanding.

T Tenacious
We are determined in community, corporate and sporting endeavours.
Discouragement affects us but generally does not erode our national psyche
to persevere.

R Realistic
There are many practical bones in every Australian manager's body. If an idea
actually works, then it is entertained. Notwithstanding the large percentage
of an intuitive preference among Australian adults (Ball 1998), realism in its
application is prized. Pure theory tends to be looked upon with disdain.

A Anti-Authoritarian
From Eureka to Breaker Morant, we do not respect authority or tradition for
its own sake. People must prove themselves on their own merits.
Competency and credibility mean more to us than status.

L Laconic
The Australian "drawl" is a distinctive accent to foreign ears. Our dry sense
of humour is a national characteristic. We have a "very keen sense of the
ridiculous" (*The Drover's Wife*, by Henry Lawson).

I Inventive
Generally, Aussie leaders are more pragmatic than creative. However, we continue to invent and contribute to world-class scientific development (such as
the "black box" or "flight recorder" on airliners).

A Achievers
While rarely "blowing their own trumpet," Australians do like to win. An
earlier advertising slogan for BHP, which was one of our largest and most
successful companies, typifies our understated ambition: "BHP — The Quiet
Achiever."

CONCLUSION

As we enter the new millennium Australia is on the brink of a transformation.
As we reconsider our place in the world, we reflect more than ever upon our
national identity and what it means to be an Australian.

▼▼▼▼▼▼▼▼▼▼▼▼▼▼▼▼▼▼▼▼▼

This age of redefinition is also reflected in a more open, creative and empowered approach to leadership. Moira Scollay is a great example of this new approach to leadership: people-friendly and yet results-oriented, decisive and yet consultative, conceptually smart and yet emotionally intelligent. In the face of intolerance and isolationism, as exemplified by One Nation, open and hope-filled leaders like Moira are more vital than ever. She is one "Tall Poppy" who must not be cut down.

As Australia ponders our place with the Asia Pacific region "down under," as we embrace the new millenium, and as we celebrate the anniversary of our federation on 1st January 2001, there is much to celebrate and much to reconsider.

REFERENCES

Avolio, B. (1996). What's all the Karping about down under? Transforming Australia's leadership systems for the twenty-first century. In K. Parry [Ed.] *Leadership research and practice* (pp. 3–15). South Melbourne, Australia: Pitman Publishing.

Ball, I. (1996 & 2000). *Current MBTI data.* Victoria, Australia: Deakin University. Psychological Type Research Unit, Faculty of Education. [Ian Ball is Manager of the Unit].

Banks, N. & Latemore, G. (1999, February). *Heart at work or just hard at work?* Workshop session for the Australian Human Resources Institute (AHRI), HR Practices Day, Brisbane, Australia.

Barratt, P., Hollway, S., & Shergold, P. (1996, September). *Improving APS leadership.* Discussion paper prepared for the portfolio secretaries' retreat for the Public Sector & Merit Protection Commission, Canberra, Australia.

Biddulph, S. *Manhood: An action plan for changing men's lives.* Sydney: Finch Publishing.

Blount, F. & Joss, B. with Mair, D. (1999). *Managing in Australia.* Australia: Lansdowne Press.

Cairnes, M. (1998). *Approaching the corporate heart: Breaking through to new horizons of personal and professional success.* East Roseville, Australia: Simon & Schuster.

Callan, V. (1992). Issues in career management. In P. C. L. Heaven [Ed.], *Life span development* (pp. 167–180). Harcourt Brace Jovanovich.

Callan, V. (1988). *From specialist to leader.* Address at the Senior Executive Leadership Program (SELP) for the Queensland Department of Public Works and Housing, Brisbane, Australia.

Chorn, N. (1995, November). Creating feminine values in organisations. *Management,* pp. 5–7.

Chorn, N. (1997). *On being a leader.* Unpublished occasional paper. Sydney.

Chorn, N. & Nurich, I. of The Centre for Corporate Strategy. (1997). *Strategic alignment: The science of aligning customers, strategy, culture and leadership*. North Carlton, Australia: Australian Psychologists Press.

Clancy, D. & Webber, R. (1997). *Roses and rust: Redefining the essence of leadership in a new age* (2nd edition). Warriewood, Australia: Business & Professional Publishing.

Cole, K. (1996). *Supervision: Management in action*. Sydney: Prentice Hall.

Colins, C. & Chippendale, P. (1995). *New wisdom II: Values-based development*. Brisbane, Australia: Acorn Publications.

Cooper, R. & Sawaf, A. (1997). *Executive EQ: Emotional intelligence in business*. London: Orion Business Books.

Cox, E. (1994). A truly civil society. *The 1995 Boyer lectures*. Crows Nest, Australia: ABC Radio National, ABC Enterprises.

Cox, E. (1995). *Leading women*. Sydney: Random House.

Dowling, T. (1998, 9th–10th May). Send in the heroes [Review section]. The Weekend Australian, p.10.

Dunne, J. (1998, May). The stuff of leadership. *Management Today*, pp. 15-18.

Dunphy, D. & Stace, D. (1990). *Under new management: Australian organizations in Transition*. Sydney: McGraw-Hill Book Company.

Dunphy, D & Griffiths, A. (1998). *The sustainable corporation: Organisational renewal in Australia*. St. Leonard's, Australia: Allen & Unwin.

Ellyard, P. (1997). *Ideas for the new millennium*. South Carlton: Melbourne University Press.

Friedman, T. (1999). *The Lexus and the olive tree*. London: Harper Collins Publishers.

Goldrick, P. (1997, April). Critical leadership skills in the changing workplace. *Management*, pp.17–19.

Goleman, D. (1995). *Emotional intelligence: Why it can matter more than IQ.* London: Bloomsbury.

Handy, C. (1994). *Beyond certainty: The changing world of organisations.* London: Hutchinson.

Harrison, R. (1972, May–June). Understanding your organisation's character. *Harvard Business Review*, 3, pp. 119–128.

Hansen, E. (1996). *Frommer's Australia.* New York: Macmillan.

Hansen, I. (Ed.). (1962). *The call of the gums: An anthology of Australian verse.* London: Edward Arnold Publishers Ltd.

Henderson, S. (1990). *From strength to strength: An autobiography.* Sydney: Pan Macmillan.

Hickman, C. & Silva, M. (1984). *Creating excellence.* London: Allen & Unwin.

Horne, D. (1976). *Death of the lucky country.* Ringwood, Australia: Penguin.

Jones, C. (1998). *An authentic life: Finding meaning and spirituality in everyday life.* Sydney: ABC Books.

Korac-Kakabadse, A. & Korac-Kakabadse, N. (1996). *The leadership challenge for the APS: An internationally comparative benchmarking analysis.* A report for the Public Service & Merit Protection Commission, Canberra, Australia.

Karpin, D.S. (Ed.). (1995). *Enterprising nation: Renewing Australia's managers to meet the challenges of the Asia-Pacific Century.* Canberra, Australia: Australian Government Publishing Service.

Kaye, M. (1996). *Myth-makers and story-tellers.* Chatswood, Australia: Business & Professional Publishing.

Kotter, J. (1995, March–April). Leading change: Why transformation efforts fail. *Harvard Business Review*, pp. 59–67.

εε

Kotter, J. (1996) *Leading change*. Boston: Harvard Business Press.

Kouzes, J.M. & Posner, B.Z. (1991). *The leadership challenge: How to get extraordinary things done in organizations*. Oxford: Jossey Bass.

Kouzes, J.M. & Posner, B.Z. (1993). *Leadership practices inventory*. (Expanded ed.). San Francisco: Pfeffer, an Imprint of Jossey Bass.

Latemore, G. (1997a, August). *Temperament and culture: Applications and cautions for the MBTI practitioner*. Paper to support a concurrent session at the MBTI at Work Conference, sponsored by Australian Psychologists Press, Melbourne, Australia.

Latemore, G. (1997b). *The twelve Rs: An approach to leading and managing change*. Unpublished occasional paper, Brisbane, Australia.

Latemore, G. & Callan, V. (1998). Odysseus for today: Ancient and modern lessons for leaders. *Asia Pacific Journal of Human Resources*, 36 (3), pp. 76–86.

Latemore, G. & Crawford, B. (1988). *People working together*. Unpublished occasional paper #1 for the Australian Institute of Training and Development. Brisbane, Australia.

Lawson, H. (1967). *While the Billy Boils* (2nd series). Sydney: Pacific Books.

Limerick, D. & Cunnington, B. (1993). *Managing the new organisation: A blueprint for networks and strategic alliance*. Chatswood, Australia: Business & Professional Publishing.

Littler, C. Dunford, R., Bramble, T., & Hede, A. (1997). The dynamics of downsizing in Australia and New Zealand. *Asia-Pacific Journal of Human Resources*, 35 (1), pp. 65–79.

Lombardo, M. & McCauley, C. (1988–1994). *Benchmarks*. Center for Creative Leadership.

McBride, T. (1979). *The dreamtime of the Aborigines and present day Australia with special reference to the role of the healer*. Unpublished doctoral dissertation, C.G. Jung Institute, Zurich.

Mackay, H. (1993). *Reinventing Australia: The mind and mood of Australia in the 90s*. Sydney: Angus & Robertson.

Mant, A. (1996). *Intelligent leadership*. St. Leonard's: Allen & Unwin.

Margerison, C. & McCann, D. (1990). *Team management*. London: Mercury Books.

Mitchell, S. (1984). *Tall poppies: Successful Australian women*. Ringwood, Australia: Penguin Books.

Moodie, A. M. (1998). *Local heroes: A celebration of success and leadership in Australia*. Sydney: Prentice Hall Australia Pty. Ltd.

Moss, S. (1991). Introducing type: *An Australian handbook on Jungian type theory and the MBTI*. Brisbane, Australia: DMP Publications.

Murray, L. (1983). First essay on interest. *The people's otherworld*. Sydney: Angus & Robertson.

Murray, W. (Ed.). (1998). Future tense: Australia beyond election 1998. *The Australian* with Paul Kelly and the National Affairs Team. St. Leonard's, Australia: Allen & Unwin.

Parry, K.W. (Ed). (1995). *Leadership research and practice: Emerging themes and new challenges*. South Melbourne: Pitman Publishing.

Reynolds, H. (1998). *This whispering in our hearts*. St. Leonard's, Australia: Allen & Unwin.

Richardson, R. Previous Treasurer, New Zealand. (1995, 11th May). Interviewed on The World Today, ABC Radio 4QR, Brisbane, Australia.

Rintoul, S. (1999, 8th–9th May). Hanson thrives in social chasm (from A fair and decent place), Australia Unlimited [special article]. The Weekend Australian.

Rundle, S. (1997). *Managerial responsiveness: Flexibility, adaptiveness and responsiveness (FAR-ness) as the key success factors in market entry in the South East Asiangrowth wedge-Indonesia, Malaysia and Singapore*. Unpublished doctoral dissertation, Monash University, Victoria, Australia.

Sarros, J. & Butchasky, O. (1996). *Leadership: Australia's top CEOs-Finding out what makes them the best.* Sydney: HarperCollins

Shappiro, E. (1993). *Fad surfing in the boardroom: Reclaiming the courage to manage in the age of instant answers.* Sydney: HarperBusiness.

Sheldrake, P. (1998, June). Challenging corporate illusions. *The Qantas Club,* pp. 6–10.

Sinclair, A. (1998). *Doing leadership differently.* Melbourne: Melbourne University Press.

Stace, D. & Dunphy, D. (1994). *Beyond the boundaries: Leading and re-creating the successful enterprise.* Sydney: McGraw Hill Book Company.

Steketee, M. (Ed. National Affairs). (1998, 13th June). Whole world watches one nation. The Weekend Australian, p. 1.

Stokes, P. & James, J. (1993). *So now you're a leader: 10 precepts of practical leadership.* Sydney: McGraw-Hill Book Company.

Tacey, D. (1993). *Edge of the sacred: Transformation in Australia.* North Blackburn, Australia: HarperCollins Publishers.

Thomson, K. (1998). *Emotional capital.* Oxford: Capstone.

Wannan, B. (1977). *Great book of Australiana: Folklore, legends, humour, yarns.* Melbourne: Curry O'Neil Publishers, Melbourne.

Willmot, E. (1987). Australia: The last experiment. *The 1986 Boyer Lecture.* Crows Nest, Australia: ABC Radio National, ABC Enterprises.

Wilson, R. (Ed.). (1997). *Bringing them home: Report of the national inquiry into the separation of Aboriginal and Torres Strait Islander children from their families.* Canberra: Australian Government Publishing Service.

EPILOGUE

"This is really a wonderful Colony; ancient Rome in her imperial grandeur would not have been ashamed of such an offspring."

Letter from Charles Darwin (1836)
(Cited in Hansen 1996: 21)

"This land was never given up.
This land was never bought and sold.
The planting of the Union Jack
Never changed our Law at all."

("Treaty" by the Aboriginal rock group Yothu Yindi)

ACKNOWLEDGMENTS

The author wishes to acknowledge the helpful comments of:

• Professor Victor Callan, Head, Graduate School of Management, The University of Queensland,Brisbane.
• Dr Norman Chorn, Director, Centre for Corporate Strategy, North Sydney.
• Ms Moira Scollay, CEO, Australian National Training Authority, Melbourne.

BULGARIA

Vasselina Russinova
Institute of Psychology, Bulgarian Academy of Sciences
Eliana Pencheva
Institute of Psychology, Bulgarian Academy of Science

EDITOR'S NOTES. The Bulgarian chapter begins with a contrast between two academic leaders. Dr. Eliana Pencheva introduces us to an academic entrepreneur who seeks improvement in the delivery of education by establishing a private school. A second leader, who seeks to change the educational system from within, is then profiled.

It is interesting to note that within countries of the former Soviet Union, the collective was emphasized at the cost to the individual, a stark contrast to the Western emphasis on the individual at the expense of the team. In such circumstances, individuals who excel may be subject to social criticism. To avoid potential problems, Dr. Russinova and Dr. Pencheva elected to limit the identification of the leaders they profiled. Next, Dr. Vesselina Russinova provides us a comprehensive review of Bulgarian economic and political history and current status. Dr. Russinova completes her section of the chapter with a summary of leadership models from within the Bulgarian experience. With this comprehensive foundation, Dr. Eliana Pencheva explores leadership within the more specific setting of the Bulgarian educational network.

TWO ACADEMIC ENTREPRENEURS/LEADERS

P. N. (age forty-seven) passed through the entire professional hierarchy of the secondary education. He was a teacher for seven years, school principal for four years and school inspector for four years. He was very experienced and knew all elements of the school system.

In the late 1990s, together with several colleagues, he founded a private elementary school (1–5 grade). This was a small school, with small classes and good equipment. As compared to the low payment of other teachers, those in his school were well paid.

The students were primarily the children of the school founders and owners. P. N. specially chose the school staff. Despite the common lack of educational motivation, the students displayed strong achievement, a result of the encouragement by their ambitious parents. The school policy was subsequently relevant — students were ranked according to their marks.

Two of the students left the school voluntarily, since they did not succeed in satisfying the school requirements. We may say that P. N. displayed a job-centered leader's behaviour, but at the same time, he did his best to create a favorable climate for teachers' work. He held monthly encounters with parents that had rather the form of consultations. Moreover, he most often organized meetings of the school personnel, discussing educational problems and achievements. Note that despite all this, the teachers refrained from talking about the personal problems they met when interacting with the students. Such behaviour may be classified as a pedagogical helplessness.

At first glance, the educational process seemed to develop normally, satisfying students and parents. Half a year ago P. N. employed a school psychologist. Leaving her some time for orientation, he asked her to find out what made the teachers insufficiently involved and motivated for their job, not doing their best to fulfill the educational tasks. He expressed his hope that the school psychologist might solve this problem.

M. B. (forty-three years old) was an accomplished leader even before taking the post of school principal. For example, he was a functionary of the Bulgarian Young Communist League (The Comsomol). He had also been a successful principal of a special school for ten years (1-12 grades). The school was "uncommon" for Bulgaria at that time, since the teachers taught humanitarian, business and law courses.

M. B. hired a number of school counselors and university lecturers to teach different subjects. One specific educational feature was that students were free to choose their subjects. Moreover, their relations with peers, parents and teachers were informal.

As a principal, M. B. was a very controversial figure. He invented the school's innovative style, gave the staff great freedom, but at the same time demonstrated authoritarian behaviour. For instance, he proposed a number of essential school problems for group discussion. He was ready to listen to all opinions but imposed his own. He himself often proposed creative ideas but monopolized most of the discussion time, revealed his ideas in detail, but chaotically. Meetings with the school personnel continued too long, boring and tiring M. B.'s collaborators. Yet, they were not brave or bold enough to interrupt him.

Another unpleasant feature of M. B.'s character was that he always took one man's decision, despite the opinion of the other educators. They discussed their dissatisfaction but nobody opposed the principal. The fulfillment of routine management tasks was chaotic — anyone (student, teacher or outsider) would visit any time M. B.'s office, stating his problem. M. B. would interrupt the running meeting by starting a talk with the visitor. Many educators left the school dissatisfied with the principal's policy. Those that stayed had the full freedom of developing creative initiatives within the scope of their professional tasks.

The position of school principal is very competitive at present in Bulgaria, and is organized by the Bulgarian Ministry of Education. Hence, there is another candidate for M. B.'s occupation. The school staff is concerned with M. B.'s eventual replacement, for it is interesting to note that people are ready to protest if this happens.

LEADERSHIP AND TRANSITION IN BULGARIA

Following the collapse of the Soviet Union during 1989, a process of political, economic and social change commenced in Bulgaria. In the beginning, attention was turned to the political changes: pluralism; replacement of the totalitarian regime; settlement of parliamentary democracy; and efforts to create new legislation.

The necessity of managing the growing economic crisis came to the forefront. Markets and raw materials had decreased, state enterprises had run into debt, and existing technologies and techniques had become outdated. Consequently, some of the state enterprises went into liquidation, while others reduced production.

Changes in the laws regarding ownership of property and a restructuring of the economy were necessary, particularly legislation that advocates the conversion of a planned economy to a market economy. Such dramatic and far-reaching change processes take a long period of time, during which unemployment grows and the income of the population plummets dramatically. While we are implementing such changes, foreign investments remain insufficient, and most of the banks go bankrupt.

A great amount of the financial capital is removed illegally out of the country. Criminality increases substantially. All these events create unfavourable conditions for economic enterprise.

Two positive factors exist for the future economic development of Bulgaria: the great number of specialists in different fields, and the high competency and low wages of working people. These factors can be used for economic development after the creation of a favourable framework: a legislation that gives priority to economic growth, lower taxes and stability. The processes of social changes are going very slowly.

Another challenge to economic prosperity is the fact that Bulgarian people have attitudes towards passivity and security. During the whole period of the planned economy, the people relied on work in state enterprises and organizations — there was no private enterprise. Some time is needed to change values, attitudes and standards of behaviour. Moreover, people need information about how to achieve success in the new situation.

Bulgarian leaders have had to work in this unfavourable situation for state economic organizations. Recently, however, the state firms have been in a process of privatisation. Some of the privatisation transactions are ineffective. There are few international and private Bulgarian firms, and unfortunately, most of them are commercial firms that do not contribute to the economic growth in our country.

MANAGEMENT AND LEADERSHIP IN BULGARIA

A critical issue in Bulgaria is the professionalism of our leaders. Indeed, we need to make the conceptual leap from managers, or those who maintain the status quo, to leaders who transform an organization. We have plenty of managers but precious few leaders.

As opposed to the focus of requirements and skills needed for professional positions in economically developed countries — which stress a knowledge of human resources management and development, organizational psychology and market economy — before 1989, professional requirements consisted mostly of a high educational and technical expertise level in the field where the enterprise operates. There was a lack of knowledge about the more "human" and strategic aspects of business.

Regardless of the achievements of an enterprise, it was funded for political profit. In the new conditions, the state tends to withdraw from subsidizing losing enterprises. This makes it difficult for those in charge to make decisions about the future development of the enterprise. The large state economic organizations are ruled by boards, where younger people are included who are entering the sphere of market economy but don't have enough experience.

Management education is complex. Besides specialized knowledge about techniques and technologies of production, our new generation of leaders in Bulgaria has to be familiar with economics, market relations, personnel management, psychology, administration and documentation.

At the present time, knowledge in these fields is insufficient, and specific skills and experience are needed. Now in our country, secondary special schools in management are opening and some attempts are being made to broaden the programs about computer and information competency, foreign languages and human resource management. This kind of education is extended in economic high schools. Nevertheless, it is still insufficient as the Bulgarian teaching lecturers in these fields are few and many of these lecturers don't have much practical experience.

PERSONALITY AND LEADERSHIP

It is necessary to mention the role of personality traits in building up a leader and an effective manager. In many research studies of predictors of success, the following traits are some of those that were identified: intelligence, decisiveness, self-dependence, persuasiveness, decision-making skills, stress, tolerance, etc. Later it was found that it is not sufficient simply to possess these traits, but to demonstrate them in behaviour and have a leadership style able to be adapted to different situations.

Leaders have to be able to persuade other people to follow them in the performance of a certain task. The achievement of this purpose depends strongly on the ability of a leader to transmit his or her visions, goals and enthusiasm to the team.

Stoyneshka & Peev (1996) make a distinction between the terms "leadership" and "management." There are common characteristics for leadership and management, as both terms are connected with the categories of "influence" and "power."

The leader is usually a member of a group and he influences the behaviour of the other members. We may say that he is an informal leader. His authority is due to his personality traits. A manager is an officially nominated person who performs administration and organization of work; he is responsible for its successful realization and has to deliver the interests of the organization. He exercises power over his subordinates; it may be stated that he is a formal leader.

The best case is when the formal manager of an organization possesses the characteristics of an informal leader. This is not always possible, for the reason that a manager has to attract informal leaders and join them to work for the interests of the organization.

STYLES OF MANAGEMENT LEADERSHIP

A very important condition for a successful manager is to have an adequate style of management. The most adequate style of management is chosen in connection with the main functions of management, which are:

1) to organize, coordinate and regulate the basic processes of work,
2) to guide people with the aim of accomplishing organizational goals.

The style of management is revealed to a great extent in the process of human resource management. The style of a manager is expressed in: his approaches and means for achieving goals and resolving managerial tasks; his coordination between personal and common interests; and his interactions with the staff and with other managers. The style of management may be defined as a relatively stable individual configuration of management activity related to the personnel. It depends on some factors among which are the following:

1) some personality characteristics, such as authority, dominance, anxiety, sociability, aggressiveness, self-dependence, extroversion etc.;
2) knowledge and skills in management;
3) characteristics of work activity;
4) specificity of work situation;
5) specificity of the personalities, level of qualification and work experience.

As the style of management depends on so many factors, it may be supposed that there are different kinds of styles. Some theories differentiate particular styles according to different criteria.

According to the criteria for "way of decision-making," Kurt Lewin (1944) defines styles as authoritarian, democratic and liberal. It is assumed that the democratic style is acceptable, as the value of personality is highly respected in it. Subordinates have the right to take part in making managerial decisions. To what extent would democracy contribute to the success of the organization? This depends mainly on the characteristics of the personnel and also the work activity situation. From literature it is well known that the democratic style is highly effective with an educated and qualified personnel, while in the case where subordinates are without qualifications and experience, some elements of authoritarianism are needed.

The work situation is also important. In a crisis or war situation where the exact norms and rules are not well established, some elements of authoritarianism are imposed.

Fleishman (1953) defines styles of management according to "task-orientation" or "personnel-orientation." The so-called "managerial set" is created and, by using it, any manager may be appraised in the matrix of styles if we know his attitudes

▼▼▼▼▼▼▼▼▼▼▼▼▼▼▼▼▼▼▼▼▼▼

about work and about the people he guides. It is assumed that orientation to only one of the parameters leads to a one-sided ineffective style of management.

Likert (1967) defines four types of styles according to the attitudes towards subordinates:

1) exploitative, authoritarian;
2) friendly, authoritarian;
3) consultative;
4) participative or democratic.

According to this author, if the style of a manager develops from first to fourth, the organization is more effective and people in it are more satisfied.

In the so-called "contingency model" of Fiedler (1967), the style of management is effective when it fits the situation. Fiedler argues that a favourable situation is that in which: faith exists between people in the group; tasks are strictly defined; and the manager has the power to stimulate or sanction specific behaviours. Each manager, according to his personality characteristics, knowledge, experience and information uses a certain style of management. A manager who is able to change his style quickly and flexibly in accordance with the changes of the requirements of work environment is expected to be most effective.

At present, the specifics of the situation in Bulgaria are those of a crisis, related with uncertainty and rapid changes. These characteristics require flexibility. On one side, work morale is not on a high level, wages are very low and the system of stimulation does not function. On the other side, in most of the enterprises work qualified people who demand more democracy in their relationships with the managers. The lack of sufficient knowledge and experience about management, the unfavourable economic and political situation, and the rise of private business in a risk situation combine to create possibilities for using mainly an authoritarian style of management. This is the style directed mostly to task performance and achievement of the goals of the enterprise.

Much has to be done for improving the style of management in Bulgaria. It may start with appropriate education and with selection of managers who have to perform leading functions. An introduction of competition for the different levels of management would be useful. The main criteria for selection could be knowledge and communication skills, and besides that, ability to lead and influence subordinates, decision-making skills and persuasiveness. Education and training should be accomplished not only before holding a position, but also periodically during work.

TYPES OF LEADERS/MANAGERS

In connection with the level of management, and also with the kind of work activity, we define several types of managers: high level or top managers; medium level managers; and operative or primary managers.

1. Top managers (high level of management) rule a whole organization; they define its aims and strategies and present it to other organizations.
2. Managers on a medium level are responsible for the fulfillment of the decisions about politics and the strategy of the organization.
3. Operative managers rule and coordinate the activity of workers and employees. Managers from all the levels perform connections and coordination up and down, vertically as well as horizontally, in an organization and out of it. This requires good communication skills, which are very important in management activity as a whole. Every unit in the organization, depending on the object of activity, has its managers. There are managers with specific functions:

- managers in marketing who deal with the realization of the product of activity;
- financial managers who govern resources, investments and bookkeeping;
- production managers who create, organize and keep the systems of production;
- human resource managers who make appointments, and are in charge of selection and guide evaluation, stimulation, qualification and promotion of the personnel;
- managers in specialized fields, for example, organizing and leading research and development activity, external economic relations, etc.

These kinds of managers exist in bigger organizations. In the private enterprises, the different levels of management rarely exist. Usually the owner of the firm realizes all kinds of management activities.

The requirements towards managers are in connection with the specificity of their activity. I am not going to fix here on activities related to accounts, budget control, marketing, etc., which are not connected directly with guiding people. I intend to examine only some of the basic activities concerning personnel management.

The administrative function of management usually includes the following activities: inquiry, planning, organization, coordination and control. Armstrong (1993) widens this list including selection and education of employees, estimation and stimulation, leading relationships in a team, resolving conflicts, crises and problems, and organizing vertical communication. These activities are connected with influences that may increase or decrease work motivation. They may build up positive or negative attitudes towards the organization and loyalty or disloyalty to work goals and their fulfillment.

A manager should contribute to creating active work behaviour in his subordinates, to the qualifications of workers and formation of work habits, and last but not least, to maintaining overall health and productivity. By means of these influences on employees, a manager practically contributes or does not contribute to the fulfillment of organizational goals.

People who live and work in similar social conditions tend to demonstrate similar models of behaviour in many aspects. The influence of external factors on behaviour is indisputable, but it is refracted by a number of personality characteristics. In order to be of benefit to the organization, behaviour has to be in accordance with the organizational goals. Organizational goals are externally fixed and are predominantly economic: increasing of production; increasing of profit; and decreasing of expenses. The realization of these goals is done through effective use of all kinds of resources (financial, technical, technological and human).

The achievement of social goals in our situation practically remains in the background. This fact is in connection mainly with the lack of professionalism in management and also with the big economic crisis in Bulgaria. Managers and leaders do not realize that the creation of conditions that satisfy the needs of the subordinates, including professional realization, would contribute to higher work motivation and joining to organizational goals.

In order to work systematically for the achievement of these goals, a manager should know exactly the criteria for their attainment and should have the means to do it. Periodical examination of these criteria (including those that cannot be objectively evaluated) is one of the main tasks for a manager. The results of such examination should be made popular in order to motivate aspirations to achievement of certain standards.

Some managers confess that people work to satisfy their needs, but the fact that satisfaction of needs does not join them to organizational goals is not clearly realized. The most widespread opinion is that organizational goals should be higher than those of working people. Different goals are put together usually through sanctions. Most managers rely on the fact of high unemployment and that subordinates will agree to work for low wages.

In Bulgaria there is a weak relation between work outcomes and the stimulation for work motivation. The principle of wage levelling is a reality. People are paid for position, length of service and education. The extra pay for length of service and education is minimal. In cases of additional payment for the purpose of stimulation, the objective results are not fully considered. There are simply no other kinds of work stimulation except payment.

The organization of assessment and promotion is not on a high level. Now some organizations start seeking ways of constructing real criteria for assessment. Such a procedure still has not become a real means of influencing and managing work motivation. In most cases, assessment is done formally without any methodological and/or organizational preparation. It is known that nothing can decrease a willingness to work more than an unfair negative appraisal and ignoring one's contribution to common positive outcomes.

Regardless of the fact that in Bulgaria, the assessment procedure is well known, it is not done according to scientific requirements. Testing as a selection procedure for revealing important professional qualities is done only in cases of application for chauffeurs, engine drivers, aviators and operators in risky occupations.

The proper organization of communication processes is not a serious concern. These processes go chaotically, and managers are not prepared in advance for it. Very often, willingly or unconsciously, important information that may be useful for joining organizational goals is hidden. Information usually spreads downward — managers are not seeking feedback information. Training in communication skills for managers is rarely done. Most managers think they can do without it and under-

▼▼▼▼▼▼▼▼▼▼▼▼▼▼▼▼▼▼▼▼▼

estimate the usefulness of training programs. Younger managers are more interested in training, but very often they cannot go through it for financial reasons.

Career development is not considered to a needed extent. Career advancement may be done only in some specific institutions — for example, in universities and research institutes. Most managers ignore the importance of this activity. One reason for this may be job uncertainty for managers who often change their occupations. Promotion of managers is connected predominantly with private relations, with political uniformity, and not so much with real work outcomes or with competitions.

Many studies on organizational relationships reveal conflicts and dissatisfaction. In most cases, interactions on horizontal and vertical levels are sources of occupational stress. Managers in our country do not include resolving conflicts in their duties; on the other hand, they are not prepared enough to manage such kinds of problems.

It may be fairly concluded that the development of people is done to a great extent chaotically and it is not connected with the success of the organization. Having in mind that skills and qualities are normally spread in a given sample, we assume that there are managers (predominantly among younger people) who will show great interest towards personnel management. They would be aimed at individual education and specializations abroad.

PSYCHOLOGICAL STUDIES ON LEADERS/MANAGERS IN BULGARIA

The activity of managers working in state and in private firms differs in some aspects. K. Manolov (1995) studied work motivation of managers in private and in state firms. According to this author, economic motivation includes motives like, "make more money" and "be economically independent." Such motives prevail in 48.3 percent of managers studied. Motives of professional realization — "to develop professionally" and "to do appropriate work" — prevail in 50 percent of them. On a third place are motives of power — "to have influence on people" and "to make important decisions" — which are reported in 25.9 percent of subjects.

TABLE 1		
Parameters of Stress	**X**	**SD**
Job Satisfaction	3.741	0.337
Psychological Health	3.483	0.145
Physical Health	2.986	0.13
Type A behaviour	3.227	0.063
Locus of control	3.000	0.062
Sources of Stress	3.340	0.253
Coping strategies	4.372	0.173
Means and standard deviations of the parameters of occupational stress in managers		

Comparatively, economic motivation dominates in 85.2 percent of cases of managers from private firms. In managers from state firms, the motivation of professional realization predominates in 70.1 percent of cases. In both groups of managers, power motivation is in third place. The fact that managers of private firms (who often are the owners) demonstrate economic motivation may be explained by the aim to acquire private property, which gives stability, freedom and certainty. Managers in state firms usually see their future in their career development. They consider management activity as a basis for higher incomes. These managers hold power without having private property, and so logically, they are aimed at having a big career.

From all written above, it becomes clear that management as professional activity is very complex, complicated, responsive and to a great extent, risky. It is connected with many different kinds of contacts with people, with decision-making under the restraints of a time deficit and/or without enough information, and with persuasion and administration. If we add the heavy economic situation and the unfavourable framework on the macro level in which manager's work in Bulgaria, we may suppose that their activity is connected with many stress situations. In work and organizational psychology, the so-called managerial stress is studied.

A study on stress was made which includes ninety managers from economic organizations. The Occupational Stress Indicator (OSI) was used, a method proposed by C.L. Cooper which has a Bulgarian version (Russinova & Vassileva 1994). Some parameters of the model of occupational stress indicate relatively high scores (see Table 1).

▼▼▼▼▼▼▼▼▼▼▼▼▼▼▼▼▼▼▼▼▼▼

Parameters	Managers on high level		Managers on medium level		F	P
TABLE 2						
	X	SD	X	SD		
Job Satisfaction	25.93	5.57	22.58	5.40	5.66	0.02
Satisfaction with the organization	22.00	6.58	17.65	5.49	7.74	0.05
Health	61.21	9.45	66.24	10.16	3.92	0.05
Locus of control	15.00	2.92	16.51	2.21	5.15	0.02
Workload	17.96	5.30	21.10	6.33	4.42	0.03
Control as coping	29.50	3.98	26.79	4.47	6.26	0.01

Mean scores, standard deviations and statistical significance of difference in evaluation of the parameters of occupational stress between managers of high and medium level

Results on job satisfaction and coping with stress are of special interest. Managers studied show high job satisfaction and think that they successfully use different ways of coping with stress. Most often they use "control over the situation" and "support seeking" as coping strategies. At the same time, the evaluation of physical health has a lower position on the scale. This is connected with the great strain in working in unfavourable conditions (Russinova 1998).

There is a difference between managers on high and medium levels in the evaluation of different parameters of stress (Table 2).

The sample* consists of 248 Managers (151 men and 97 women) at the high and medium levels. Those at the high level are participants in a managerial board of directors and executive managers, while the medium level are those managers who are technical experts or run different branches of the organization. The analysis of variance is used for statistical interpretation of the results. The evaluations of the parameters of stress are more unfavourable in managers of medium level.

TABLE 3		
Value Dimensions	X	SD
Individualism	3.020	1.980
Power Distance	3.440	2.060
Masculinity	3.070	2.370
Future Orientation	2.850	1.670
Uncertainty Avoidance	2.870	1.440
Means and standard deviations of value dimensions in Bulgarian managers		

TABLE 4				
Parameters of values and stress	Men M (N = 51)	Women M (N = 26)	F	P
Individualism	11.63	10.77	3.18	0.07
Job Satisfaction	23.65	21.63	4.37	0.01
Satisfaction with organization	21.57	18.94	3.18	0.00
Personal responsibility	28.58	30.70	2.02	0.04
Gender differences for individualism, satisfaction with organization and personal responsibility				

An interesting issue concerns values revealed in a group of managers studied (Russinova 1998). Hofstede's theory of values and culture and his method were used (Hofstede 1980). The results on value dimensions are presented on Table 3.

Power distance, individualism and masculinity are more clearly expressed than the other value dimensions. Managers are probably aimed at being more independent, which is one of the basic requirements to them. Future orientation is also significant for the profession but it is connected with a close perspective. These tendencies are regarded as typical characteristics for different groups studied in Bulgaria. Nevertheless, it is not desirable for managers as it is connected with working more for oneself than with working for others and for the society. Management work very often demands ignoring private interests and taking risks. I would not like to assume that most of our managers are aimed only to their career making.

L. Vassileva (1998) reveals the level of expression of the value dimensions according to Hofstede (Table 4).

▼▼▼▼▼▼▼▼▼▼▼▼▼▼▼▼▼▼▼▼▼▼▼

The results presented on Table 4 indicate that significant differences between men and women in values exist only in individualism, where men have higher scores. An interesting fact is that men are more satisfied with their work and with the organization than women. It is necessary to note that women managers have higher personal responsibility. Very often women are unfairly underestimated in their work regardless of the work outcomes.

A CROSS-CULTURAL COMPARISON ON PERSONALITY CHARACTERISTICS AND ON THE PARAMETERS OF OCCUPATIONAL STRESS IN MANAGERS

In the framework of a large cross-cultural study of values to Hofstede's theory and of the parameters of occupational stress according to Cooper's model, 248 Bulgarian managers and 330 Japanese managers were studied. In Bulgaria, the study was done by a research group from the Institute of Psychology, Bulgarian Academy of Sciences, and was directed by Dr. Vesselina Russinova; in Japan it was done in the University of Nara City under the guidance of Professor Satoru Shima. The same research methods were used in both studies. The aim of the comparative study was to outline the parameters of stress that may depend on cultural traditions and on work conditions that exist in both countries. The results are shown on Tables 5 and 6.

From the results it is clear that more hassles exist in the Bulgarian organizations. However, the Japanese managers also have stressors in their occupations, experiencing to a comparatively higher extent personal responsibility, home/work balance and the managerial role as stressors than Bulgarian managers. The latter evaluate their job satisfaction significantly higher. This result may indicate that creating work organization in leadership positions is not as high of a demand for Bulgarian managers. Interestingly, they more often use control to cope with stress.

As it is shown on Table 6, Bulgarian managers who prefer a bigger power distance apparently insist more on their independence than the Japanese do. Bulgarian managers also demonstrate comparatively higher individualism and masculinity. Japanese managers show higher uncertainty avoidance, drive, impatience and internal locus of control. These characteristics undoubtedly contribute to their work.

TABLE 5						
Parameters of Stress	Bulgarian Managers		Japanese Managers		T	P
	M	SD	M	SD		
Sources of Stress:						
Workload	20.36	5.912	21.73	5.21	3.17	0.002
Home/Work Balance	18.01	6.61	20.38	4.85	4.70	0.000
Managerial Role	12.32	3.56	13.04	3.05	2.62	0.000
Personal Responsibility	14.15	4.05	15.21	3.52	3.42	0.001
Hassles	13.50	3.90	12.64	3.13	2.93	0.004
Coping Control	27.79	4.86	23.54	3.97	11.71	0.000
Job Satisfaction	25.18	5.19	22.43	5.49	6.17	0.000

Differences on the parameters of occupational stress between groups of Bulgarian and Japanese managers (only significant differences are presented)

TABLE 6						
Characteristics	Managers		Managers		T	P
	M	SD	M	SD		
Power Distance	13.77	2.06	10.056	2.04	21.66	0.000
Future Orientation	11.73	1.67	11.64	2.35	—	—
Individualism	12.09	1.98	8.88	2.44	11.72	0.000
Masculinity	12.28	2.37	9.90	1.99	13.31	0.000
Uncertainty Avoidance	11.98	1.44	13.38	1.86	13.39	0.000
Type A						
Impatience	9.67	3.51	11.14	2.44	8.02	0.000
Drive	8.86	3.30	11.59	2.59	11.44	0.000
Locus of control	48.10	8.81	58.56	6.51	16.38	0.000

Significant differences on personal characteristics between Bulgarian and Japanese managers

▼▼▼▼▼▼▼▼▼▼▼▼▼▼▼▼▼▼▼▼▼▼

The studies presented are fractional and they do not give a complete image of the Bulgarian manager in the period of economic and social transition. Nevertheless, these studies demonstrate the tendencies of the unfavourable interactions between the crisis situation and some characteristics of managers. The way out of the heavy economic crisis is not only through changing the conditions — economic and financial — but also through improving competency and the style of management.

Note that some changes in the results on the tables are due to the larger sample that we investigated.

Let us now explore a more specific setting for an application of leadership theory within Bulgaria. Leadership will be examined within the Bulgarian secondary school system.

SCHOOL LEADERSHIP, TYPE AND VALUES

The Bulgarian secondary education continues the tradition typical for the Bulgarian national revival, and provides serious and profound knowledge. According to Bulgarian laws, the students are given equal chances of getting a free secondary education. Now, new ways for gradual reorientation of the Bulgarian school are sought which will for modern market relations and civil society. Specific steps are taken in this direction, such as the restoration of school boards of trustees, the competitive selection of school principals and the development of school autonomy. However, the radical social, economic and political changes that developed recently in Bulgaria affect significantly the school as an institution. The accompanying demographic collapse, immigration and urbanization and the economic and spiritual crisis yielded a slowing of educational progress. Hence schools are to be closed and teachers are to be discharged due to the decreasing number of students. In addition, the equipment is poor and some schools break up for irregular holidays, since central heating of the classrooms has been cut. All this outlines a growing tendency of students leaving schools, and the motivation for learning and teaching is decreasing.

Note that the Bulgarian school inherited an authoritarian, centralized and strongly ideologized structure, being typical for the totalitarian regime. However, in contrast to its high quality, our secondary education system has a serious defect, that is, the process of learning emphasizes memorization whereas knowledge itself is somewhat abstract in character. So, it does not focus enough on living reality and does not pay enough attention to students' emotions and creativity. The Law of People's Education arranges the autonomy of the Bulgarian school, but there is disparity between this lawful act and the legislative norms at lower levels. Thus, the law seems to be practically senseless, since its application is hampered. All these failures, together with the low payment, explain the lack of school principal candidates and a number of posts remain vacant.

The school management is a process, directed toward the achievement of educational goals by using an effective and efficient planning. It should organize, lead and control human, physical, financial and informational resources. To realize such an activity, the principal makes numerous and highly varied professional contacts with social and occupational groups of different kinds and structures. Those are students, educational and administrative personnel, superior bodies, parents and the public. The specific characteristics of his professional activity prove that the principal's communications are of the highest frequency, as compared to those of other occupational groups, engaged in education. Hence, his professional roles are within wide ranges. The activation, integration and direction of the school personnel's efforts to achieve the general goals of education link with leadership, since it is one of the basic functions of management.

LEADERSHIP AND LEADERSHIP STYLE

As one of the basic management functions, school leadership means motivation of and influence on the school staff in order to achieve the educational goals.

Considering the fifty-year-old tradition of an authoritarian leadership style, the Bulgarian teachers developed a strong necessity of dependence, expressed in their expectations that someone else should be responsible for their activities. On the other hand, "communication with the superiors" is one of the most frequently shared deficits when identifying the problems of teachers' professional interactions in the course of their in-service training. This "problem with the authority" is typical for them (Pencheva 1993).

There are no specialized schools for graduate training of education management in Bulgaria. There is an in-service training in the Sofia University, where the principals gain qualification in educational management by attending different courses. They get knowledge on leadership and motivation in classes on psychology. They also participate in group-dynamic training for developing respective attitudes and interpersonal skills. Principals find this part of the training as the most interesting, because as they debate amongst themselves, the training gives them new ideas for interpretation, understanding and accepting the relationships at school. They are also very deeply impressed by the practical techniques for dealing with people. So the participants are highly motivated to acquire theoretical and technological competence which, corresponding to the specific situation, would enable them to realize appropriate leader's behavior. At the same time, they are so strongly accustomed to control-oriented behaviour, that they cannot easily accept new more people-oriented approaches. When discussing case studies or taking part in simulating games, a great number of the participants are more inclined to prefer directive and manipulative leadership styles, regardless of the situation. Moreover, they look for various arguments and explanations to justify and promote them, referring to the Bulgarian cultural context.

For instance, B. L., a long-term principal of a school in the town of P., explained during a training course for group decision-making that he always knew the right solution of any particular problem in his school. So he posed the question in a group discussion and floated very carefully his idea, using his authority to direct the teachers to it. Then he encouraged them to articulate the solution, convincing them that they had generated it by themselves and pretending that he accepted the idea because of their solid arguments. Similarly P. R., a teacher from Sofia, shared how his boss used to propose an idea to one or several members of the pedagogical staff. He then persuaded them to claim during the personnel meeting that the idea was their own, thus simulating a democratic decision-making.

Although highly qualified, school managers are still deeply attached to the ideology of control that was pervasive among the educational administration. The majority of them apply authoritarian and directive leadership styles, corresponding to their beliefs, pre-service education and cultural patterns. The principals' behaviour today might be characterized on one hand as an interesting and very controversial mixture of ambitions to acquire modern human technologies, and on the other hand as different acts of resistance towards them. This is a natural and understandable reaction, considering the transition conditions in Bulgaria. One may generalize the reasons for resistance of the school leaders toward change as follows:

1. The principals cannot still fully believe that more democratic relations between them and other participants of the education process could be successful in today's Bulgaria. They claim that Bulgarian national psy chology, as well as the global crisis of the society, demands a strong hand inschool management

2. Although aware of the theoretical differences between democratic and liberal leadership style, the principals tend to equalize both of them when interpreting case studies, so they worry that the application of a democratic leadership style may disturb the order and discipline at school.

3. It seems that certain principals are unaware of their real professional behaviors and their influence over the school climate. They declare and seem to be deeply convinced that their own leadership style is people-oriented.

4. Some trend to manipulative behaviors exists, but the administrators tend to interpret them as a participative leadership style, using very well "particpatory rhetoric." This yields the declared belief that they have a competence and could apply different and situational specific leadership styles in practice.

Obviously, such a resistance is based on several factors-principals' low tolerance to uncertainty, the indefiniteness and complexity of the problems and barriers that the transition period states, and principals' fear that they could not succeed to satisfy modern requirements and could lose their influence. As part of a greater study, we assess how those observations on school administrators refer to their personality characteristics.

PSYCHOLOGICAL TYPOLOGY OF SCHOOL PRINCIPALS

The Myers-Briggs Type Indicator, based on Jung's theory of psychological type, is one of the most popular instruments, administered for studying the relationship between vocational choice and personality differences. It is comprised of four dichotomous scales that address certain personality preferences. Those are:

Extraversion (E) – Introversion (I)
Sensing (S) – Intuition (N)
Thinking (T) – Feeling (F)
Judging (J) – Perceiving (P)

Many researchers find specific personality characteristics among school principals, when considering them as a category. Most often Judging is indicated as typical for them (Myers & Myers 1993, Di Tiberio 1996). Other publications outline the combination of Sensing and Judging (Meisgeier et al. 1996). Myers and McCaulley (1985) conclude that administrators at all levels of the educational system prefer Thinking and Judging. We find similar data in many other researches (Gardner & Martinko 1996). The psychological pattern ESTJ is outlined as a modal type of the school principals (Hoffman 1986). It is interesting to see what is the type distribution among Bulgarian educational administration. Is there any cultural specificity of our school principals or do they demonstrate similar personality preferences as colleagues in other countries? To test this hypothesis, we examined by the MBTI (Form G) a sample consisting of 88 school principals. We compared the sample with two other groups. One of them was a general Bulgarian population — 256 persons, including students at high school, students at the university studying different subjects, and people with different occupations. The other one is comprised of 276 principals from the CAPT database.

Comparison with the Bulgarian general sample. Table 1.a,b gives Selection Ratio Type Table (SRTT) analysis. Consistent with the cited research, the principals' sample is overwhelmingly more Sensing (I = 1.74), more Thinking (I = 1.44) and more Judging (I = 1.69), all of them at the p = < 0.001 level of significance. Those data are relevant to the findings that the preferences for Sensing, Thinking and Judging are typical for managers at different levels and organizations, and that one may characterize nowadays the "managerial culture" in type terms with these three preferences. One may also describe it as practical and results-oriented (Walck 1997). It is interesting to find that school managers are more Introverted than the general population, although the difference is not statistically significant.

Source of data	Group	MBTI Type Table
Bulgarian school principals	Tabulated	Center for Applications of Psychological Type.
	88 school principals	Legend: % = percent of total choosing this group who fall into this type.
	N = 88	I = Self-selection index; Ratio of percent of type in group to % in sample

					N	%	I
				E	44	50.00	0.96
ISTJ *	ISFJ	INFJ	INTJ	I	44	50.00	1.04
				S	61	69.32	1.74 *
N = 29	N = 0	N = 1	N = 12	N	27	30.68	0.51 *
% =32.95	%= 0.00	% =1.14	% =13.64	T	84	95.45	1. 44 *
I = 2.34	I = 0.00	I = 0.22	I = 1.40	F	4	4.55	0.14 *
				J	84	95.45	1.69 *
				P	4	4.55	0.10 *
ISTP	ISFP	INFP "	INTP	I J	42	47.73	1.53 #
				I P	2	2.27	0.14 *
N = 1	N = 0	N = 0	N = 1	E P	2	2.27	0.09 *
% =1.14	%= 0.00	% = 0.00	% = 1.14	E J	42	47.73	1.88 *
I = 0.32	I = 0.00	I = 0.00	I = 0.22	S T	60	68.18	2.18 *
				S F	1	1.14	0.13 "
				N F	3	3.41	0.14 *
ESTP	ESFP	ENFP #	ENTP #	N T	24	27.27	0.78
				S J	58	65.91	2.45 *
N = 1	N = 1	N = 0	N = 0	S P	3	3.41	0.26 "
% = 1.14	% = 1.14	% = 0.00	% = 0.00	N P	1	1.14	0.04 *
I = 0.22	I = 0.58	I = 0.00	I = 0.00	N J	26	29.55	1.0
				T J	81	92.05	2.14 *
				T P	3	3.41	0.15 *
ESTJ	ESFJ	ENFJ	ENTJ	F P	1	1.14	0.06 *
				F J	3	3.41	0.25 #
N = 29	N = 0	N = 2	N = 11	I N	14	15.91	0.62
% = 32.95	% = 0.00	% = 2.27	% = 12.50	E N	13	14.77	0.43 *
I = 3.83	I = 0.00	I = 0.53	I = 1.19	I S	30	34.09	1.53 "
				E S	31	35.23	2.00 *

Note concerning symbols following the selection ratios:
" implies significance at the .05 level, i.e. Chi-square > 3.8;
implies significance at the .01 level, i.e. Chi-square > 6.6;
* implies significance at the .001 level, i.e. Chi-square > 10.8.
_ (underscore) indicates Fischer's exact probability used instead of Chi-square.
Base population used in calculating selection ratios;
Bulgarian general population
Base total N = 256. Sample and base are independent.

TYPE DISTRIBUTION OF BULGARIAN SCHOOL PRINCIPALS AND SRTT COMPARISON WITH THE GENERAL BULGARIAN SAMPLE

▼▼▼▼▼▼▼▼▼▼▼▼▼▼▼▼▼▼▼▼▼▼▼

TABLE 1b

* * * * Calculated values of Chi-square or Fischer's exact probability * * * *

Type table order

				E	0.1000	IJ	7.7685	SJ	42.6742	IN	3.5761
15.2518	0.2067	0.1280	1.0222	I	0.1000	IP	0.0004	SP	0.0139	EN	12.1329
				S	22.8195	EP	0.0000	NP	0.0000	IS	4.8468
0.3091	0.2067	0.0282	0.1280	N	22.8195	EJ	15.2470	NJ	0.0006	ES	11.8517
				T	0.0000	ST	37.0104	TJ	63.8715		
0.1280	0.6963	0.0034	0.0034	F	0.0000	SF	0.0227	TP	0.0000		
				J	0.0000	NF	0.0000	FP	0.0000		
30.7770	0.3341	0.5280	0.2542	P	0.0000	NT	1.8369	FJ	0.0092		

TYPE DISTRIBUTION OF BULGARIAN SCHOOL PRINCIPALS AND SRTT COMPARISON WITH THE GENERAL BULGARIAN SAMPLE

According to Table 1, TJ (93 percent) and SJ (66 percent) are clearly the modal administrators' preferences in this sample. People with the preferences to the first pair are known in literature as "logical decision makers," and those with preferences to the second combination — as "realistic decision makers."

Note that two psychological types are over-represented among school head-masters — ESTJ (I = 3.83; p < 0.001) and ISTJ (I = 2.34; p < 0.001). This result is consistent with the cited researches on such a contingent. Note also that the absolute numbers in the two types are equal, but the ratios are different. There is a fact of special interest: six types are missing in the principals' sample — ISFJ, ISFP, INFP, ENFP, ENTP, ESFP — and five of them are Feeling types. For three of the types, there are statistically significant differences from the general population. Those are the Intuitive types — INFP (p < 0.05), ENFP and ENTP (p < 0.01). Review some of the characteristics of the two types that are most frequently found among our educational administration. The first one is ESTJ. Those are people who tend to be practical, realistic, matter-of-fact, decisive and quick to implement decisions. They organize projects and people to get things done, focus on getting results in the most efficient way possible and take care of routine details. They often have a clear set of logical standards, systematically follow them and want others to also, and may be forceful in implementing their plans. The second one is ISTJ. Those people are known as quiet, serious, earning success by thoroughness and dependability. They tend to be practical, matter-of-fact, realistic and responsible. They decide logically what should be done and work toward it steadily, regardless of distractions. They often take pleasure in making everything orderly and organized — work, home and life. They value traditions and loyalty (Myers et al. 1998, p. 64).

Intuition is the common feature of the three underrepresented types. This function is connected with perceiving patterns, interrelations and envisioning future possibilities. Feeling is the function characterizing two of them. It is connected with warmth, sympathy and consideration of people's needs.

Comparison with the principals' group from the CAPT base data. Selection Ratio Type Table analysis (SRTT) points out that the two samples are similar to one another as a whole, but at the same time they could be differentiated in terms of some typological characteristics (Table 2.a.b). Bulgarian principals are more Thinking (I = 1.23; p < 0.001) and Judging (I = 1.12; p < 0.001), than their

▼▼▼▼▼▼▼▼▼▼▼▼▼▼▼▼▼▼▼▼▼▼

foreign colleagues. Very impressive is the significant difference between the two samples for the TJ dimension (I = 1.31; p < 0.001). This ratio is due to the fact that all four types in this group are more frequent among Bulgarians. Note that they are significantly underrepresented in ISFJ and ESFJ (p < 0.05), which are actually vacant. The brief description of the two missing types is the following:

> ISFJs tend to be quiet, friendly, responsible and conscientious. They are committed and steady in meeting their obligations, and are often thorough, painstaking, accurate, loyal and considerate, frequently noticing and remembering specifics about people who are important to them. They are concerned with how others feel and strive to create an orderly and harmonious environment at work and at home.
>
> ESFJs tend to be warm-hearted, conscientious and cooperative, and want harmony in their environment, working with determination to establish it. They like to work with others to complete tasks accurately and on time, and tend to be doggedly loyal, following through even in small matters. They notice what others need in their day-by-day lives and try to provide it. They want to be appreciated for who they are and what they contribute (Myers et al., p. 64).

We may conclude that as a whole, Bulgarian school principals possess the common preferences, typical for managers in general, and in particular for school managers in other countries — they are overwhelmingly STJ and predominantly ESTJ and ISTJ. This was confirmed by the comparison with the general Bulgarian population. At the same time we may note that in spite of these similarities, Bulgarian principals differ from their foreign colleagues in a specific aspect. What is it?

Source of data	Group	MBTI Type Table
Bulgarian principals	Tabulated	Center for Applications of Psychological Type.
Data from CAPT	Bulgarian principals	Legend: % = percent of total choosing this group who fall into this type.
Atlas, p. 231	N = 88	I = Self-selection index; Ratio of percent of type in group to % in sample

					N	%	I
				E	44	50.00	0.97
ISTJ	**ISFJ** $\underline{\ }$	**INFJ**	**INTJ**	I	44	50.00	1.04
				S	61	69.32	0.98
N = 29	N = 0	N = 1	N = 12	N	27	30.68	1.05
% =32.95	%= 0.00	% =1.14	% =13.64	T	84	95.45	1.23 $\underline{*}$
I = 1.30	I = 0.00	I = 0.52	I = 1.57	F	4	4.55	0.20 $\underline{*}$
				J	84	95.45	1.12 $\underline{\ }$
				P	4	4.55	0.31 $\underline{\ }$
ISTP	**ISFP**	**INFP**	**INTP**	I J	42	47.73	1.17
				I P	2	2.27	0.31
N = 1	N = 0	N = 0	N = 1	E P	2	2.27	0.30
% =1.14	%= 0.00	% = 0.00	% = 1.14	E J	42	47.73	1.08
I = 0.45	I = 0.00	I = 0.00	I = 1.05	S T	60	68.18	1.21 "
				S F	1	1.14	0.08 $\underline{*}$
				N F	3	3.41	0.43
ESTP	**ESFP**	**ENFP**	**ENTP**	N T	24	27.27	1.28
				S J	58	65.91	1.07
N = 1	N = 1	N = 0	N = 0	S P	3	3.41	0.38
% = 1.14	% = 1.14	% = 0.00	% = 0.00	N P	1	1.14	0.20
I = 0.52	I = 0.63	I = 0.00	I = 0.00	N J	26	29.55	1.25
				T J	81	92.05	1.31 *
				T P	3	3.41	0.47
ESTJ *	**ESFJ** $\underline{\ }$	**ENFJ**	**ENTJ**	F P	1	1.14	0.15 $\underline{\ }$
				F J	3	3.41	0.23 #
N = 29	N = 0	N = 2	N = 11	I N	14	15.91	1.22
% = 32.95	% = 0.00	% = 2.27	% = 12.50	E N	13	14.77	0.91
I = 1.26	I = 0.00	I = 0.90	I = 1.23	I S	30	34.09	0.97
				E S	31	35.23	0.99

Note concerning symbols following the selection ratios:

" implies significance at the .05 level, i.e. Chi-square > 3.8;

\# implies significance at the .01 level, i.e. Chi-square > 6.6;

* implies significance at the .001 level, i.e. Chi-square > 10.8.

_ (underscore) indicates Fischer's exact probability used instead of Chi-square.

Base population used in calculating selection rations; Principals—CAPT; Base total N = 276. Sample and base are independent.

Type distribution of Bulgarian school principals and SRTT comparison with principals from the CAPT database

▼▼▼▼▼▼▼▼▼▼▼▼▼▼▼▼▼▼▼▼▼▼▼

TABLE 2b

* * * * Calculated values of Chi-square or Fischer's exact probability * * * *
    Type table order

				E	0.0877	IJ	1.2565	SJ	0.5308	IN	0.4624
1.9425	0.0439	0.6892	1.8277	I	0.0877	IP	0.1217	SP	0.1071	EN	0.1169
				S	0.0569	EP	0.0814	NP	0.0840	IS	0.0326
0.6855	0.2028	0.5811	1.0000	N	0.0569	EJ	0.3348	NJ	1.2789	ES	0.0023
				T	0.0002	ST	3.9889	TJ	17.0967		
0.6892	1.0000	0.3425	0.5761	F	0.0002	SF	0.0009	TP	0.2228		
				J	0.0144	NF	0.1564	FP	0.0358		
1.5697	0.0267	1.0000	0.3869	P	0.0144	NT	1.3177	FJ	0.0041		

Type distribution of Bulgarian school principals and
SRTT comparison with principals from the CAPT database

Obviously, our school leaders prefer more frequently TJ than FP in comparison to the same professionals from CAPT's research. Both underrepresented types are SFJ. It means, in other words, that our sample confirms the established tendency that the position of school administrator is not very attractive for the people with F preference. Moreover, it seems that this tendency is stronger for Bulgaria in comparison to other studied countries. As Myers and McCaulley (1985) suppose, the tough-minded TJ types among the school administrators at all levels of the educational system can easily become so caught up in the technical aspects of administration, that they overlook the importance of a) creating structures that facilitate communication and teamwork, and b) recognizing and appreciating contributions of faculty in the daily stresses of coping with school tasks.

According to our findings, this trend is stronger among the Bulgarian executive educators, because the TJ configuration is more concentrated in their group in comparison to the same professionals in other countries. It means that we may think about certain Bulgarian specificity in this sample — an issue that could be confirmed or rejected by further research.

The global picture of the examined type distribution of the Bulgarian school principals shows that they all have natural predispositions for fulfilling effectively task-relevant activities. In order to become real contemporary change agents in the Bulgarian school, they have to pay much more attention to so the called "needs and relationship oriented behaviour" and to a future oriented behaviour. The principals may succeed in this field not only through the development of their own personal competence in those areas. They may also involve more teachers with preferences to Feeling and Intuition in a shared leadership, being necessary for the school democratization.

SCHOOL PRINCIPALS' VALUE PROFILE

Bulgaria's schools advance their mission of spirited growth by combining tradition and innovation. A balance between those two parts of human experience is extremely difficult to achieve in the modern age of informational exchange. The economic, social and political crises in Bulgaria are accompanied in addition by a total values crisis. It is expressed by the existence of a "value vacuum" and by the introduction of aggressive and consuming behavioral patterns in the social space.

Such a moral cataclysm, occurring in the mass consciousness, affects quite dramatically the Bulgarian educators. This is so, since moral norms involved in their educational activity play the role of professional norms, too. Being already rejected, the socialist principles are not applied in the Bulgarian educational system now. However, a new ordered ethic system of rules for professional behaviour, bound to replace those principles, still lacks. Thus, a confusion of educators' professional standards occurs. The school's personnel are not able to meet such a challenge and its productivity suffers seriously.

Principals are key figures in the process of humanization and democratization of the Bulgarian school. They are to transform themselves into change agents, which means that they should, first of all, change their own values, attitudes and beliefs. The present study aims at establishing the actual state of school principals' value preferences, studying 112 executives — eighty-nine women and twenty-three men aged from 21 to 54. The principals have previously undergone a group-dynamic training in the Central Institute for In-Service Teacher Training at the University of Sofia in the period 1994–1996 (Pencheva 1998).

Since modern methods of studying the value orientation have limited capabilities of perceiving the hidden motives of behaviour, we orient our study to the use of a simulation game, which plays part of a project test. The idea is prompted by the principal's expressed strive for socially desirable behaviour (Pencheva 1988). We apply the simulation game in the course of leadership skill training. The game consists of solving a moral dilemma under a catastrophic situation. The studied principal should choose six out of ten objects and human beings that could survive after a demolishing world war and give mankind a new lease of life. The process of decision-making develops in two stages — an individual decision and group decision, made after achieving a consensus.

The results show that principals at an individual and at a group level, chose values such as universality, benevolence and achievement, and reject values inherent to categories such as power, hedonism and stimulation, following the classification of Schwartz (Schwartz 1992). This enables one to determine the principal's general value orientation as being humanistic. However, note a specific fact within such a frame: that principals, both in their personal and group decisions, separate the couple in love included in the list, despite the lovers' definite desire to remain together. One may explain this fact by the principals' inclination to subordinate the interests of the minority to those of the majority and may interpret the result as a "collectivism-dimension," described by Triandis (1996). On the other hand, the fact that they demonstrate a willingness to overcome their ethnic prejudices for the sake of consensus achievement can be interpreted as developing in several directions. One of them is the choice of a biological criterion, which means a shift towards more masculine values (Hofstede 1991). Another direction is that toward a socially desirable behaviour, as discussed above. Here it is prompted by the ethnic tolerance, loudly proclaimed in Bulgaria. This norm is especially important for the professional behaviour of the educational personnel. The third direction is the real presence of tolerance for and pluralistic attitude to differences. It seems elementary to reduce the moral choice to one of these three logical constructions. It is obvious that all three analyzed tendencies determine the value choice, but one or another of them would prevail with different individuals.

The comparison between principals and teachers may provide an additional feature of the present value profile. Teachers' preferences can be rather determined as shifted towards the "feminine values" pole of the "masculinity-femininity" dimension. The fact that teachers, unlike principals, display a humanistic approach when dealing with young people's fate, thus showing a stronger devotion to individualistic values, deserves special attention. Hence, when solving moral dilemmas in a catastrophic situation, principals tend more to control-oriented behaviour than teachers.

A correlation between principals' value profile at an individual level and some socio-demographic characteristics is sought. Such characteristics are gender, age, work place, length of service (general and educational), subject level and level taught.

The effect of factor "gender." We study eighty-nine women and twenty-three men. The correlation between the two samples, based on this characteristic, is high ($\tau = 0.84$). The differences result from the fact that men appear to be more devoted to values, such as charity and intelligence, and have no ethnic prejudices, while women appear to accept motherhood and sexual freedom but reject a person of another ethnic group. Such a picture cannot be uniquely analyzed but proves the existence of differences in value standards when concerning gender.

▼▼▼▼▼▼▼▼▼▼▼▼▼▼▼▼▼▼▼▼▼▼

The effect of factor "age." Regarding this characteristic, the principals are divided into three groups: first group, up to the age of 30; second group, aged between 31 and 40; third group, aged between 41 and 50. Note that the strongest correlation exists between the first and second group ($\tau = 0.9$). Table 3 shows the dependence between the second and the third group ($\tau = 0.86$) and finally, the correlation between the first and the third group ($\tau = 0.85$).

The greatest difference is that between the youngest and the oldest studied persons. Hence, based on the age factor, a certain dynamic of principals' values may emerge. It shows that the value orientation of the studied principals significantly varies with age. This is expressed in the gradual decrease of the ethnic tolerance, until its entire absence in the group of the oldest principals. However, note the increase of female presence in the group of chosen candidates, the humanization of the attitude to younger people and the stronger respect for the value, "love."

The effect of factor "work place." Here the studied persons are divided into two groups — eighty-nine people working in town and nineteen in village. The ranking correlation between the choices of members of those groups is very high ($\tau = 0.96$). Although weak, the differences show a more humanistic orientation in principals of town schools as compared to those managing village schools.

The effect of factor "educational qualification." The examined participants are divided into two groups with respect to this characteristic — eighty-four persons with higher and twenty-eight persons with lower educational qualification. The ranking correlation between the answers of the members of these groups

TABLE 3	
Age	**Number of Participants**
Up to 30 (1st group)	19
31–40 (2nd group)	58
41–50 (3rd group)	35
Total	112
Distribution of participants regarding factor "age"	

shows significant differences (τ = 0.70). The principals with higher education accept sexual freedom and ethnic differences, but parallel to this, tend to control the behaviour of young people. Unlikely, principals with lower education display a humanistic approach to others and respect religious values. Considering Bulgarian people, this fact, however, is extremely interesting to note, since during the last fifty years, the Communist regime rejected religion. Obviously, the head-teachers with lower educational level turn to the church moral principles. It means that they are going to rely on religious norms during a situation of spiritual crisis.

The effect of factor "length of service." Here the effect of general and educational length of service is sought, while the studied persons are divided into three groups: first group, up to sixteen years of length of service; second group, service length of six to fifteen years; and third group, service length of sixteen to twenty-five years. The sample does not include principals with larger service length.

A. General length of service. The correlation analysis shows that a relatively high relation exists between the first and the second group (τ = 0.72). The relation between the second and the third group slightly increases (τ = 0.76), while that between the first and the third group significantly decreases (τ= 0.61). See Table 4 below.

Hence, the most significant is the difference between the value choices of principals with general service length up to five years and of principals with length of service sixteen to twenty-five years. What does this difference prove? Principals with the shortest experience rather prefer values of "masculine" type, as well as a

TABLE 4	
General length of service	Number of Participants
up to 5 years (1st group)	8
6–15 years (2nd group)	58
16–25 years (3rd group)	46
Total	112

Distribution of the studied contingent with respect to the general length of service

▼▼▼▼▼▼▼▼▼▼▼▼▼▼▼▼▼▼▼▼▼▼▼

dominant and control oriented approach, when dealing with other people's fate. On the contrary, principals with the longest experience are rather oriented towards feminine values and are inclined to respect young people's personal interests. Probably the longer service moderates some authoritarian role tendencies or increases the striving for socially desirable choices.

B. Educational length of service. Regarding this characteristic, the studied contingent is divided as follows in Table 5.

Here the differences between separate groups are much more expressed. The correlation analysis shows that the relation between the first and the third group is comparatively high (τ = 0.78). However, note that the other dependencies are moderate. So, for the second and third group, τ = 0.67, and for the first and third groups, its value significantly decreases and becomes τ = 0.53. Hence, principals with the longest educational service differ significantly from the principals with the shortest length of service.

How could these results be interpreted? The increase of educational service length yields a decrease of principals' affinity to other ethnic groups and to a non-standard sexual behaviour. The choices in the group with the longest service are characterized by feminine presence, humanistic attitude towards the young couple and their love, as well as a turn to religious values.

The effect of factors "subject matter and level taught." Regarding this factor, the principals are divided into three groups: the first group consists of persons

TABLE 5	
Educational length of service	**Number of participants**
up to 5 years (1st group)	33
6–15 years (2nd group)	53
16–25 years (3rd group)	26
Total	112

Distribution of the studied contingent with respect to the general length of service

who teach humanities (such principals are called "humanitarians" in the study); the second one, persons teaching science, technical and industrial disciplines (i.e. "technocrats"); and the third group, principals who manage preschools and elementary schools. See Table 6.

Following this division, the second and the third groups are the closest ones with the respect to the proposed solution — the relation between them is significant ($\tau = 0.73$). A slightly weaker correlation is the dependence between technocrats and humanitarians ($\tau = 0.72$), while still weaker is the dependence between humanitarians and principals of preschools and elementary schools ($\tau = 0.65$).

The comparison, based on this characteristic, shows extremely interesting differences between the three groups. It seems that the orientation of pre- and elementary school principals is most humanistic. This is indicated by the displayed respect for the individual preferences of the couple in love and by the prevailing number of women in the group of people, chosen to continue the existence of mankind. On the other hand, they show ethnic intolerance. Humanitarians have an authoritarian approach when dealing with human fates, but they are the only ones who show preferences to religious values. This is a contradiction, which cannot be uniquely explained. The respect of religion can be definitely linked with the character of the subject matters they teach, being based on humanistic values. It is surprising, however, that these values do not determine humanitarians' attitudes to the fate of the couple in love. The technocrats, on their side, display the

TABLE 6	
Subject matter/level taught	Number of participants
Humanitarians (1st group)	34
Technocrats (2nd group)	41
Pre-school and elementary school (3rd group)	26
Total	112

Distribution of the studied contingent with respect of subject matter and level taught

strongest preference toward biological criteria, as compared to the other two groups. At the same time, however, they do not demonstrate ethnic prejudices.

The analysis of the group process outlines three main mechanisms of attaining a consensus when solving a moral dilemma. The first one is that the majority prevails over the minority, the second one is the unification of the group members in accepting the most persuasively presented choice and the third mechanism is searching for a new, original solution, achieved as a result of group member cooperation. The comparison to the teachers' group shows that the principals are more inclined to take an active part in the process of solving a moral problem, than to accept a ready solution. As expected, the process of group decision making displays a large range of effects with different signs. Analyzing the positive effects, we may note, for instance, the observed mobilization of the group motivation and cognitive resources, being so necessary for the task fulfillment. Those phenomena are described by a number of authors (Bandura 1991, Martoccio & Dubelon 1994). The identification of the individual with the group is another fact of great importance, being a characteristic of the simulation game. Such identification takes place most intensively during the transformation of the individual choice under group pressure and during the acceptance of group norms (Van Knippenberg 1994).

Considering the negative effects, the study registers all deformations that occur during information exchange. The majority effect, and, conversely, the effect of the most powerful group member are two examples of such distortions. The most curious one is the observed phenomenon, "groupthink," in which a group is more interested in consensus than in the consideration of alternative possibilities during group decision making. Groupthink occurs most often during crises (Janis 1982). The discussed situation, although experienced as a simulation by the studied persons, is a catastrophic one. The evidence shows that the group context in principle, and that the search for consensus in solving moral problems in particular, are also useful for developing an effective strategy of school management. Moreover, they provide wider perspectives for in-service principal training in this field.

The context and the process analysis of individual and group solutions for moral dilemma in a catastrophic situation is an attempt for a projection of some value preferences of Bulgarian school principals. The established value profile can be interpreted in several aspects. The first one is the proof of a tendency to a difficult transition from material to post-material values in Bulgaria — one of the post-communist countries. As shown by a number of researchers, it is the most important characteristic of the cultural transformation towards a democratic society (Perlaki 1994, Hamberger 1997). The second aspect takes into account the national specificity of value transition, tackled here only within the narrow frames of the studied contingent. This specificity consists of many controversial tendencies. The general direction of the value transformation is humanistic. However, a number of other tendencies occur within such a background and they can be related to different and natural forms of resistance during a period of radical change.

One of them, established by the present study, is a process which we call a "seeming change" of values. What is characteristic for such a tendency? This phenomenon, in its visible form, follows the outlined trend towards democratization and humanization of attitudes and values. In its hidden form, however, it can be treated as a deepening of the devotion to principles of the past. Hence, behind the facade of a modern value orientation, some outdated stereotypes are visible. One of the most common mechanisms of our principals' value modification is expressed in the search for and finding of justifications needed to promote authoritarian behavioral models in the school. They are considered as the only arguments to suit the contemporary Bulgarian conditions.

The third aspect accounts for some school manager deficits that may disturb the pluralistic picture of their value orientation as a whole. Those are prejudices against some categories of people, rooted in the traditional Bulgarian moral structure. However, they also bear the stamp of conservatism, characteristic of people involved in education.

The method of this study does not allow for deriving general conclusions, but rings a bell for the existence of shadow spots in the value reorientation of Bulgarian school principals. It outlines the existing resources, as well as the available weaknesses of humanizing the school environment.

Future ideas for improving school management involve administering of the psychological type model for principal in-service training and consulting. This would encourage type-appropriate ways of developing modern values and technologies for managing secondary education in Bulgaria, corresponding to the European standards.

REFERENCES

Armstrong, M. (1990). *A handbook of human resource management*. London: Kagan Page Limited.

Armstrong, M. (1983). *How to be an even better manager*. London: Kagan Limited.

Bandura, A. (1991). Social cognitive theory of self-regulation. *Organizational Behavior and Human Decision Process*, 50, pp. 248–287.

Bulak, J. (1980). *Motivacia k praci a riadenia*. Bratislava. Praca.

Di Tiberio, J. (1996). Education, learning styles and cognitive styles. In: A. Hammer [Ed.], *MBTI applications* (pp. 123–166). Palo Alto, CA: Consulting Psychologists Press.

Dimitrov, P. (1992). Psychological business of manager. (In Bulgarian). Sofia: Institute of Marketing.

Fiedler, F.E. (1967). A theory of leadership effectiveness. New York: McGraw Hill.

Fleishman, E. A. (1953). Leadership climate, human relations, training and supervisory behaviour. *Personnel Psychology*, 6.

Gardner, W. & Martinko, M. (1996). Using the Myers-Briggs type indicator to study managers: a literature review and research agenda. *Journal of Management*, 22 (1), pp. 45–83.

Hamberger, A. (1997). Inter-ethnic contact as a predictor of blatant and subtle prejudice: test of a model in four West European Nations. *British Journal of Social Psychology*, 32 (Part 2), pp. 173–190.

Hoffman, J. (1986). Educational administrators: psychological types. *Journal of Psychological Type*, 11, pp. 64–67.

Hofstede, G. (1980). Culture's consequences: International differences in work-related values. *Cross-cultural Research and Methodological Series*, 5. London: Sage.

Hofstede, G. (1991). *Cultures and organizations: Software of the mind.* London: McGraw Hill.

Janis, I. (1982). Groupthink: psychological studies of policy decisions and fiascoes, (2nd ed.). Boston.

Lazarus, R. (1966). *Psychological stress and coping processes.* New York: McGraw Hill.

Lewin, K. (1944). Dynamics of group action. *Educational Leadership, 1.*

Likert, R. (1967). *The human organization.* New York: McGraw Hill.

Manolov, K. (1995). The new Bulgarian management in the period of change. (In Bulgarian). Sofia: Acad. Press.

Martocchio, J., Dubelohn, J. (1994). Performance feedback effects in training: the role of perceived controllability. *Personnel Psychology,* 47 (2), pp. 357-373.

Meisgeiger, C., Hermond, D. & Norris, C. (1996, March). Implications of psychological type and measures of creativity for the preparation of educational administrators. In M. Fields and J. Reid [Eds.], *Proceedings of the Second Biennial International Conference on Education of the Center for Applications of Psychological Type.* Gainesville: Center for Applications of Psychological Type.

Myers, I. & McCaulley, M. (1985). *Manual: a guide to the development and use of the Myers-Briggs Type Indicator.* Palo Alto, CA: Consulting Psychologists Press.

Myers, I. & Myers, P. (1993). *Gifts differing.* Palo Alto, CA: Consulting Psychologists Press.

Myers, I., McCaulley, M., Quenk, N., A.Hammer (1998). MBTI Manual: A guide to the development and use of the Myers-Briggs Type Indicator, (3rd ed.). Palo Alto. Consulting Psychologists Press.

Pencheva, E. (1988). *Professional and personality profile of the school principals (theory, studies, qualification),* (In Bulgarian). Sofia: MSCE.

Pencheva, E. (1993). *Effective school management.* (In Bulgarian). Sofia: Personal-Consult.

Pencheva, E. (1998). *School, values and change.* (In Bulgarian). Sofia, University publishing house "St. Kl. Ohridski."

Pietrasinski, Z. (1968). *Psichologia preveducichpracovnikov.* Bratislava.

Russinova, V. (1998). *Work values and occupational stress in managers.* Paper presented on ISSWOV Conference, Istanbul.

Russinova, V. (1980). *Psychological factors for labor effectiveness.* (In Bulgarian). Sofia: BAS.

Russinova, V., Vassileva, L. (1995). Occupational stress: A theoretical and experimental model of C. L. Cooper. (In Bulgarian). *Bulgarian Journal of Psychology*, N 4, pp. 39–49.

Schwartz, S. (1992). Universals in the content and structure of values: Theoretical advances and empirical tests in 20 countries. In M.Zanna [Ed.], *Advances in experimental social psychology*, Orlando, 25, pp. 1–65.

Semov, M. & Tonchev, G. (1992). *Business and moral.* (In Bulgarian). Sofia: Union of Inventors in Bulgaria.

Shopov, D. & Atanassova, M. (1995). *Management of staff.* (In Bulgarian). Sofia: University of National and World Economy.

Stoineshka, R., Peev, I. (1996). *Economical psychology.* Varna.

Todorov, K . (Ed.). (1992). *Leadership in organization.* (In Bulgarian). Sofia: Informa-Intellect.

Triandis, H. (1996). The state of modern studies on individualism and collectivism. (In Bulgarian). *Problems of Sociology*, 1, pp. 5–17.

Van Knippenberg, D. (1994). Social categorization, focus at attention and judgment of group opinion. *British Journal of Social Psychology*, 33, (Part 4), pp. 177–489.

Vassileva, L. (1998). *Work related values in managers on different levels*. Paper presented on ISSWOV Conference

Walck, C. (1997). Management and leadership. In C. Fitzgerald & L. Kirby [Eds.], *Developing Leaders*, pp. 55–79. Palo Alto: Davies-Black Publishing.

FINLAND

Vesa Routamaa
University of Vaasa

EDITOR'S NOTES. Dr. Routamaa explores leadership from the perspective of two CEOs who managed key industries of historic importance to Finland. First we follow the progress of Kari Ruusunen as he restructures the Piikkio Works to achieve a position of profitability, while at the same time, establishing progressive operational core values. We then explore the entrepreneurial approaches of Kirsti Paakkanen as she innovatively leads Marimekko back to its historic role of importance in the Finnish fashion industry.

Following the profiles of these dynamic leaders, Dr. Routamaa provides us with the recent history and demographics of Finland. He then covers the introduction of the MBTI in the Finnish academic and private sectors. Dr. Routamaa's approach to introducing psychological type and the MBTI serves as an excellent model for others to follow.

▼▼▼▼▼▼▼▼▼▼▼▼▼▼▼▼▼▼▼▼▼▼▼

Mr. Kari Ruusunen, CEO
Kvaerner Masa-Yards Inc. Piikkiö Works

PRELUDE

Shipbuilding has historically been one of the most important industries in Finland. In ancient times, the craftsmanship of wooden ships was already well known and the export of wooden ships was one of the main export businesses of Finland, where the forest was the main natural resource. Actually, when they exported tar, they always built a new ship for shipping and sold both products on the same business trip.

After the Second World War, in spite of a successful and heroic defence of its independence, Finland had to pay an enormous amount of war compensation to the Soviet Union. Despite the fact that the serial production of ships delivered to the Soviet Union did not necessarily represent the newest technology, the extensive shipbuilding industry was re-established. Later, the Soviet Union was an important (paying) customer, asking for high quality tankers and icebreakers, among other things. Special tankers and ro-ro ships were important products in developing the knowledge level of the shipyard industry in the 1970s. Since that time, the Far East has been the main mass producer of tankers and loose cargo steamers. To illustrate the importance of the bilateral business with the Soviet Union in the shipyard industry, it may be mentioned that 70 percent of the ships produced in Finland between 1945–1989 were delivered to the Soviet Union.

Icebreakers, car ferries and cruisers have been the most famous products of Finnish ship building. The market share of Finnish cruisers was 35 percent of the world markets, and the share of the car ferries was 14 percent in 1992. Recently, the biggest gas tank ships in the world are an example of the Finnish key competence in this sector. Because of the state subsidies in most competitive countries, and the low state support and high labor costs in Finland, the Finnish shipyards have had to invest especially in research and development, quality and single products. Tailored special ships have been the competitive strategy to succeed in the tight world competition.

Kvaerner Masa-Yards Inc. is a Finnish shipbuilding company with long traditions of producing high-quality ships. During the last ten years over 25 percent of the world's large cruise liners (e.g., M/S Sensation and M/V Crystal Symphony) and passenger ships have come from the Helsinki and Turku Yards. Kvaerner Masa-Yards offers creative design skills based on a wide-ranging knowledge of the cruise business and professional ship production. The company is today part of the Shipbuilding Division of the international industrial Kvaerner ASA business group.

Masa-Yards builds cruise liners and passenger ferries, LNG carriers, cable ships, icebreakers, ice-going tonnage and all types of special technology vessels, such as special tankers, research vessels and floating storage and production units. Kvaerner Masa-Yards operates two highly modern new building yards, Turku New Shipyard and Helsinki New Shipyard. It may be mentioned that Kvaerner Masa-Yards' Turku New Shipyard is building two mega-size cruise liners for Royal Caribbean International for delivery in 1999 and 2000. The "Project Eagle" vessels have a gross tonnage of more than 130 thousand GT and a passenger capacity of 3,600 passengers. The cruise liners are thus the world's largest. Kvaerner Masa-Yards Piikkiö Works' factory produces pre-fabricated cabin and bathroom modules. Kvaerner Masa-Yards Technology covers research and development, concept design and engineering services, shipyard and welding technology, after-sales services, and includes the Arctic Technology Centre (MARC) in Helsinki and the Welding Technology unit in Turku. Kvaerner Masa Marine Inc. in Vancouver B.C., Canada, and its affiliate company in Annapolis, Maryland, USA, are engaged in marine consulting engineering and marketing primarily in North America.

Kvaerner Masa-Yards' website offers more information: http://www.kvaerner.com/ship/masa-yards/.

WARTSILA MARINE

Wartsila Marine was one of the biggest shipyards in Finland until 1989. In the late 1980s, oil production went down, the economy of the Soviet Union began to change, the worldwide production of ships sank 20–30 percent compared to the level of 1983, and the Finnish Mark was strongly overvalued. Receiving new orders was a tough job. At the same time, the management of Wartsila Marine tried to establish reorganization and new work forms.

To achieve decentralization, flexibility, MBO, higher capacity utilization, etc., a product based profit center organization was planned. In addition, to avoid the disadvantages of strictly divided work and salary categories, which prevented flexible use of labor, there was an intention to establish the use of multi-skilled employees and team-based production. However, the union did not accept the reorganization. The organization was a giant with numerous profit centers and staff departments. The management had to spend most of their time on internal meetings to coordinate the differentiation. In autumn 1989, Wartsila Marine went bankrupt. It was the end of an institution that had a prominent position in the Finnish economy. Marine's fall made even the big boys cry.

THE NEW AGE OF SHIPYARDS:
THE BIRTH OF MASA-YARDS

After the bankruptcy, a new company, Masa-Yards, was established. The new president, Mr. Martin (Masa) Saarikangas, was an important figurehead. He succeeded in getting rid of the old personnel policy and the conflicts between union and management. In the previous company, the interaction between management and workers was formal, and the union played a central role, using strikes as a normal way of discussion. Contrary to the traditional remote and cool leadership culture, President Saarikangas wore overalls, climbed onto the ship framework with welders and demonstrated the new values and working principles.

Saarikangas established direct contact with workers and shop stewards. Some would misuse this direct connection to avoid middle management. This period of great changes in the Finnish economy as well as the bankruptcy of Wartsila Marine helped to carry out the reform that had failed earlier. Reorganization of work transition from piecework to time wages, and empowered leadership became realizable (Routamaa 1998). Instead of the former tight division of labor, the idea of multiskilled employees and team-based production was accepted; workers, foremen and engineers could work together. Different groups of staff also got their representatives on working parties and management teams.

Ownership arrangements of Masa-Yards were temporary and narrow for a business like shipbuilding; thus after a couple of years, the company was sold to Kvaerner Inc. At the moment, because the global economy, especially in Asia, has continued to weaken and poor trading conditions had a corresponding negative impact on profits, the results of Kvaerner are not at their best.

KVAERNER MASA-YARDS INC. PIIKKIÖ WORKS

Kvaerner Masa-Yards' Piikkiö Works is responsible for manufacturing cabins and bathroom units for ships. It is an independent profit centre, specializing in the manufacture of ready-to-install modular cabins and bathroom units for ships, off-shore platforms and hotels. The Piikkiö Works employs approximately 220 people and is located at Piikkiö, in southwest Finland.

In a new situation after Wartsila Marine had gone bankrupt, Piikkiö Works had to indicate its ability to answer the challenges of competitive work. When Masa-Yards was established, all employees were fired. Even though the start-up phase of the new company was confused, Senior Vice-President (later called the CEO) and Plant Manager of the Piikkiö Works, Mr. Kari Ruusunen (ENTJ), who served the previous company from 1988, had an opportunity to have a clean table to begin. "Compared to the shipyard's hierarchy, it was easier for me to make big changes... I downsized quite a lot, one third off of the staff and mostly from the top," stated the CEO. He hired most of the employees back, with the exception of half of the clerical, administrative and managerial personnel. As he said, "We didn't select only the pets, but also so-called difficult people. Differences teach understanding; it forces one to change and develop. It is easier to analyze and solve problems when different opinions and points of views come up in the team" (Honkonen & Routamaa 1997).

From the beginning, CEO Ruusunen did not imagine that he could autocrati-cally solve the problems. First, he chose one of his colleagues to take care of the customers. This colleague was an older shipbuilder knowing the customers of his age. The CEO himself took the responsibility especially for internal relations. Together, they decided to manage the new situation differently. They collected a group of five to ten key persons with whom they began to discuss who would be capable to join the organization, people who would be able to discuss and make decisions. In that way, people who earlier contended and dug the ground from under each other, formed up into a team.

Starting restructuring the from top level, CEO Ruusunen discontinued the management group, decentralized decision-making, and destroyed the bureauc-racy. No department boundaries were maintained, and staff easily changed over from one job to another. According to the CEO, the members of the old management group were good fellows, but the group weakened individual responsibility, and the subjects brought up to be dealt with were more and more curious. When there is no management group, the managers have to learn to make decisions themselves. In addition, the staff used to think that the management group was all bad. Closing up the management group produced fear as one could not turn to or blame the group, but it also produced enormous motivation.

As praised by the CEO, "A positive explosion broke the hierarchical, pyramid organization and changed it into an amoeba organization. The teamwork goes so well now that you always can pass to an empty position and you know that someone will fill it. We can talk using symbols and unfinished sentences. We understand each other."

The executive team decided that communicating with staff members through written memos was ineffective. As problems arose, the CEO and/or the executive team would call everyone together and conduct a briefing. The goal was to ensure that staff members did not learn about developments impacting the company through television or newspaper coverage. As the company was under a media magnifying glass, it was important that staff members perceived the executive team as being on top of things.

Prior to the reorganization, the production of the cabins was based on divided jobs and individual piecework. The employees could only do the work belonging to their own salary category. The CEO set up a team organization and disposed of the barriers. As often, the foremen did not like the idea. "When a group from the plant, by chance, visited some team event, foremen came back, their cheeks glowing red, and said that this team bustle won't do," recalled CEO Ruusunen. However, he did not give up. The commitment must be gained on the shop floor. The pilot team consisted of a line where the workers had the biggest social problems. "We stated that if this team will be successful, they all will be," said the CEO, who often spoke of "us," even though it could be interpreted that he was the mastermind behind most of the reforms.

Actually, immediately after launching the teams, the salary costs increased because they closed down the salary categories. But owing to increased productivity, shortened turnaround, decreased costs per unit, etc., total costs decreased. "There is no limit to the greediness," and that is why they had to agree on dividing productivity. CEO Ruusunen stopped the teambuilding for a short while:

"If I give it all (the whole profit) to you, after some years there is nothing to divide. We must give a share to the customer, a share to the employer, and a share to you," Ruusunen recounted. "After this wrangle over profit-sharing, the teambuilding process took its own course in a year," smiled the CEO contentedly.

As crystallized by a team member: "When somebody gets ill, the situation is under control by the shorthanded team because everybody is helping each other. Why didn't they already start the teams many years ago?"

All in all, the reorganization succeeded; the results doubled, and the staff has been decreased by third. The group has always remained intensive, and turnover of the labor force has been slight.

At every level, the behavior and learning have been unconscious. The CEO speculated, "It is the team; they do not understand what really has been done during the last eight years. We have an organization chart, but we do work on the basis of informal organization, that is the way to illustrate the behavior. This has been a hell of a heavy experience for former managers and foremen. All such ancient barricades based on organizational status do not mean anything any more. Motivation and orientation must be based on something other than a position on the hierarchy, it must be based on the job content." The flat organization means that interaction is genuine but straight, and working is chaotic. When the business is doing fine, positive chaos creates new energy, which follows from continuous improvement of products, process and organization. That is difficult for perfectionists, for those who want everything planned and for those who want to feel in control.

Their method of management is process management and continuous learning, as the CEO calls it. It is continuous learning also regarding products. The basic idea is that all forces should be concentrated on serving the shipyards and the customers in such a way that the customers can see it. The goal is enthusiastic and creative research and development that proactively anticipates future problems. Actually, the product is not purely the cabin — they sell more than cabins, they sell "command of the business" in terms of (physical) space. Every product is a prototype tailored to the needs of the customer, a solution to the customers' space problem.

To launch the process management, to get the staff to understand that they are not making cabins but solving problem, was not that easy. Some of the office staff insisted that they should make systems and certify the procedures — ISO 9000 and things like that were in fashion. However, when a new project starts, prerequisites for its realization will be uniquely created in the office. CEO Ruusunen persisted in avoiding excessive bureaucracy. Afterwards he was supported by the example of Ericsson, a company that had yards of shelves of certificates and procedures until they started teamwork. After that, they had only a five-inch file.

In launching the change, CEO Ruusunen's leadership philosophy was based on his earlier work history as well as intuition. He had earlier been employed by smaller enterprises in different regions, in rural Finland. As he stated it, "In such separate units I had learned, as you know, that you must solve problems yourself. That was a great skill when the crisis arose. The bankruptcy arose right on cue; it was a positive exploitation. I thought, hi there! There are many familiar elements here! The procedures started off intuitively. For example, beforehand, I had not an idea that the management group could be closed down. If an opportunity presents itself, don't let the chance slip. As regards my vision, it is related to the Marine's bankruptcy. It was a damn big possibility even though it was an enormous disaster. I saw a good starting point. I had a feeling that even though these shipyards around us never could start up, at least we are doing well."

A great man
is made up of qualities
that meet or make
great occasions.

— James Russell Lowell

THE NEW BASIC VALUES OF KVAERNER MASA-YARDS INC. PIIKKIÖ WORKS

The enthusiasm of the dynamic start-up phase must be consolidated in order to avoid old organizational life creeping into the staff's mind. That is why the new basic values were launched. The values are as presented in Figure 1.

According to CEO Ruusunen, successful teamwork is based on the member's flexibility, humility, difference, sensitivity, innovativeness and courage. Further, this kind of work form is a way to open, interactive, cooperative and decisive goal oriented organization capable of aspiring to its vision. "I manifest an awful lot of this value management... On the other hand, it is terribly risky if your own activities are something else than what you are talking about," considers CEO Ruusunen.

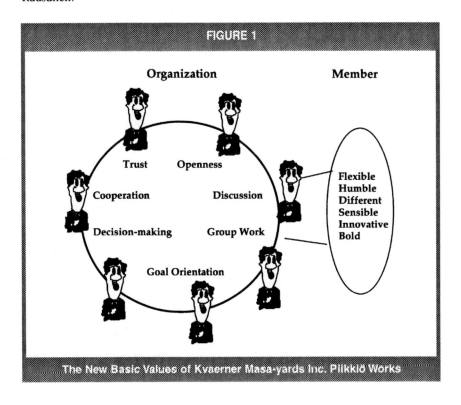

The New Basic Values of Kvaerner Masa-yards Inc. Piikkiö Works

▼▼▼▼▼▼▼▼▼▼▼▼▼▼▼▼▼▼▼▼▼▼

A leader is above all things an animator. His thought and faith must be communicated to those he leads. He and they must form as one at the moment of executing a plan. That is the essential condition of success.

— Ferdinand Foch

He believes that leadership must be based on openness and trust. "Of course intriguing belongs to everyday life, but if there are colleagues who behave against our values and play too much, our team lets them realize it."

The flat organization means that subordinates have great freedom of action. He sees that his main personal input in the company, in percentage terms 80 percent, is to cause pressure for change and development. At the office, from 8 A.M. to 4 or 5 P.M., the work is social interaction and, as he puts it, he has "restless feet." He is not that type who needs to be involved in everything but he has the will and feeling to walk around the company now and then to see if things are all right. "Here you grow accustomed to getting comments straight to your face when you are not authoritarian, but still you are if need be," considers the CEO, who in spite of that seems to carry out MBWA (management by walking around).

Open interaction makes it possible to create commitment with great dedication not only based on money. "To be a soft leader in difficult matters is a hell of a challenge compared to being tough, remote and cool when it is easy to make decisions. It is even more difficult to be genuine and open when a crisis has been lived through, whereas in a crisis, people accept it easier. Anyway, you cannot appeal to everybody — you don't even need to," reasons the CEO.

Illustrating his lifestyle, CEO Ruusunen states that he is obviously "that sort of a plodder... I always strive for better and better results, and the aim is to find out new viewpoints, as it were, unconventional viewpoints. When the going gets tough, I... see things more clearly, more calmly... I stand stress quite well. It has been very useful for me when I have gone around and worked in different firms, worked with really different people... have learnt to understand the weak signals." He works from Monday morning to Friday evening, 7:00 to 7:00 committedly. When he has a holiday, he really has it, and when he comes back, he does not remember phone numbers. "I don't lose my nerve... I do not worry, but I wonder and consider" (Routamaa & Honkonen 1998).

His work as the CEO is to act as internal consultant in active social interaction. That is why, in the evenings at home, it is nice to sit quietly in an armchair and not have to talk with somebody. Luckily, his wife has also a social job in the field of customer service. Of course, the small town environment has its expectations as regards participation, that is, the well-to-do family's social pressures are not limited to office hours.

Kirsti Paakkanen, CEO
Marimekko®
Passion Management in a Creative Brand

PRELUDE

The year is 1960. On the front cover of *Sports Illustrated*, United States presidential candidate John F. Kennedy is in the limelight together with his wife. What a beautiful couple! They look relaxed and sporty when they smile at the camera. Jacqueline Kennedy, who earlier had been seen wearing expensive Parisian fashions, is now dressed in a sleeveless cotton dress. The plain, simple cut does her slender figure justice. New fashion? Yes. The dress is a real Marimekko, a Finnish design garment. The trailblazer in Finnish clothing industry, Marimekko was impressively washed ashore in a Cape Cod resort. Marimekko has surprisingly found a fashion model which is followed by the whole world.

Mrs. Kennedy was only one of those many people who found that this Finnish design was something different. People will rather wear a dress designed by some well-known designer, but, wearing Marimekko, it is enough that it is a real Marimekko. The name has always been a trademark of quality, a guarantee of good work and of a well-designed product. The history of Marimekko is as unconventional as its products.

Marimekko was established by an entrepreneurial couple, Mrs. Armi Ratia and Mr. Viljo Ratia, in 1951. Marimekko's purpose was to produce all kinds of clothes and clothing accessories, including made-to-order wholesale and retail, import and export. From the very beginning, the company was not a conventional clothing factory, and it still differs from the companies in the field. CEO Armi Ratia was especially a very creative and original person. Marimekko was her idea, and by means of the company she carried her visions into effect.

▼▼▼▼▼▼▼▼▼▼▼▼▼▼▼▼▼▼▼▼▼▼

After the start-up stage, the latter half of the first decade saw rapid growth and expansion. At the end of 1960 the plans to expand abroad were wild; for example, there were plans to establish factories in Spain and in the United States. CEO Ratia managed the company with intuitive skill and through personal relations. She did not easily submit her creativity to the economy, and only the rational bank managers represented on the board of the company restrained her ambitious plans.

In its established phase, Marimekko emphasized especially the role of design personnel; the whole company was subjected to the design function. It may be mentioned that in a study of the clothing industry (Routamaa 1980, 1985), the structure of Marimekko radically differed from the general structure of clothing companies; the number of non-production personnel was highly over-represented in relation to the industry in general. For a few years, Mrs. Ratia did not carry out the CEO's duties when the company was reorganized. In 1971, Mrs. Ratia came back and remained in charge until her death in 1979. In 1985, her children sold the company to Amer Group Ltd, a Finnish conglomerate.

Amer Group is a leading sporting goods manufacturer, with its Sports Division representing approximately 90 percent of the Group's likely net sales. It includes Wilson Sporting Goods Company, one of the leading global sporting goods companies (golf, racquet and team sports equipment) and the Atomic Group (skiing equipment under the Atomic, Dynamic, Koflach and Ess brands; snowboards and inline-skates under Oxygen brand). Amer also includes Finland's largest cigarette manufacturer, Amer Tobacco. Amer shares are listed also in London and are available through an ADR facility in the US. Their net sales in 1996 were $94 billion US dollars. They have a personnel of 4096 employees, and in the 1980s, Amer Group was also a car importer and printing house, among other things.

Being in Amer Group's possession, Marimekko drifted step-by-step into a situation where Mrs. Rafia's original business idea had nearly totally disappeared. While CEO Ratia had emphasized creativity and free visionary enterprise, the Amer Group's take-over led to hierarchy and bureaucratic organization. There were managers at the top of the hierarchy whose will guided the designers. In Armi Ratia's time, the designers had liberty of action, they were on the top. The Amer Group turned the organization topsy-turvy, changed the leadership style to emphasize control, and despite their efforts to make Marimekko a profitable, strong brand, they failed. A personified company could not work under faceless ownership. The products and trademark were still there, but the spirit was gone. The trailblazer, a creative model for the whole of Finnish design, could not be just any clothing.

Marimekko was losing money; there were too many managers and other employees, foreign units were too big and unprofitable. The recession of the early 1990s put the economy of Marimekko to the test, as well as that of Amer Group. Rumor had it that Marimekko would be closed down, split up or sold out totally. This chaotic situation paralyzed the company further. The staff had lacked confidence; it was a situation where anybody inside the company seemed to be replaceable, far from a situation in which they could show creativity.

NEW LIGHT ON MARIMEKKO'S SHADOW: ENTREPRENEURIAL LEADER COMES ON THE SCENE

Amer Group sought for a way out and a new owner for Marimekko. The salvation appeared in the shape of a strong, smart, visionary leader. Kirsti Paakkanen (ISFJ) came to Marimekko in September 1991.

When Amer Group offered Marimekko to Paakkanen the first time, she declined. The company was in bad condition and needed restructuring. Amer Group reduced the staff many times so that, in the end, it was half of the original size. Then Ms. Paakkanen accepted the offer and bought Marimekko with the goal of restoring the original Marimekko. A hopeless situation, everyone had said to her about the company — it was losing money because its former reorganization had failed and was struggling with the recession, like the whole country. However, the new owner and chairperson of Marimekko, CEO Paakkenen, trusted her own instincts and the power of the brand.

In order to understand the origin of CEO Paakkenen's principles, values, business ideas and her way to realize those ideas, the background on which these are largely based will have to be described. When, at the age of fifteen, she left her poor and dear home in the middle of the Finnish forests for Helsinki, she got a good head start in life: self confidence and fairness. That is all her parents, who had no means to school her, could give her. Confidence and fairness are the most important of resources, and they cannot be replaced with money. She loves the guiding principle: treat me well, treat me badly, treat me right, but not as a

▼▼▼▼▼▼▼▼▼▼▼▼▼▼▼▼▼▼▼▼

façade — always fairly. She is ready to fight for fairness, whether she is fighting for herself or others. Maybe on the basis of these experiences, every newcomer in her business, regardless of education and future position, begins "behind the counter."

She started going to evening school, worked daily as a salesclerk in a milk store, and at night cleaned forks and knives in hotels. Later, she took classes in advertising and marketing, studied the Finnish language and began her job in the world of advertising. In that way, she learned to understand the meaning of determination, industriousness and dreams, the importance of the quality of work at every level, and the meaning of personal relationships. She had found the guidepost that guided her to success. On the way to success, one needs also humility, such that one does not walk over anybody. Thus, even in the smallest duties Kirsti Paakkanen wanted to exceed both her own expectations and the expectations of others.

Responsibility and power are gifts that CEO Paakkanen is willing to share. The value of those gifts Kirsti Paakkanen learned at home. When she had packed her few things in a cardboard box in order to leave home, her father tried to stop her. She said to her father, "Dear Dad, I now take my life in my own hands." It was not only assuming responsibility and power, but also giving responsibility and power, a show of trust by her dad. Everybody should go their own way, their own gifts as their resources, using their own feelings as their power. Kirsti Paakkanen believes strongly in her own intuition, which comes from her life experience and philosophy of life.

Some people do something for a living, some people live their work. CEO Paakkanen belongs to the latter group. Before Marimekko, Ms. Paakkanen had an outstanding career as the owner and CEO of Womena, an advertising agency. In 1969, when she started the business, there were already more than one hundred advertising agencies in Finland. She showed her wealth of ideas when she boldly developed a creative and brand new concept and profile for her firm. She had not much money, but she had style and ideas.

The first task of the agency was self-evident: marketing itself and having an impressive air. She rented a beautiful apartment in the middle of Helsinki, built herself all the furniture, and put twigs of forest in vases. She hired only women who were equal, no titles, and the job descriptions were flexible, comprehensive. She found the principle in the story of the Creation: according to her, the first sales talk was that in which Eve persuaded Adam to eat the apple in paradise.

Persuading a customer was allowed, too, but pressing him was not permitted. This principle was used when she found her first customers. She mailed 600 green apples packed in beautiful, white boxes with a text on them: today "omena" (apple), tomorrow Womena. The next day, they sent a splendid letter that introduced the agency, its principles, and the know-how of the staff. They got thirty-five customers. In addition to an excellent sense of beauty and style, CEO Paakkanen had already acquired the ability to appeal to customers' feelings. The company started without debts, and during the twenty years owned by Ms. Paakkanen, the company never operated at a loss or was in debt.

Womena was a success. In 1988, Ms. Paakkanen sold the agency to The Interpublic Group of Companies, Inc., a major American agency. After serving three years in Womena as agreed, she built a home in Nice, France. The free, lazy life proved to be strange to her responsible and thorough temperament, and she steered her black Jaguar back to Finland, Sinatra's "My Way" playing on the car radio, and took the opportunity and bought Marimekko.

HOW SHE MADE IT:
ENTREPRENEURSHIP — BACK TO BASICS

Marimekko Ltd, founded in 1951, is a Finnish textile and clothing company engaged in the design, manufacture, retail and wholesale of ladies' apparel (knitwear, woven fabric garments, cotton jerseys), printed interior textiles, canvas and nylon bags and other accessories. The turnover in the 1997 fiscal year was 23.4 million US dollars; licensed production (retail/the USA and Japan) yielded 60 million US dollars. In Finland, Marimekko clothes, interior textiles and accessories are sold in Marimekko's own shops and by authorized retailers. The most important export markets are Germany, Switzerland, the United States, the Netherlands, Norway, Sweden and Denmark. Exports account for about 30 percent of net sales. The company's trademarks are Marimekko and Decembre. The licensed production in Finland is paper napkins and tablecloths, glassware and notebooks; in the Unites States, it is bedding, bathroom textiles, wall coverings and fabrics and children's clothes; in Japan, it is bed linens and home textiles. The Marimekko website — www.marimekko.fi/nutshell.html — provides further information about the company.

▼▼▼▼▼▼▼▼▼▼▼▼▼▼▼▼▼▼▼▼▼▼▼

When Ms. Paakkanen took possession of Marimekko, she first analyzed what Marimekko was yesterday, is today and will be tomorrow. She did not use consultants because she wanted to learn herself the strengths and weaknesses, problems and failures of Marimekko. She analyzed the economy, organizational culture, staff, interest groups, customers and markets. She found out why the company had succeeded, and why it had once gone downhill. Because she was a novice in the field of clothing, she felt it necessary to learn the important issues first before carrying out any change.

Without deeper analysis here, it may be emphasized that she really changed the customary courses of action and strategies demonstrating the failures in product policy, production methods, selling methods and marketing values. After the reorganization by Amer, there was "one department where there were five managers and one worker...the manufacturing of [Marimekko's] products had been given up...instead of our expensive design products, cheap novelties imported from Asia...Affiliated companies had been scraped together...Stores were running at a loss; they sold some yards of fabric or some cheap tricot and the rent and salaries overdrew the daily register...Sales people waited for the customers instead of going to them or inviting them to the company..." This was something the CEO wondered at. She made new product, production, selling and marketing strategies for Marimekko.

> Leadership involves remembering
> past mistakes,
> an analysis of today's achievements,
> and a well-grounded imagination
> in visualizing the problems of the future.
>
> — Stanley C. Allyn

At first, in order to communicate priorities to put the economy right and to arrange the order and steps of the efforts, the CEO named the first key years: Start year 1992, Innovation year 1993, and Culture year 1994. She had a vision, and she told her plans to the staff. Always, when something new happened she called the staff together, told them the news, and tried to raise the spirit. Once the company had clarified its goals, and had trust in tomorrow, she called in some outside help. They gave lectures about resistance to change, creativity, burnout; they were, among other things, not conventional consultants, but included a philosopher, a psychiatrist, a psychologist, etc. Among the staff, there were always some who recalled the old "good times" — "...like this and like that we did in Armi's time..." One of the ideas of those lectures was to get those recollections to be forgotten, unlearned.

Also in Marimekko, she used the principles that had guided her through her whole life. The principles that work also in today's business are: self confidence, respect, fairness, creativity, knowledge, feelings, enthusiasm, care, rewarding, positive thinking, quality and service. In a way, her philosophy is quite simple: just remember that in business you always have another human being in front of you. Too often business will be separated from normal life; one behaves as though the rules of normal socializing would not be valid. She does not want to emphasize femininity; a good manager is good regardless of gender.

MANAGEMENT BY PASSION:
THE KEY CAPTIVATES THE CUSTOMER

Feelings and emotions are key attributes of CEO Paakkanen's leadership. She likes to talk about management by passion (MBP), and "feeling-marketing" as the first issue of her management philosophy. Management by passion is not a softy management suitable only in boom conditions. The reverse side of management by passion is narrow-minded task management, to take charge of affairs. That is, feeling management does not mean getting emotional or becoming indifferent to impersonal fact analysis.

In the first days, because of the rumor that Marimekko would be closed down, the orders were few. The middle management reported to CEO Paakkanen that a part of the staff should be laid off, which was quite a usual procedure at that time. CEO Paakkanen gathered the management and announced that tomorrow the middle management will be laid off if there are not enough orders. The next day the managers reported that there were enough orders so that the workers should not be laid off.

Hierarchy and titles are not important in Marimekko. All the staff aim at a common goal. Feeling-marketing and management by passion together create

▼▼▼▼▼▼▼▼▼▼▼▼▼▼▼▼▼▼▼▼▼▼

opportunities for customer orientation. That is, passion is the key to conquer the hearts of the customer. In order to clarify CEO Paakkanen's philosophy, she relates an example from her time at the advertising agency. She shows two ways of dealing with creative input from a client.

One day, a customer brings a bottle of juice to the agency and says, "Please, you should make a product, a brand of this. You should launch the product on the market." A frustrated manager's style would have subordinates do the work: The manager takes the bottle, gathers the staff to the conference room and snorts, "Now that idiot brought up this kind of disgusting dishwater. Pink juice, not even colorful, and we should make a product and trademark of it. And we only have one week's time."

But what if the manager really loves her or his work? Perhaps the scenario might unfold in this way: "Dear colleagues, please come to the conference room. Our marvelous customer gave us a challenge, a huge challenge! Oh, we are privileged! Please, come on! I have on my own bought you some cakes, lighted candles and decorated the table with flowers to celebrate the occasion. Please, have a look at what our customer brought us, wonderful juice, pink as strawberry juice. We are permitted to make a product of this. We can name and launch it. The customers trust us; we really are competent and fantastic. We have a lot of time, a whole week."

The spectacle in the latter case is only natural in CEO Paakkanen's management practice. But management by passion is not a spectacle without a cause. She has manifested the following theses:

- Commit yourself: When something has been decided together, stand behind the decision even though you originally had disagreed.
- Search: Let us search for something new. Let us do a drama for every season, with a manuscript. It must serve from the design to the store. The manuscript must be made known to everybody.
- Identify: Identify, locate and eliminate the sources of problems; do not simply take care of the symptoms.
- Sort the situation out: take care that everybody knows where we are going. Find out what you yourself understand and know, and make sure that others understand and recognize where we are going in the drama.

- Respect the customer: Marimekko cannot afford to fail any more. The most important thing is to respect the customer. That is where our success will start. From now on, Marimekko does not play without a manuscript in any project, not without dress rehearsal.
- Be an example: Marimekko is today an example. Whatever you do, be an example. Every act we perform is watched. Your acts speak louder than your words. Today, we are trend-makers, but we are also vulnerable to our customers' wear and tear behavior. This is a great responsibility.
- Inspire: You must be the most enthusiastic player. We need a team pulling together completely so that we are able to set an example for other companies. The results of an exemplary team will be rewarded according to the shared outcome.
- Develop: As a supervisor, delegate the decision-making to the level in the organization where they have the best knowledge. The supervisors show the direction. Trust is a good thing, but also control is important.
- Certify: Your duty is to certify that every job you delegate will be correctly realized. It is an excellent idea that you have as wide a team as possible around you but you must always check who is responsible for the realization and that the job keeps its fixed course.
- Focus on relationship oriented marketing: The values have changed. Re-familiarize yourself with your customer. Reassess first yourself, and forget your old attitudes.

The image of Marimekko was badly faded during the phase of Amer Group's ownership, and was in the rear of the Finnish company list. To follow the improvement of its reputation, the company has been continuously involved in image surveys. The standing has been radically improved, and the CEO has continually small wins to report. She can credibly assure the staff that Marimekko really is an example today.

As mentioned, CEO Paakkanen believes strongly in her own experience and instinct, also abroad. CEO Paakkanen has reorganized exports and licensed production that showed a deficit in the era of America. When she had a sales drive in America for the first time, she asked the Finnish Foreign Trade Association's advice. She got a bundle of handouts and leaflets. She did not understand a word of them. The trip failed. She decided to act and succeed in her own way the next time, and succeeded. In Chicago, to the door of a chain of sixty-two stores glided two very long limousines. Both were stuffed full of Marimekko stuff. "Literally, I brought the shop to the spot. They told me, they had never seen a performance like that. Today, Marimekko has twenty successful licensed customers in the States." She rubs her hands and smiles contentedly in her always black and elegant dress.

Finally, it may be mentioned that CEO Paakkanen's management by passion also touches society, that is, she emphasizes also the responsibility of the company for society. Too many entrepreneurs, she says, are ready to empty the register and, at the same time, ask for public support; however, the company is a part of society and it should support society, by way of taxes and social premiums, among other means.

> Today's business leader
> cannot justify his existence
> by profit statements alone.
> He must also render service to his local,
> national, and world community.
>
> — Dorothy Shaver

Today, the results of her leadership style are on display to all. According to the classification of creditworthiness in 1997, Marimekko is located in the best financial solidity and solvency grade (AAA). The profitability of Marimekko has improved continuously. The loss of 40 million US dollars during the period of the former owner has changed to profit. All units have reached their goals. Exports have increased significantly and licensed production has expanded. Recently, the export to and the production in the United States has again really taken off — DelGreco sells and has printed Marimekko fabrics in New York, and DelGreco Textiles distributes the fabrics to Canada, the United States and Mexico.

Paakkanen underlines the ethical responsibility of the company. Money should not represent power but responsibility. A company is also always responsible for its staff, and indirectly for their families. The staff cannot be a question of expenses as is often the case. It may be mentioned that society also respects Paakkanen's values. She has been given several honourable awards and titles, and she is a sought-after speaker.

FINLAND

How to characterize Finland? Finland's terrain is made up of 188,000 lakes, 180,000 islands, 5,100 rapids, a 338,000 square-kilometer (131,000 square miles) area, of which 69 percent is forest, 8 percent is land under cultivation. It has 1,500 kilometers of coastline to the south and west and 1,269 kilometers (788 miles) of common frontier with Russia. Other neighbours are Sweden and Norway, and Estonia behind the Gulf of Finland. According to the latest statistics, Finland has a population of 5.1 million people, which averages 17 people per square kilometer (43 per square mile); 93 percent speak Finnish, 6 percent Swedish, and we have a 100 percent literacy rate. Eighty-six percent of Finnish people are Lutheran and 1 percent Greek Orthodox. It has been a sovereign parliamentary republic since 1917. At least 70 percent of the people have cellular phones. Such is Finland.

In the 1980s, Finland was generally called the Japan of Europe. This was because of the country's exceptional economic performance and growth. In many statistics, Finland was among the top countries of the world. The unemployment rate was very low, 2–3 percent, and yet in practice, there was a lack of workforce. The Finnish Mark (FIM) was very highly rated. Firms, including the small to medium enterprises, took a considerable number of loans in foreign currency. The export rate was high; about 27 percent of the export was directed to the Soviet Union, on a bilateral basis, metal and engineering as well as textile and clothing industry products being among the top exports.

All in all, the main exports were paper, machinery, ships, timber, chemicals, clothing, wood pulp and petroleum products, not to mention cellular phones and telecommunications in general. Growth in the stock market continued, and especially Finnish banks began to play stock markets games. In Finland, it has been typical that the main bank institutions have an extensive control over the biggest companies, playing a dominant role on the boards of the companies; unfortunately, management and business skills have not been in keeping with the willingness to control the companies.

▼▼▼▼▼▼▼▼▼▼▼▼▼▼▼▼▼▼▼▼▼▼

At the end of the 1980s, shadows began to gather over the heated Finnish economy. Pressure on the highly rated Finnish Mark and the instability of Eastern Europe gave signs of trouble, but the short-sighted politicians, bank managers and business managers did not see beyond the curve; unrealistic expectations of ever-continuing growth in the stock markets made the bank sector management blind. The strong Mark policy bluffed the government, and the traditionally high export rates to Eastern Europe had deteriorated the sensitivity and abilities of business people to design products for new export markets.

Along with the collapse of the Soviet Union in 1990, Finnish export had decreased by about a quarter; the devaluation of the Finnish Mark and its effect on the foreign debts of small to medium enterprises among other things, strongly deepened the recession of the early 1990s. There were new records in the number of bankruptcies as well as in the unemployment rate, both of which had usually been very low in Finland. It should be mentioned that the debt incurred from the large proportion of Finnish exports to the Soviet Union had not yet been paid by the Russian government.

The recession caused a restructuring of the formerly conservative bank sector as well as of many fields of the metal industry and even ruined temporarily many other businesses, e.g., the textile and especially the clothing industry. A new problem was the collapse of bigger companies; that is why the unemployment rate reached an ultimate record. The stock market game played by the main banks destroyed a huge amount of Finnish capital forever.

In the early 1990s, great changes took place in Finnish economy. The long economic boom of the previous decade was followed by an exceptionally deep recession which brought about a strong need for a change in working and business life. A great number of small to medium enterprises fell, but incredibly, also many big companies, even banks, went bankrupt. To revitalize bankrupt estates and unprofitable companies called for exceptional leadership and entrepreneurial efforts.

The survival of the economy and business demanded a new government policy, restructuring of many industries, and rethinking of work and organization forms. The process of change has been rapid but the reorganization faces many barriers such as strict labor rules, exaggerated welfare subsidies including internationally record-breaking unemployment support, high labor costs and one of the highest income taxes in the world. For example, Finland has the highest amount of paid holidays in the Organization for Economic Cooperation and Development (OECD). As well, there are not many countries where average families' available incomes are nearly the same irrespective of whether the parents are employed or not.

High labor union membership, on average 80 percent, assures that the previous interests will be protected. The Nordic welfare society has been kept running by making foreign and domestic debts; everybody, perhaps with the exception of members of parliament depending on elections every fourth year, can image that this is not a wise policy. This kind of policy surely does not improve free enterprise and initiative. The dilemma is that there are still a record number of unemployed people compared to earlier decades and, at the same time, there is a lack of labor in many industries. This is the case especially in high tech businesses, in spite of the fact that Finland educates more engineers in relation to population compared to any other country in the world. By the way, the lack of engineers is at least partly due to the fact that too many engineers are employed as general managers, instead of performing the duties connected with engineering skills.

Despite this exceptionally high economic boom at the moment, the unemployment rate decreases very slowly, because of changed industrial structures as well as the increased efficiency of production. In addition, the high income tax level together with the obligations of the welfare society are obstacles to increasing entrepreneurship as a key to self-employment and decreasing unemployment.

However, as mentioned, after the latest recession, the Finnish economy has done well. Finland joined the European Union in January 1995; this required quite a healthy economy. In 1996, with regards to the GDP per capita, 24.178 US dollars, Finland was among the top countries. Forest, paper, metal, electronics and information technology are the major industries. The two last mentioned, with NOKIA as the flagship, have already passed paper and forest in importance, and now anchor the Finnish economy. As a curiosity, it may be mentioned that in density of cellular phones per capita (in excess of 50 percent), Finland is clearly number one. As the most wired nation in the world, Finland has also the highest rate of internet users, approximately twice as many as the United States.

In Finland, nearly 70 percent of the women are employed outside the home. Together with Canada, Finland is the leading OECD country to invest in education, spending 7.4 percent of GNP on education. Accordingly, 53 percent of the population have completed post-secondary education. In order to better develop and market products and services in a very competitive world market, the government will raise the R&D funding from 2.5 to 2.9 percent of GNP before the year 1999. Because 99.7 percent of all enterprises are small to medium (<249 employees), the internalization of small to medium enterprises is of key importance. In all, it may be said that the infrastructure and management create good possibilities for success for business in Finland. Actually, sometimes when waiting at the red traffic lights in the middle of the night in an empty village it feels that in the country of a handful of people we have an infrastructure of a superpower.

According to the World Competitiveness Yearbook (1998), Finland is the fifth best country for business. In more detail, Finland was also first in the introduction of new technology, in developing and applying technology, technology cooperation, R&D, research financing, access to international financing, enterprise training, trustworthy companies, trustworthy management, and extent of working women. No doubt, the infrastructure is favorable to business. Leadership skills, however, are another matter. On the one hand, referring to the very high labor cost in the country, and, on the other hand, to the fact that, for example, knowledge and technology are easily to be copied or imitated, leadership and human resource management are key attributes of a company's competitive advantage. That is why leadership skills both in transition and in keeping competitiveness are ultimate factors of survival.

THE MBTI IN FINLAND

GETTING INSPIRED

After finding the trait view of personality too static and irrelevant, for instance, in leadership and team development, I became attracted to brain dominance views in late 1980s. However, the theoretical base, the construction and the usage of these tests seemed ambiguous. That is why I reviewed the situation and searched for all sorts of views to be compared to each other. Finally, in 1992, my team and I compared empirically some measures including brain dominance, systematic-intuitive views and the MBTI. Even though our initial efforts with the MBTI were based on an informal translation, it proved to be workable and most interesting.

Although inspired by this first overview, it was our participation in an advanced MBTI workshop conducted by Dr. Mary McCaulley and Gerald Macdaid of the Center for the Applications of Psychological Type (CAPT), attendance at CAPT's First Multicultural Research Conference, visits with MBTI experts at Mississippi State University, and collaboration with Ms. Jamelyn Johnson of CAPT's staff in January 1993 that finally convinced and inspired the team to continue its journey in the fascinating world of psychological type. Could such interactions have had any other result?

THE DEVELOPMENT OF THE FINNISH VERSION OF THE MBTI

Until 1991, the use of the MBTI in Finland had depended on individual trainers or psychologists who used informal translations of the instrument. No scientifically significant research results could be found. The first Finnish draft of the MBTI, Form F, was studied for research purposes by the researchers at the University of Vaasa in 1991. In 1994, the author was asked by the Consulting Psychologists Press (CPP) to attend to the validation and distribution of the Finnish version.

The procedure of the validation was based on three points: on linguistic and cultural fine-tuning, on research covering different topics, tests and samples and on the evaluation based on the feedback discussions with those who have taken the MBTI. The tentative translation was made by a psychologist familiar with the theory on which the MBTI was built. This version was strongly revised by the Finnish translation team consisting of researchers of organizational behavior, psychology and linguistics. A psychologist involved in the translation of the Swedish MBTI worked with the Finnish translation team.

Next, the team revised the translation in 1996. That revision was based on statistical analyses as well as on a back-translation by a bilingual American lecturer at the University of Vaasa. This version was further analysed.

At every third phase, a sample of 400–600 observations was collected. Even though the resulting version of the MBTI is working well, some finishing touches

▼▼▼▼▼▼▼▼▼▼▼▼▼▼▼▼▼▼▼▼▼▼▼

are still under way. Also, a Swedish version of the MBTI Form F for the Swedish speaking Finns is in preparation and there are a number of MBTI related teaching materials currently being developed and translated in Finnish.

THE RESEARCH

In connection with the research and training projects arranged by the author, also validation data was collected. The data has been used in studies concerning especially leadership, strategic thinking, creativity, careers and occupational expectations, team building and entrepreneurship, among others. A number of graduate as well as post-graduate students have been dealing with those subjects.

Leadership study, one of the main topics of the Finnish team, has not been concerned so much with the role of personality and cognitive styles in leadership behavior. The progress from the trait theory through behavioral approach to the situational leadership view may have turned the conversation to more simple factors than type. The importance of type has been, maybe implicitly, neglected. That is why the leadership study from the point of view of type, a personality approach to the leadership, has been developed. The personality approach to leadership is associated with the strategic thinking of managers (Gallén 1997, 1999), and with creativity (Asikainen & Routamaa 1997).

In order to educate and recruit competent leaders, it is important to examine the relationship between the MBTI and work expectations of students, as well as the success of the students in their studies and careers after the studies. That is why comprehensive projects of career expectations (Honkonen 1998, 1999, 2000; Honkonen & Routamaa 1996a, 1996b) and follow-up of study and career success of different students has been established. Similarly, psychological types and lifestyle among managers and business students (Routamaa & Pehkonen 1999) has been studied in order to find out the extremes of different types (e.g., situational leadership behavior).

From the point of view of the national cultures, the study has been extended to leadership styles in the cultural context in order to clarify the interaction between culture and type as predictors of the leadership behavior. Further, the study of expatriates' experiences (Suutari 1996, 1998, Suutari & Brewster 1998) has been extended to analyze the association between type and cultural sensitivity. Of course, stress and change management (Routamaa & Honkonen 1996, 1998) are associated with the points of view of leadership concerned.

Leaders have the strongest impact on organizational culture that creates or creates not the prerequisites for intrapreneurship, internal entrepreneurship. It may be said that leadership and entrepreneurship are an end of the same dimension. Keeping this in mind, and the role of type in general, entrepreneurship in terms of networking attitudes (Routamaa & Varamäki 1998), international orientation (Routamaa, Vesalainen & Pihlajaniemi 1996) and stress (Routamaa & Honkonen 1998), among others, has been studied.

As indicated above, the meaning of a personality approach to leadership behavior is comprehensively covering the association of type and leadership. At the same time, when added to our understanding of type and leadership, the reliability of the MBTI in general and especially the validity of the Finnish translation has been proved.

OTHER APPROACHES TO THE STUDY OF LEADERSHIP

Which leadership strategy or style could work in a transition phase? Considering leadership at the collective or organizational level, transformational leadership has often emerged when change has been required. Vision and charisma may play important roles in managing change and transition. Visionary and charismatic leadership has been seen as a fundamental built-in element of transformational leadership here, even though they have sometimes been considered separate leadership styles or views, too (House 1977, Conger & Danungo 1987).

As Pierce and Newstrom (1995, 195) put it, "Many organizations are struggling with the need to manage chaos, to undergo internal cultural change, to reinvent business, to restructure their organizations, to adopt or invent new technologies, to empower organizational members, to reduce organizational boundaries, to discover paths to continuous improvement, and to invent high involvement organization and management systems. In the face of such challenges, the transformational and charismatic leader represents a style of leadership that may be capable of navigating organizations through chaos and into the 21st century." Transformational leaders may inspire their followers through charisma, they may

▼▼▼▼▼▼▼▼▼▼▼▼▼▼▼▼▼▼▼▼▼▼

meet their emotional needs through individual consideration, or they may intellectually stimulate them by stirring within them an awareness of problems, insight
into solutions, and the passion to bring about resolutions (Bass 1985, 26–40, Pierce
& Newstrom 1995, 196). That is, especially in transition, transformational leadership may be effective to create necessary efforts from the edge of an abyss.
Concerning charisma, Bennis and Nanus (1985, 224) stated, however, "charisma is
the result of effective leadership, not the other way around."

Along with the development of leadership approaches from trait to behavioral,
and further, to situational approaches, the importance of a leader's personality had
somewhat faded. Transformational leadership associated with charismatic and
visionary leadership has brought the meaning of the leader's person more into
focus. The author and his team have restored the meaning of type in leadership
behavior (Routamaa & Ponto 1994, Routamaa, Honkonen, Asikainen & Pollari
1997, Routamaa & Pollari 1998; Routamaa & Pehkonen 1999). As regards personal characteristics and leadership behavior, a personality perspective to leadership
has emerged (Routamaa & Ponto 1994, Routamaa & Pollari 1997).

A manager's personality functions as a filter when the manager interprets what
kind of style the subordinate needs. And more importantly, the supervisors' types
distinctly affect the leadership style as interpreted by subordinates (Roush 1992;
Routamaa, Honkonen, Asikainen & Pollari 1997).

In contrast to the transformational leadership, for example, Bass (Bass &
Stogdill 1990) defined transactional leadership style where something is offered by
the leader in exchange for something wanted from the subordinate. Transactional
leadership (or should one rather speak of management?) is quite a conventional way
to try to keep the wheels in motion, maybe suitable for steady conditions.
According to practical conclusions, it could be said that many times "what transactional leadership produces, that transformational leadership will mend."

> It is not only paying wages, and giving commands,
> that constitute a master of a family;
> but prudence, equal behaviour, with readiness
> to protect and cherish them, is what entitles man
> to that character in their very hearts and sentiments.
>
> — Richard Steele

To mention some of the transformational leadership or related views, examine the four strategies of leadership presented by Bennis and Nanus (1985): (1) attention through vision; (2) creating meaning through communication; (3) creating a climate of mutual trust, including that the leader's own actions are consistent with the vision and its attendant values; and (4) deployment of self. The last strategy refers to the ability to know one's strengths and weaknesses and using the former to good effect, constantly learning and reflecting on one's experiences. Kouzes and Posner (1987) identified five practices of successful leaders: (1) challenging the process; (2) inspiring a shared vision; (3) enabling others to act; (4) modelling the way; and (5) encouraging the heart. Summing up briefly, in launching the change a successful leader evaluates the prevailing situation, then formulates and communicates the vision and resources by modelling the way-building trust, for instance, by his or her own example and taking risks (Figure 2). This kind of leadership results in intense teamwork, fewer conflicts, common values, cohesiveness, commitment to a leader and the goals of the organization, and high performance.

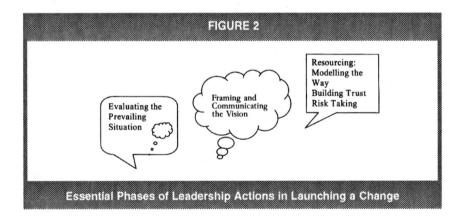

FIGURE 2

Evaluating the Prevailing Situation

Framing and Communicating the Vision

Resourcing: Modelling the Way Building Trust Risk Taking

Essential Phases of Leadership Actions in Launching a Change

SUMMARY

To summarize the common features of the two successful leaders illustrated, the following common actions could be identified:

- radical evaluation of the prevailing situation — chances, organization and resources, institutional limitations;
- envisioning something different from the former operations and communicating the new values and courses of action, promoting unlearning;
- emphasizing the example of the CEO, taking risks;
- building trust, manifesting values, favoring team building, communicating the wins, softening rank differences
- being open and equal, but decisive.

Both of the leaders profiled in this chapter quite explicitly carried out the essential phases of leadership actions in launching a change, as summarized earlier (see Figure 2).

The ENTJ (shipyard) leader uses more often firm actions, for example closing up the management group, controlling the share of profit to assist in teambuilding and launching new practices, among other things. The ISFJ (Marimekko) leader emphasizes more management by passion, both in speech and actions. She uses the philosophers and other speakers as well as written theses to promote unlearning whereas the ENTJ leader more clearly urged others to move ahead, marching himself in front. In spite of the fact that the foremen did not like it, at least in the beginning, he used job enrichment and job enlargement in terms of teamwork to motivate the shop floor workers, and, at the same, he made it possible to lighten the hierarchy considerably.

The ENTJ leader respects openness and trust, and prefers management by walking around, and yet avoids too much involvement in the followers' problems. The ISFJ leader emphasizes similar values whereas she is more personally involved in the affairs at every level, taking care of the people and customers. As an ISFJ entrepreneur, she is also more deeply involved in current affairs. For her, the business is a lifestyle, and for him, it is more a profession. She was also skillful in using charisma to have extraordinary and profound effects on followers, customers and general public. She considered especially the emotional needs (MBP) using, however, written principles and goals to secure the course. He destroyed the formalities and preferred to stimulate intellectually the followers by stirring within them an awareness of problems (e.g., causing pressure, asking what really is the product), insight into solutions and the passion to bring about resolutions. Undoubtedly, they are perfect illustrations of transformational leaders.

Transformational leaders recognize the challenges, and make decisions about the changes their companies must make in order to survive and be successful. Referring to the challenge of change in organizations, both leaders carried out most of those steps of the successful journey (phases 2–4) to success listed by Barger and Kirby (1995: 13–14). What they had to abandon were:

- inflexibility
- paternalistic structure, autocratic decision making
- "boxes" (prescribed work roles)
- turf issues
- security and dependence
- the Florence Nightingale image
- whining

What the essentials were — the requirements for making it through the journey and succeeding in the future:

- energy and enthusiasm
- a sense of humor
- creativity and ingenuity
- team orientation
- adaptability and flexibility
- perseverance
- mutual respect
- realistic goals and expectations
- ethical principles

What they needed to make it through "the desert of old culture":

- information, information, information
- recognition
- courage and strength

▼▼▼▼▼▼▼▼▼▼▼▼▼▼▼▼▼▼▼▼▼▼

- hope and vision regarding the future
- guidance and encouragement
- perseverance
- unity/cohesiveness
- resourcefulness and adaptability
- trust/bonding
- administration support — global directions and boundaries
- incentives — celebrations, small victories — some fun!

As could be seen in the stories about these two leaders is, both of them approach tasks differently — he, largely based on intuition and experience, she, more based on feelings and values — and yet both have quite literally expressed most of the steps mentioned above. She has more entrepreneurial grip accompanied by passion whereas he is more tuned to new ideas and possibilities. As could also be found out, they have been successful in rescuing the companies from difficulties, up to now.

REFERENCES

Aromäki, J. (1988). Kirsti Paakkanen — Tunnemarkkinoinnilla hyvää tulosta [Passion Marketing — a Way to Good Results]. *Economica*, 2 (2), 7-10.

Barger, N.J. & Kirby L.K. (1995). The challenge of change in organizations. Palo Alto, CA: Davies-Black.

Bass, B.M. (1985). Leadership: Good, better, best. *Organizational Dynamics*, 13, 26-40.

Bass, B.M. & Stogdill (1990). *Handbook of leadership: Theory, research and managerial implications.* New York: The Free Press

Bennis, W. & Nanus, B. (1985). *Leaders: The strategies for taking charge.* New York: Harper & Row.

Conger, J.A. & Kanungo, R.N. (1987). Towards a behavioral theory of charismatic leadership in organizational settings. *Academy of Management Review 12*, 637-647.

Donner, J. (1986). Dreams and Reality. In P. Suhonen & Pallasmaa [Eds.], *Phenomenon Marimekko* (pp. 8-18). Espoo: Weiling & Göös.

Gallèn, T. (1997). The cognitive style and strategic decisions of managers. *Management Decision*, 34 (7-8), 541-551.

Gallèn, T. (1999, April). The cognitive style and strategic thinking. *Proceedings of the Third Biennial International Conference on Leadership of the Center for Applications of Psychological Type* (pp. 25-30). Gainesville, FL: Center for Applications of Psychological Type.

Honkonen, M. (1998, January). Personality and work expectations of Finnish students: An application of J. L. Holland's perspective. In M.U. Fields (Ed.), *Psychological Type and Culture — East and West: A Multicultural Research Symposium* (pp. 17-27). Honolulu, Hawaii, January, 1998. Gainesville, FL: Center for Applications of Psychological Type.

Honkonen, M. (1999, April). Psychological type and career anchors of future managers. *Proceedings of the Third Biennial International Conference on Leadership of the Center for Applications of Psychological Type* (pp. 37–42). Gainesville, FL: Center for Applications of Psychological Type.

Honkonen, M. (2000). Personality preferences and career expectations of Finnish business students. *Forthcoming in Career Development International Journal (67).*

Honkonen, M., & Routamaa, V. (1996a). Personality types and occupational expectations: Finnish graduates' vocational hopes related to Holland's occupational groups. In R. A. Moody (Ed.), *Proceedings of the Second Multicultural Research Symposium of the Center for Applications of Psychological Type* (pp. 151–160). University of Hawaii, January, 1996. Gainesville, FL: Center for Applications of Psychological Type.

Honkonen, M. & Routamaa, V. (1996b). Finnish graduates' personality and favorite occupations by temperaments. *Proceedings of the 4th International Type User's Conference: Diversity, Change & Development*, September 9–11, 1996, Sandton, South Africa.

Honkonen, M. & Routamaa, V. (1997). Psychological types and teamwork effectiveness: A study of production teams in industry. *Proceedings of the Second Biennial International Conference on Leadership of the Center for Applications of Psychological Type* (pp. 79–86). Gainesville, FL: Center for Applications of Psychological Type.

House, R.J. (1977). A 1976 theory of charismatic leadership. In J.G. Hunt & L.L. Larson (Eds.), *Leadership: The Cutting Edge*. Carbondale: Southern Illinois University Press.

Jylhä E., Paasio, A. & Strömmer, R. (1997). *Menestyvä yritys* [A successful enterprise]. Edita Helsinki: Edita.

Kouzes, J.M. & Posner, B.Z. (1988). *The leadership challenge*. San Francisco: Jossey-Bass.

Lawrence, G. (1993). People types and tiger stripes (3rd ed.). Gainesville, FL: Center for Applications of Psychological Type.

Niemeä, J. (1996). *Ammattirajoista tiimityöskentelyyn. Työnjaon ja työelämän suhteiden muutos Suomen telakoilla 1980- ja 1990-luvulla* [From profession boundaries to teamwork: The change of labor of work and public relations in the Finnish shipyards in the 1980's and 1990's]. Turun yliopiston julkaisuja, Sarja Cosa 127. Turku: Turun yliopisto.

Pierce, J.L. & Newstrom, J.W. (1995). *Leaders & the leadership process: Readings, self-assessments & applications.* Chicago: Irwin.

Roush, P.E. (1992). The Myers-Briggs Type Indicator, subordinate feedback, and perceptions of leadership effectiveness. In K.E. Clark, M.B. Clark & D.P. Campbell (Eds.), *Impact of Leadership.* Greesboro, NC: Center for Creative leadership.

Routamaa, V. (1980). *Organizational structuring: An empirical analysis of the relationships between structure and size in firms of the Finnish shoe and clothing industry.* Vaasa: Acta Wasaensia, No 13.

Routamaa, V. (1985) Organizational structuring: An empirical analysis of the relationships and dimensions of organizational structures in certain Finnish companies. *Journal of Management Studies* (22), 5, 498–522.

Routamaa, V. (1991). Human resource management in the context of strategic management. In J. Näi (Ed.), *Arenas of Strategic Thinking* (pp. 235–253). Helsinki: Foundation of Economic Education.

Routamaa, V. (1998). *Is the time ripe for releasing enthusiasm, creativity and cooperation abilities?* Newspaper University Forum. http://www.uwasa.fi/taky/nuf/english/autumn97.html

Routamaa, V., Honkonen, M., Asikainen, V., & Pollari, A-M. (1997, April). Psychological type and leadership styles: Subordinates' point of view. *Proceedings of the Second Biennial International Conference on Leadership of the Center for Applications of Psychological Type* (pp. 271–278). Gainesville, FL: Center for Applications of Psychological Type.

Routamaa, V., & Honkonen, M. (1998, January). Psychological type and stress. In M. U. Fields [Ed.], *Psychological Type and Culture — East and West: A Multicultural Research Symposium* (pp. 91-100). Honolulu, Hawaii, January, 1998. Gainesville, FL: Center for Applications of Psychological Type.

Routamaa, V., & Pehkonen, H. (1999, April). Psychological types and lifestyle among Finnish managers and business students. *Proceedings of the Third Biennial International Conference on Leadership of the Center for Applications of Psychological Type* (pp. 109–115). Gainesville, FL: Center for Applications of Psychological Type.

Routamaa, V., & Pollari, A-M. (1998, January). Leadership styles in the cultural context: A comparison of Finnish and South African managers. In M. U. Fields (Ed.), *Psychological Type and Culture — East and West: A Multicultural Research Symposium* (pp. 59–67). Honolulu, Hawaii, January, 1998. Gainesville, FL: Center for Applications of Psychological Type.

Routamaa, V., & Ponti, V. (1994, January). Situational leadership and the MBTI types of certain Finnish managers. *Proceedings, The Myers-Briggs Type Indicator and Leadership: An International Research Conference* (pp. 189–197). College Park, MD: University of Maryland.

Routamaa, V., & Ponti, V. (1994, January). Situational leadership and the MBTI types of certain Finnish managers. *Proceedings, The Myers-Briggs Type Indicator and Leadership: An International Research Conference* (pp. 189–197). College Park, MD: University of Maryland.

Routamaa, V., Vesalainen, J., & Pihlajaniemi, E. (1996). Meeting the challenges of export markets: Entrepreneurs' personality and international orientation. Proceedings of the 7th ENDEC World Conference on Entrepreneurship (pp. 479–487). Singapore: Entrepreneurship Development Centre, Nanyang Technological University.

The Forbes leadership Library (1995). Thoughts on Leadership. Chicago: Triumph Books.

World Competitiveness Yearbook (1998) Lausanne: IMD.

BIBLIOGRAPHY ON RELATED ISSUES

Asikainen, V., & Routamaa, V. (1997, April). The relationship between the MBTI and the creativity orientations of managers. *Proceedings of the Second Biennial International Conference on Leadership of the Center for Applications of Psychological Type* (pp. 11–16). Gainesville, FL: Center for Applications of Psychological Type.

Murto-Koivisto, E., Routamaa, V. and Vesalainen, J. (1996). The prerequisites for different types of successful interfirm cooperation in the SME-Sector. *Journal of Enterprising Culture* (4), 2, 109–122.

Routamaa, V. & Honkonen, M. (1996). Psychological types and organizational change, Proceedings of the 4th Type Users Conference, South Africa.

Routamaa, V. & Vesalainen, J. (1987). Types of entrepreneur and strategic level goal setting. *International Small Business Journal* (5), 3, 19–29.

Suutari, V. (1996). Variation in the leadership behaviour of western European managers: Finnish expatriates' experiences. *The International Journal of Human Resource Management* (7), 3, 678–707.

Suutari, V. (1998). Leadership behaviour in eastern Europe: Finnish expatriates' experiences in Russia and Estonia. *The International Journal of Human Resource Management* (9), 2, 235–258.

Suutari, V. and Brewster, C. (1998). The adaptation of expatriates in Europe: Evidence from Finnish multinationals. *Personnel Review* (27), 2, 89–103.

HUNGARY

Ilona Erös
Anima-Reason Consulting Ltd.

EDITOR'S NOTES. Dr. Ilona Erös introduces us to an extraordinary Hungarian entrepreneur named Ildikó Magyar. While Magyar achieves economic success, she is also very candid in revealing the difficulties she faced in balancing the needs of her business versus the needs of her family. Once she realized there was a substantial disparity, Magyar took the lessons learned and incorporated them into her business operations. You will be fascinated as you learn the histories of her workforce.

Dr. Erös provides us with an extended history of Hungary. She then thoroughly reviews the use of psychological type and the MBTI, along with other assessment approaches, in Hungary.

ILDIKÓ MAGYAR

The house, in a suburb of Budapest where the conversation takes place, is 900 square meters and it is not only a flat, but also the site of her company. On this warm September afternoon we are sitting outside the house, on the balcony. In front of our eyes we can see family houses and peaceful hills as we recall the decades that have passed by. Darkness falls on the hills, and we escape the cool breezes coming down from the neighboring hills, continuing our conversation in the hall of the house, sipping a glass of wine.

Ildikó was born in a Budapest family. Her father left Hungary after the war and they did not know anything about him. Her mother could never really disregard this and, when Ildikó was five years old, committed suicide. Following that tragedy, Ildikó's grandparents raised her.

One of her first deep impressions was connected to some relatives who were living in a huge flat with eleven rooms. This flat was later nationalized, when nine rooms and the bathroom were given to a large family. The relatives piled up all the remains of an old bourgeois golden age in those two rooms, while the rest of the house was bare and poor.

Unfortunately Ildikó was not allowed to visit these relatives for long, because once her leg was poured with hot water by accident, and her grandmother, feeling that she was not secure there, did not let her go there any more. With this decision she cut Ildikó from all the beauty she could hear and see there.

In 1956, the year of the Hungarian Revolution, her family was deeply influenced as some former taboos were openly discussed. She had heard before a number of times this sentence: "It is better if the child thinks it was like that." She realized that her family used to live a much different way of life. She also learned that her father was alive, as he sent her new clothes, which were very different from the ones that could be bought in Hungary.

During her childhood she first realized that she was different from others. A long-lasting experience was the service done for the Pioneer Railway. Children got used to independence, discipline, team building and responsibility there. It was a privilege to work there — only the best pupils could become members of Pioneer Railway. She also loved gymnastics, and was excellent at school, too. She remembers her grandfather saying to her as he took her to school for the first time in her life, "You must always be number one." Her grandparents would not let her do both school and gymnastics, therefore she had to quit gymnastics.

Ildikó had a number of favorite teachers, including one who had only one half-leg; the other one was totally missing. Still, he was enthusiastic to take the children hiking, mountaineering. She was impressed by the efforts of this man, and all that he did against his own limitations.

Once during her primary school years, Ildikó was diagnosed with pneumonia, and was taken to a sanatorium for half a year. Afterwards she was accepted into one of the most famous, highest quality secondary schools. She was a good achiever, especially in mathematics. She liked going to school, even though her obesity prevented her from becoming fully accepted by the other students. The feeling of the lack of belonging to a community was significant during all her childhood and adolescence.

When her grandparents died (she was sixteen), her aunt exchanged the grand-parents' flat and put her up. When she was seventeen she moved to a classmate's house. This was possible financially because she received pension from the state, after her grandfather died. Here once again she was surrounded by beautiful objects and was exposed to a better way of life. But after her final examination, on the beginning of her adult life, she had no flat of her own, and was without any help. The depressing feeling of homelessness was accompanying her all through her life, and now, when she is living in better financial conditions, she is "collecting" flats, if not for herself, then for her sons. That is a way for her to save the boys from similarly sad experiences.

The main point for Ildikó in deciding which university to go to was where she could get student hostel accommodation. She ended up at the Budapest Technical University's electrical engineering facility. The choices she made during the university years were not always motivated by strict professional considerations. For example, when she chose to specialise in microwave technology, she was motivated by the sympathy she felt for the dean.

During her university years she got to know a young man who later became her husband. The boy's mother was dying scarves and Ildikó could work for her. She was working during all her university years to complement her low stipend.

Ildikó graduated with good results. The friends of her fiancé accepted her, even though she was a woman. Still, those five years at the university did not leave too many traces in her soul.

Ildikó received her first professional job at the Experimental Institute of the Hungarian Post and Telecommunication Office. Her first choice — ground stations for satellites — is still her field of work today. However, in those days it was a unique field.

Ildikó's first son, Tamás, was born in the beginning of the 1970s, while she was working at the Experimental Institute. While her son was young, she got her second degree as an economist-engineer. She also learnt to speak French. Two-and-a-half years later her second son, András, was born.

Once one of her workplace officers told her that there would be an opportunity to spend six months in France on a scholarship, and since no one at the company except Ildikó spoke French well enough to earn the appointment, she decided to take the opportunity.

That scholarship changed her ideas about work, results and, essentially, the rest of her life. She learned the basics of digital switching technology, and she could also watch the farsighted planning, implementing and measuring policy of the French government, which they did in order to improve the telephone system and strengthen the nation's industry. This had a deep impression on her, because she could not see anything similar in Hungary. When she came home, she was not able to communicate what she had learnt, in part because there were no correct expressions for these, and because nobody was interested in how these lessons could be used in Hungary.

Ildikó maintained her contacts in France and visited the country several times. After seven years she moved to a new job with a foreign trade company. She worked there as an internal consultant, and she got to know the Hungarian industry. Later, Ildikó moved back to the Documentation Bureau of the Post and mostly she translated documentation from her home. Translation was her main additional earning until the 1990s, because her salary and the salary of her university lecturer husband were not enough to support her family. Actually, the weekends were mostly spent with translating.

In 1981 Ildikó was appointed to be the head of the Documentation Bureau for one year. In this position she got to know the life of an organization from a management position. Another important experience gathered here was cooperation with and managing of others. Wherever she went during her site visits, she experienced the desperate need to improve things.

During the late 1980s Ildikó's employer undertook a cooperative project with an Austrian firm to install special equipment that would connect scarcely populated areas into the telephone network. It was a revolutionary and important step, as many small villages had little to no telephone connections. During this project she focused on the buyer-seller relationship. She discovered that when equipment arrived in Hungary, people started using it exactly in the same way they used the old equipment, just like using a vacuum cleaner together with a dustpan. Her colleagues were not prepared for using this up-to-date technology. Today Ildikó clearly sees that if one wants to use new equipment effectively, one needs a new kind of knowledge, and therefore has to invest time, energy and money.

It was a dramatic experience for her to work with a Canadian company and observe their high degree of professionalism. The employees always completed their work according to the need of the client. This was a highly unusual experience for her. Learning from that experience, she decided that one day, when she set up her own company, it should work with the highest professionalism.

The Post authorized her to work as a representative of a foreign company, Philips, from the very end of the 1980s. This meant a higher salary, more freedom and more challenges in sales than in professionalism. While on this assignment Ildikó's husband made extra money at university by researching alternative ways to substitute the equipment included in the COCOM-list. When this list ceased to exist, Ildikó's family had to look for new income.

Ildikó embarked on her entrepreneurial venture by setting up a technical company. Eleven relatives, friends, colleagues joined her. Their first job was to set up the first microwave base-station in Hungary. They worked enthusiastically to make something totally new in the middle of dramatic political changes. They worked day and night, sometimes neglecting their families, to make a go of it.

Ildikó soon realized that it was not only the industry standards that mattered, but like the Canadian firm she had encountered earlier, also the individual needs of the customer. This was the era of privatization in Hungary and many foreign investors were interested in the country. Ildikó's company provided them with information, organized business meetings, and networked with prospective foreign

▼▼▼▼▼▼▼▼▼▼▼▼▼▼▼▼▼▼▼▼▼▼

suitors. This activity made the company's name known to professionals without even spending money on public relations. Most of their profit was reinvested into the company.

Ildikó's role has remained mostly the same through the times within the company: think-tank and technician in one person. But ideas and implementation changed radically. The development of the company was not planned; it just naturally evolved.

Ildikó ensured that the company's activities were governed by two things: learning and development. The company adapted to changes quickly and effectively, and with sensitivity to quality. All this could help them to become the first company in their trade to acquire the ISO certificate.

Ildikó never undertakes innovations without participation from her employees because she knows she has to do it all together with them. It was clear to her that it was impossible to use the knowledge of other countries in the same way they do. This is why she usually does not jump into something new before getting feedback from her staff.

Today the company employs about seventy people. In 1993, when there were only twelve of them working at the company, she asked them whether they wanted to become owners. Five of them said yes. Since then, two of them left the company. The other three stayed and they are quite satisfied with their decision, because they make much more money now than before as employees.

Problems in her private life stopped the success story of company foundation and development. Her elder son was conscripted in the army for the compulsory one-year national service right before going to university. There he was treated exceptionally, because he was a very good handball player, and he did not have to obey most of the regulations, which the others had to. With some of his friends they started trading across the border. They made huge sums of money.

Once the boy was over with the national service he seemed only to be interested in making money. He was working for a company that bought wrecked cars abroad, then fixed them in Hungary. This was a good way of making a lot of money. However, the police became suspicious of his employer and took her son into custody for three months. The police inspector called her in several times each week, and made her watch her son walk in handcuffed. Probably they tried to pressure him by this to make a satisfactory confession. Finally they had to release the boy because of lack of evidence. Ildikó was shocked by this experience. Only her boyfriend was able to keep her together. She could not rely on her husband. He never visited his son in the prison even though only the parents were allowed to go in the prison visitation area. Ildikó and her husband divorced in 1998.

Meanwhile, the younger son was about to fail in school in drawing, and a psychologist recommended that Ildikó should take the son out of school for one year. He thought the son was clever and would want to go back afterwards. On the contrary, he did not want to. One night he went out to a disco with some friends and was taken into custody for three days. Since he was a minor he was left in solitary confinement to prevent him from learning bad things from the older kids. He was deeply disturbed by the solitary confinement as it caused him to feel like a caged beast. Afterwards, he took occasional employment and began boxing. One time, he met one of the criminal celebrities, who realized how well he was boxing and attempted to bring the kid with him.

Following this incident, Ildikó decided she had no other choice but to escort her son everywhere, to organize his boxing career and to help him avoid getting into trouble. The kid has become a prime boxer, receiving three international champion titles: WBC in 1997, WBU in 1999 and WBO in 2000. Thanks to his French trainer, he speaks perfect French. People around him also seem to have changed for the better, but Ildikó is still afraid of some of the dubious characters in his life.

Today, Ildikó protects other friends of her son and other kind-hearted boys who have lost the ground from below their feet. When such a young man appears, he gets a job at her company and learns how to work steadily. The employees at the company help and teach these kids and also accept the fact that sometimes such a kid gets a salary even though he has not made any profit for the company. Today, a couple of such patently trained kids work enthusiastically for the company, and they have already become beloved and respected members of the community. There is another group of employees in the company who have been unemployed for a long time or life has been tough to them in other ways. Ildikó provides the same patient and nurturing environment for this group, helping them get back on their feet.

As far as Ildikó knows, her husband has never discussed their divorce with their sons. Ildikó still does not know what he thinks about all this, besides that once he mentioned that he was fed up with the family. This statement led to their divorce, which they mutually agreed upon. Ildikó interprets her sons' different steps during the last ten years as experiments to attract their father's attention. The things that have happened to the boys, those family crises, led her to meditate on why she was so successful in work and not experiencing much success in her private life. Why was it that she could influence the people surrounding her, yet not have a comfortable marriage? Maybe work was only a way to escape the problems and conflicts, which seemed to be without solutions.

She realized that her personal life was as important to her as work. She decided to change, to learn from her experience, and to make her life more complete. Ildikó started to see her successes and failures more consciously. This decision led her to train herself more in management and personality development. At the same time, she became aware that her aim was not only to do the best technician work in Hungary, but also to build a community. And building a community is not possible with the traditional way of management. New knowledge and new consciousness were needed.

Now Ildikó is accepting those who are marginalized despite their good intentions. For some people, being in this organization means they can forget about their problems in their private lives. There are some employees who had some affairs with the police. But Ildikó can really understand those who, all of a sudden, in a young age get into trouble without any bad intentions. Even now, almost nobody has abused the company's help and caring.

Ildikó has had to learn management development to make it easier to accept these people and formulate a real community from them. She thinks that at the present she does not have the right tools needed for this task. She feels the need to study and use the knowledge of professionals in order to realize the organizational development that she would like to reach, and do it more consciously. The wish to see, listen, understand and act in a deeper, more conscious way took her to a two-year change management course, an MBTI workshop and other encounter courses.

It is hard for Ildikó to follow the daily routine of managing people. Her task, managing the company day by day, does not mean much professional challenge to her. Her objective is to prepare her sons within the next six to eight years to become good owner-managers. Today she can reasonably expect, after ten years of struggle, that her sons will manage their own companies successfully.

During the next three to four years new technology will use wide-band radio solutions. The company has to get prepared for the developments of the following three years now, with the implementation of mobile services. But it is not even sure what the future will bring. It seems sure that wireless telecommunication will be optimal for long-time development because of its flexibility. She is preparing her company for these changes. The training that taught her to focus on the future and dream it vividly also helped her to realize surprising things. Ildikó thinks that this realization supported them to build the company site within half a year instead of four whole years. She is convinced that if she can take this way of thinking into her company, it will be even more effective and not only for the owners but also the employees. When all this is done, she will draw back from management but remain an owner and look for other, more exciting tasks.

Ildikó's whole life, her struggles and experiments through the peaceful and hectic phases of her life, are an example that is important not only in this part of the world, but everywhere. Her example reinforces the need and possibilities for finding your own ways, encountering yourself and others around you, accomplishing your own potential and being persistent in realizing it.

Those creative solutions, which are aimed at overtaking our arrears, are vital for the future of Hungarian society. The managers, who are similar to Ildikó Magyar, are playing an important role in our historic times in Central Europe.

HUNGARY

Hungary is located in the heart of Europe in the Carpathian Basin. It was part of the Roman Empire, for a short while, as the province of Pannonia. The famous Hun king, Attila, operated his powerful but short-lived empire from the River Tisza. Then Germanic and Turkish (Hun and Avar) tribes attacking from the East appeared in the region.

The true origin of the Hungarians, dating back thousands of years, has never been fully clarified by science or historians. One of the prevailing theories, that their ancestral home was located on the Asian side of the Ural Mountains, and that their predecessors belong to the Finnish-Ugric family of the Ural people, is

▼▼▼▼▼▼▼▼▼▼▼▼▼▼▼▼▼▼▼▼▼

linguistically verifiable. They may well have established contact with Turkish peoples, as the Turkish word *onogur* is where the word *Hungar* comes from.

Legend has it that prior to the great venture, the occupation of the new homeland in the Carpathian Basin, the heads of the seven Hungarian tribes, espousing Eastern customs, cemented their alliance with a treaty sealed in blood, and, in the person of Árpád, chose a prince from among themselves. Árpád was successful in carrying out the huge task facing the tribes-people. Archeological finds confirm that the organized resettlement of about 500,000 Hungarians in the Carpathian Basin was achieved at the cost of relatively few casualties.

Árpád's great grandson, Géza (died 997 A.D.), had himself christened, but according to chronicles he continued to make sacrifices to heathen gods, although he made his son, the later Saint Stephen, a genuine Christian ruler. Géza achieved his goal, and his son, King Stephen I (997–1038), pursued his father's policies, building up a strong, Western-style Christian state in the Carpathian Basin.

Of Stephen's successors, László I (1077–1096) and Kálmán I (1096–1116) imposed stringent laws to ensure their subjects respected the authority of the State, ownership relations and Christian values. The relatively steady progress was interrupted in 1240 and 1242 by the dramatic incursion and ruthless ransacking of the country by Tartar (Mongol) forces, who swept across the country, scorching the land and forcing the king and his court to flee to the Adriatic.

The Árpád dynasty died out in 1301. The Anjou dynasty emerged triumphant from the rivalry between European dynasties, and snatched the Hungarian crown. Charles I managed to consolidate his grip on power. In 1335, he called together the kings of Bohemia and Poland, and at the so-called Visegrád Summit, established the first Central European alliance by initiating political and trade cooperation.

Legendary commander János Hunyadi prevented the fall of Hungary to the Ottoman Empire. From a small noble family in Transylvania, János Hunyadi grew to become one of the most powerful lords thanks to his outstanding capabilities as a commander. He organized an army from the revenues of properties he was granted in exchange for his military successes, in which army soldiers from all peoples in the Balkans threatened by Ottoman rule fought alongside one another.

In 1456, the outcome of the battle waged for Nándorfehérvár (now Belgrade) was closely watched by the whole of Europe, and in the wake of the news of his victory, thanksgiving festivities were staged across the Continent. Through his victorious campaigning, the further expansion of the Ottoman Empire was warded off for another century.

His son, Mátyás (Matthias) Hunyadi, thanks to the prestige of his father, was elected king in 1458 when still a teenager and grew up to become one of the greatest monarchs of medieval Hungary. King Matthias established a strong centralized monarchy with stable revenues, a highly qualified clerical staff under his personal supervision, and a powerful and reliable army of mercenaries (the "black army"), at the head of which he conquered Moravia, Silesia and a considerable part of Austria with Vienna.

Matthias died prematurely and without a legal successor in 1490. The powerless rulers from the Jagellô dynasty that followed bought the benevolence of more unbridled lords by granting them concessions. The international role of Hungary was wasted, its political stability shaken and social progress was deadlocked. Matthias' conquests of Moravia, Silesia and part of Austria were lost.

After the defeat at the battle of Mohács the country was torn into three parts: the central section, the so-called Conquered part, was occupied by Turkish forces; the western and northern parts, known as Royal Hungary, were governed by Ferdinand of Habsburg who took the Hungarian throne; and east of the river Tisza, a new state was established, the Transylvanian Principality.

It is thought largely due to the anti-Ottoman unity that denominational strife during the Reformation and Counter-Reformation was resolved peacefully in Hungary, despite the fact that the new ideas influenced all sections of society.

As early as the 17th century — and in line with the strengthening of the Habsburg Empire — Hungarians were forced to protect their interests not only in the face of the Ottomans but also against the Austrians. The tyranny applied by Austria following the expulsion of the Ottomans elicited unprecedented resistance, and, in 1703, led to an eight-year freedom fight. The leader of the movement was Ferenc Rákôczi II, an offspring of Transylvanian princes, who tried to render the enfeebled country combat-ready by introducing social reforms and pursuing a tolerant religious policy. Following initial successes, his attempts failed and he was forced into exile with his followers.

Among the Habsburgs, Maria Theresa and her son Joseph II (1780–1790) belong among the more striking representatives of European enlightened absolutism. They intended to modernize and strengthen the empire by engaging in more proficient

▼▼▼▼▼▼▼▼▼▼▼▼▼▼▼▼▼▼▼▼▼▼▼

public administration, by pursuing an economic policy relying on scientific progress, and a more humane social policy — and in the case of Joseph II, by introducing anticlerical measures.

The Hungarian people, like other people in the region, crossed the threshold of the 19th century with a structure relying on social and economic reforms. Count István Széchenyi (1791–1860), the greatest representative of Hungarian noble liberalism who followed English ideals, realized that the feudal system, and not subordination to Vienna, was the prime cause of Hungary's backwardness. With his highly influential theoretical works and modern practical activities, he gained everlasting fame by reforming the predominant view at the time. He sacrificed much of his private property for public goals. The name Széchenyi is associated with the foundation of the Hungarian Academy of Sciences (1825), river regulation, steam shipping and rail transport in Hungary, and the initiation of the first permanent bridge connecting Buda and Pest, the Chain bridge. Lajos Kossuth, his prime political debating partner, justly called him the greatest Hungarian.

Between 1832 and 1848 the opposition dominated by Kossuth wrested major achievements at "reform national assemblies," and in 1847, the now formally established Opposition Party openly set itself the goal of forming a modern, responsible and representative government in Hungary, rid of the tutelage of Vienna and of feudal bonds. It was in this heady intellectual and excited political atmosphere that the 1848 European wave of revolution washed over Hungary.

In the wake of news about the revolutions of Palermo and particularly in Paris, the opposition sitting at the Pozsony Diet in March 1848 exerted ever more pressure on the royal court to get its reform proposals accepted. The exciting news of the revolution in Vienna then provoked the revolution in Pest on March 15, 1848. Sándor Petofi, one of the greatest Hungarian poets, and his associates headed an enthusiastic crowd in ignoring censorship and having their Twelve Points printed, which contained the essence of the liberal reform programs.

The heroic War of Independence continued with varying military fortune for nearly a year. Its fate was finally sealed by the alliance of Emperor Joseph Francis I with the Russian czar. Hungarian forces were unable to resist the overwhelming strength of the combined Austrian and Russian forces. The last major Hungarian army laid down its arms on August 13, 1849. Hungary was merged into the

Habsburg Empire to be governed by a common, centralized bureaucracy, and the backward character of an agricultural society and the associated hierarchic relations remained practically unchanged. The Hungarian political elite attempted to hamper the operation of the repressive machinery by adopting a so-called policy of passive resistance and by rejecting all offices.

The situation in the 1860s was ripe for compromise with the Habsburgs. Negotiations aimed at reaching reconciliation began at the initiative of Ferenc Deák, the "wise man of the homeland." As a result of the talks, the Habsburg Empire transformed into a dualist state federation comprising Austria and Hungary in 1867.

The next near half a century saw an unprecedented economic and cultural boom in Hungary accompanied by political stability. World War I put an end to the prosperity. The ethnic problems of the Habsburg monarchy became an ace in the hands of its rivals, the Entente powers, which gave shelter to the emigrant national councils of the minorities and recognized them as their allies. In the autumn of 1918, the military collapse of the German-Austrian-Hungarian military alliance elicited a threat to the territorial integrity of historic Hungary: Transylvania was demanded by Romania, the Southern countries by the forming Yugoslav state, and Upper Hungary by the Czechoslovak state.

At this critical juncture, a revolution broke out in Budapest in October 1918. A republic was proclaimed, headed by Count Mihály Károlyi. The discontent of the masses was fomented further by Bolshevik agitators freshly trained and just back from Russian prison camps. Mihály Károlyi found himself in an impossible situation, and finally handed over power in March 1919 to the Communist Hungarian Republic of Councils headed by the Bolshevik Béla Kun. During its short three-month rule, the Republic of Councils aimed to implement its social programs through nationalization and revolutionary terror, while continuing its struggle for the territorial integrity of the country. Czech and Romanian intervention elicited its collapse.

Hungary lost two-thirds of its original territory, and more than half of its population. As opposed to its new neighbors, Hungary became a virtually homogenous nation state, while one-third of the Hungarian population — in total more than three million Hungarians — became an ethnic minority in several neighboring successor states.

Reforms introduced by the deeply conservative Horthy regime, which retained essential parliamentary elements, did little to modernize the backward social structure. Hungary's reward for joining the Axis powers was to have the Hungarian-inhabited areas in Czechoslovakia and Romania re-annexed after the start of Nazi aggression (1938–1940). The Hungarian government showed more readiness in the war against the Soviet Union while, particularly after suffering massive defeats on the Eastern front, the traditional elite, which had harbored mixed feelings about the Nazi movement, sought an agreement with the Western powers. On learning about the true feelings of this "involuntary satellite," German troops occupied the country on March 19, 1944.

Meanwhile, the Red Army was surging ahead and the entire country was transformed into a military theater by the spring of 1945. As a result of total military defeat, the old system and state sovereignty itself collapsed and a million-strong army was stationed in the shattered country. Its leaders made promises to guarantee self-rule although, as became known later during the 1945 Yalta conference grouping, the great powers had already decided among themselves that Hungary, together with its neighbors, would belong to the Soviet sphere of influence.

The first three years after World War II saw an attempt to operate a multi-party democracy in militarily occupied Hungary. The Stalinist dictatorship introduced by Rákosi between 1948 and 1953 concluded nationalization and launched a rush program for the development of heavy industry, obliging peasants to turn in their crops and join kolhoz-type cooperatives which expropriated their lands.

Resistance to the totalitarian regime broke out with elementary force in Hungary, and led to the revolution of October 23, 1956. Imre Nagy, popular throughout the country because of the 1953 reform he had initiated, took over as head of the revolutionary government. The multi-party system was restored and Hungary quit the Warsaw Treaty, the East bloc military alliance. However, after some vacillation the Soviet government opted in favor of intervention, and on November 4, 1956, it brutally crushed the revolution. Some 200,000 refugees left a country shocked to its very core, while the era hallmarked by János Kádár, who was appointed to head the reorganized communist party as the puppet of the Soviets, entrenched itself with an unprecedented wave of reprisals.

Industrialization and collectivization were carried out peacefully. Gradually more attention was paid to the manufacture of consumer items that was encouraged by the so-called "new economic mechanism," reforms introduced from 1968 granting greater scope of operation to private enterprises. These developments brought about the terms for starting to transform the system of political institutions and the economy, terms which were conceived by the "reform communists" who dismissed Kádár in May 1988 after his resistance to any further change and who still thought they could maintain control of events.

The Hungarian Democratic Forum (MDF) came forward with a program criticizing the communist system on the basis of national traditions, and from the autumn of 1987, it organized public debates on the state of the country. The "democratic opposition" that had operated an underground press ("Samizdat") since the early 1980s established the Alliance of Free Democrats (SzDSz), while the independent organization of university students, the Federation of Young Democrats (FIDESz), also defined itself as a liberal party. At the end of 1988, beginning of 1989, parties defining the democratic era immediately after World War II were revived, namely the Independent Smallholders' Party (FKGP), the Christian Democratic People's Party (KDNP) and the Hungarian Social Democratic Party (MSzDP). The frameworks for a peaceful change of regime were established at the "trilateral negotiations" comprising the Opposition Round Table, the mass organizations, and the party-state leaders in March 1989.

An agreement and the codification of that agreement took place in the autumn of 1989, laying the basis of a constitutional state ruled by law. Shortly afterwards, the Republic of Hungary was proclaimed on October 23, 1989. The country's official old name (Hungarian People's Republic) was changed, a move which symbolically expressed the essence of the change of regime: the regaining of the country's sovereignty, and the replacement of the central plan command management and state-party system with a market economy and a multi-party democracy. Reformers in the Hungarian Socialist Workers' Party finally dissolved this party and transformed it into the Hungarian Socialist Party, contributing as catalysts in this process.

As a result of the 1990 elections, the MDF became the most powerful party in Parliament, and in coalition with the two other center-right parties, the FKGP and

▼▼▼▼▼▼▼▼▼▼▼▼▼▼▼▼▼▼▼▼▼▼

the KDNP, the president of the winning party, Jôzsef Antall, formed a government. Árpád Göncz, who had been sentenced to death for his activities in 1956, was voted president of the republic, and received a further five-year vote of confidence from Parliament in 1995. The Hungarian Socialist Party (MSzP), which gained in strength toward the end of the previous parliamentary cycle, won the elections in 1994. The SzDSz, which once again finished second in the elections, took a place in the coalition government of party president Gyula Horn.

In 1998, the previous parliamentary cycle's opposition was able to form a government again, this time under the leadership of Viktor Orbán, president of the center-right FIDESz — Hungarian Civic Party, with the participation of the FKGP and MDF. Nevertheless, despite a changeable public mood, isolated extremist forces never threatened the stability of domestic politics.

Foreign and domestic owners have mostly privatized the industry, agriculture and service. Hungary is the third country in the world having a special law on employee ownership. The economy in the first half of the decade went through a crisis, because of the collapse of the Soviet market. Now it has been increasing. At the same time, the entrepreneurship has been in bloom. Many new businesses, mostly in the service sector, have been set up.

During the 1100 years that have elapsed since Hungarian tribes settled down in the Carpathian Basin, Hungary has on several occasions felt that its adjustment and catching up were successful. Today, meeting the strict demands of economic growth, stabilization and European integration, the country once again trusts that its re-entry into the community of European countries will prove to be final this time.

THE MBTI AND OTHER HUMAN SYSTEMS DEVELOPMENT METHODS

I will now review various assessment methods gaining ground in Hungary[1] and will include several arbitrarily chosen examples.

THE PAST AND PRESENT OF THE MBTI IN HUNGARY

The MBTI first appeared in Hungary in the 1980s. The first person to work with it was Dr. Imre Lövey who applied it in organization development. He and his colleagues at Concordia Consulting Ltd. have been using it mainly in two fields. The first is research among company managers and the second is group cooperation.

RESEARCH

Lövey[2], managing partner of Concordia Consulting Ltd., conducted research[3] in 1989 among Hungarian company managers. The sample group consisted of 299 people, 75 percent of whom were men. One third were top managers; the remaining were middle managers. With respect to their ages, 42 percent were between the ages 31 and 40 years and 38 percent between 41 and 50 years.

The most surprising find was connected with the Sensing-Intuition (S-N) and Thinking-Feeling (T-F) scales: 79 percent of male and 93 percent of female managers reported a preference for Sensing. The author explains the difference between the sexes with the notion that women had to comply with the expectations of the dominant culture even more than men in order to be able to move upwards. However the significant under-representation of those with a preference for Intuition among Hungarian company managers should not make us very optimistic. Ninety-five percent of the men, who made up 75 percent of the sample group, were decision makers with a preference for Thinking. Among the women, this proportion was pronounced with 81 percent reporting a preference for Thinking. The author finds a deep contradiction between the publicly voiced humanitarian ideas of the communist regime as compared to a near total lack of those reporting a preference for Feeling. We anticipate that the same research would show different results now as a result of the fall of communism.

Mária Jobbágy[4] and Péter Takács conducted another research project. They worked on their research[5] between 1992 and 1994 with a total sample group of 471 people: 186 of them were job-searching unemployed; 149 were secondary school students; 40 were university students; and 96 were teachers. Women constituted 71 percent of the group, and 29 percent of the group were men. Their study showed about 45 percent of the sample population to have a preference for Intuition, and as for the Thinking-Feeling preference pair, 47 percent of the women reported a preference for Thinking, while it is 77 percent with the sampled men.

▼▼▼▼▼▼▼▼▼▼▼▼▼▼▼▼▼▼▼▼▼

The authors of the research focused on secondary school teachers and their students. In the case of secondary school students (aged between 14 and 18), the most characteristic was the ENFP type. It was 16 percent among the 95 girls, and 20 percent among the 54 boys. They researched teachers in two different types of schools: those who worked in traditional schools, and those who worked in experimental schools (65 and 31 people, respectively). The research came to a partly surprising conclusion — 71 percent of those working in traditional schools were Introverted and 72 percent were Sensing, compared with only 55 percent and 35 percent data in the case of experimental school teachers. Twenty-five percent of the teachers who work in traditional schools belong to the ISTJ group, and the same is true about the ISFJ group. While 19 percent of the experimental school teachers belonged to the INTJ and 16 percent to the INFP group.

A summary of this research suggests that the historical changes taking place in Hungary may empower individuals to report their best-fit preference rather than reporting what they perceive to be the more socially desirable preferences. If this hypothesis is correct then it may be possible to grab the political changes through reported MBTI types not only on a macro level, but also on the level of the individuals and organizations.

I am pleased to report that there has been extensive additional research conducted at the Budapest Technical University by my colleague, Dr. Ildikó Takács, and her colleagues in connection with student consultation. They now have a database of 1500, mostly among technically oriented men.

TRAINING

If the MBTI is used for training, it is aimed at developing self-awareness and cooperation among the members of a management team. Therefore, it takes place at companies focusing on management development. As far as we know, Imre Lövey, Júlia Mezey and the Concordia Ltd conducted the first of such programs in the 1980s. In the following decade, a number of different trainers held programs. The country became more open and the Internet became more popular, therefore these methods became available at least for those who spoke good English.

There has been some MBTI-based training for teachers, too, conducted by Mária Jobbágy and Péter Takács. They designed a program for teachers with the title, "The teacher-student relationship and the role of preferences in education," which deals with effectiveness and conflicts between the teacher-student-parent trinity based on personality types.

The same two persons also organize programs for the human services, mostly management training for managers of social institutions. During these programs, the managers get to know the theory of the MBTI and the development opportunities for the different management styles. In the program, they experience how they impact others and how the knowledge of the typological peculiarities can help them solve conflicts and problems. They also explore how they handle time, information and structure, and how they organize their work.

During the training programs for social workers, they apply the method of case-discussion groups. Here, they select group leaders based on their temperaments and study the characteristics of the different management styles and the possibilities and barriers that are implied in the differences. By sharing their experiences, it becomes possible for them to discuss the differences.

The MBTI was also introduced in higher education as a possible tool for those with the major of psychology and human resources. In this respect, the MBTI has remained an essentially theoretical subject. One of the professors who talks about the MBTI is Aranka Mészáros[6], who lectures on work and management psychology at the University of Gödöllo.

Mária Jobbágy and I hold open training for mixed groups. The majority of the members of these groups are organization development experts, but there are always one or two NGO-managers, journalists, students, entrepreneurs or government officials. Some of these programs contain basics of the MBTI: the method of speed-reading, the basic rules of ethical usage. Others are more targeted at coaching and at change management.

The same two trainer-consultants have designed and conducted a series of programs to help to manage and prevent secondary school dropouts. In this program there is training and consultation for the employees of the family-care center, and a group consultation program for the dropout kids and their parents. The program aims at recognition and appreciation of the individual differences, and helping to find a satisfying educational and life program for the boys and girls.

A number of Anglo-Saxon owned companies know or apply MBTI concepts in their management development. Quite often their managers also speak English and work with foreign consultants. Sometimes they use the type indicator found on the

▼▼▼▼▼▼▼▼▼▼▼▼▼▼▼▼▼▼▼▼▼

Internet, even though they realize the reliability of that instrument is in serious doubt. When we use the term "application of the MBTI," we are using the term in a very broad sense. Until the time of preparing this study, questionnaires translated into Hungarian were only allowed to be used for research purposes by CPP. This situation has led to an unsatisfied need for Hungarian language questionnaires in the business world. As a result, many people tried to find some kind of easy-to-apply substitute. Therefore they either made their own questionnaires, basically pulling from the original MBTI, or used another, less protected tool for this purpose. Some programs use the concept itself, others use the closely related Temperaments concept. Some trainers use questionnaires, others do their programs without them. We can expect a wider range of applications and more control over them if the Hungarian language MBTI would be validated. But there is also a need for qualifying training programs in the Hungarian language, because there are only a few qualified trainers and consultants in Hungary, who could legally buy and use the questionnaire.

BUSINESS APPLICATIONS

The need for management development has increased significantly in recent years. And if we recall the results of Imre Lövey's research, this is a very promising tendency. We think that this tendency will become even stronger in the next millennium.

The application of the MBTI in the sphere of businesses, NGOs and the government is in its childhood in Hungary, but significant growth is expected. According to our experiences, the management development methods are spreading more and more.

MBTI applications at the moment are present most in the field of human resources and consultation. Andrea Dömölky[7], HR manager of one of the most well known international telecommunication companies, uses the MBTI to evaluate the preferences of various work teams. This approach is followed by other users as well. Everybody we have talked to mentioned that his or her level of consciousness was elevated, and he or she became more open and receptive to differences.

THE FUTURE OF THE MBTI IN HUNGARY

In our opinion, there are great opportunities for the application of the MBTI. The work that was done in the 1980s and 1990s by forerunners in the business and nonprofit sectors will reach its peak in the first decade of 2000.

We expect the fastest growth in the business sphere. Although in this part of the world we get quite often impatient, we need to realize that these changes are fast and historical ones. While in the past, those with preferences for STJ could find their way to high management positions with a greater probability, in the recent several years, with entrepreneurial opportunities widened, more and more other types can successfully try to climb to top positions.

These patterns are gaining ground because they reflect success. It is striking to see that these changes are extremely radical on the level of the individual. The fact that previously proven concepts and methods are being questioned causes deep individual uncertainty and conflict. This process cannot be stopped, but with spreading the concept of the MBTI, we can help to realize and recognize the changes, and help to become successful with less inner conflict.

Besides management work, these new concepts and tools are also gaining ground in the field of human resources management. In the non-profit sector, we think the MBTI will gain ground especially in family counseling. There are certain facts indicating that the family-counseling network is becoming a customer focused service in Hungary, and the openness of the social workers to new and effective tools has grown significantly.

We expect similar tendencies in education in the first decade of the new millennium. Great efforts are being made in order to modernize the whole Hungarian education system and to introduce quality development. As a result of these we are expecting the participants of education to become real clients, and that institutions would become more fine-tuned for the needs of the customer. This would open the door for the MBTI, and on the other hand the MBTI would help in this fine-tuning.

The first steps have also been made in employment related services. As mass unemployment appeared very fast in Hungary in the beginning of the 1990s (close

▼▼▼▼▼▼▼▼▼▼▼▼▼▼▼▼▼▼▼▼▼▼▼

to 15 percent), the whole employment service had to be set up. Setting up a service system for the unemployed, it was necessary to abandon completely the obsolete previous system of handling unemployment insignificant in volume, and authoritarian in its form. This change took place with the support of the World Bank and other international organizations. The methods developed in Western countries, which have had longer experiences in dealing with unemployment, could become part of the everyday practices of the Hungarian employment network very fast. Though the MBTI does not belong to these methods yet, we see great opportunities for its applications in this field, too.

We think there are great opportunities also in training front-line people at companies who operate with a large group of customers. It does not matter if these are profit oriented or nonprofit organizations, as long as they aim at developing a more customer focused operation. We agree with one of the interviewed MBTI-users, Ms. Dömölky, who says that it will be useful to use the MBTI in Hungary in developing self-awareness and self-esteem and in more effective orientation to the world.

The MBTI can be effective in the individual development of the employees, in career-planning, training of successors, improving cooperation at the workplace and in one's private life. It can also be useful in the training of middle managers and in matching tasks with suitable persons or work groups. Experimental programs should be designed with these purposes, and the application should be further developed based on the lessons learned.

A professor of the University of Gödöllo, Aranka Mészáros teaches her graduate students with the major in human resources management. She thinks they will be able to use the MBTI during their work in job-analysis, personal selection and reducing the conflicts arising from people complying with their tasks or roles. She also sees an opportunity for using the MBTI in formulating professional teams, setting tasks for these teams, team development, performance management, creating individual development programs and training plans, care planning, organization development, and in their interpersonal relations. As we widen their knowledge about themselves, we will be clarifying and fine-tuning the requirements they set for the people with whom they cooperate.

One of the most interesting and potentially most successful areas of organization development is the reinforcement of cooperation between people, working in different areas or levels of the organization. It is well known that this can be done by developing communication. Communication has many obstacles in present day organizations — one is that we are not aware of our own personal filters, which we use unconsciously. If we can develop awareness about it, we can improve our performance by other factors unchanged. This process is helped by the MBTI in organization development initiatives.

It seems that the MBTI can gain ground in education — in not only training for teachers, but for most of the aforementioned purposes. Both students and teachers can learn and gain insight into the learning and teaching processes from using the MBTI.

The successful validation of the questionnaire can bring about significant developments generally in all types of applications and research. At the same time we can see a growing danger of the misuse of this tool. There are rumors of companies that want to use the MBTI in making decisions about their employees. Such rumors stress the importance of knowledge about the ethical application of the MBTI, both in training and publications. Through cooperation with CPP, CAPT and CEECAP, we hope to ensure the ethical use of type in Hungary.

OTHER MANAGEMENT DEVELOPMENT METHODS

We can talk about significant management development since the 1980s. The first such training was held in 1979 by Manohar Nadkarni from India with the support of UNIDO. This program focused on organization development. Later there were different programs aimed at developing efficiency in research, education and organizations. Still these programs were sporadic. Due to the relative economic stability and the demand-dominated national and regional European markets, the organizations were neither forced nor encouraged to improve their productivity and operation processes.

The dramatic political changes in 1989–90 caused significant changes in the private and organizational lives of people in the whole region. Registered unemployment went from 0–12 percent; inflation jumped over 30 percent. The multiparty political system, a grass-roots initiation, was a part of these great changes. Individual opportunities, and yet at the same time instability, grew extremely high. It is quite understandable that the previous relative stability and the radical economic and political changes forced managers to focus mainly on the

▼▼▼▼▼▼▼▼▼▼▼▼▼▼▼▼▼▼▼▼▼

present and their own survival in their positions. The company managers, who had to face a need for adaptation, were confused and kept on repeating, "we can't even foresee one year." They found themselves in a totally strange environment, losing their usual support systems, stable positions and incomes. Those managers who were able to make and execute fast and confident decisions could not only survive, but become very successful and wealthy.

The collapse of the huge but unpretentious "socialist" market in the early 1990s and the narrow access channels to the markets of the highly developed capitalist countries challenged most companies. These processes have been changing the views of company managers.

Since the middle of the 1990s, more and more organizations have been working on getting their ISO certificate, because their business partners require it from them. The TQM-culture also began to gain ground slowly. Since 1995, the National Prize for Quality (similar to the Baldrige Award) became a highly desired award to apply for at the Hungarian Center for Industrial and Commercial Quality Development[8].

From 1989 on, the change of the ownership structure of the productive potential of the country began to speed up gradually. Different views fought with each other about the issue, who should get access to state owned assets in the process of privatization. Traditional liberal views coexisted with concepts of broad-based employee ownership. This debate was the origin of the Hungarian concept of employee share ownership, which in those days all parliamentary parties supported. This support helped Hungary to become the third country in the world having a special, genuine law on employee share ownership, although in a way they are still connected to privatization. Two nonprofit organizations are working on exceeding these limitations. One of them is the Share-Participation Foundation[9], which designed and piloted a major organization development program with the aim to spread participation, empowerment and involvement, striving for the modernization of these employee-owned companies. The Foundation also has built a rich, open library that serves as a good resource for management consultants who would not otherwise have access to this kind of literature. The other organization that supports employee ownership is the National Association of Employee Owners and their Companies. It has a membership pool of 30,000 people engaged in counseling and lobbying. Despite the success of many of the 300 such companies, the legal support for the sustainability of employee ownership is still awaited.

In the last five years or so, the Hungarian economy has found its place in the new regional political and economic environment. Many of the major state-owned companies collapsed, others are just on the level of survival, while some achieved new successes in the process of privatization. An old notion is becoming popular again — planning can help reach a desired future. This new kind of planning is less for governmental administrative purposes, but involves people wanting to shape their own future. This significant change can be experienced especially in some subsidiaries of multinational companies wanting to implant their back-home practices also in Hungary.

The first experiments in empowerment were conducted in the Management Training Institute as early as the 1980s. Later, Concordia Consulting Ltd., which was set up by experts leaving the Institute, continued this approach. They helped to initiate organization development projects in a number of state owned companies.

After the collapse of the Soviet market, companies found increasingly their orientation in the Western markets. More and more owners and managers of these companies saw the key to their success in the development of their planning and management systems to meet Western standards. Some of them even reached the point that they allowed themselves to think about training programs, visioning, strategy building, action planning and implementation programs. Increasingly one finds a need for management development, effectiveness improvement, change management and organization development programs in Hungary.

The growing demand and the conditions of a free market give an opportunity for experimenting. There is hardly any management development trend that could not be seen even in Hungarian-owned or joint venture companies. Let us mention a couple of these programs, but definitively there will not be a full picture.

According to Péter Baneth, the manager of one of the consultant companies, even though we find a wide range of management concepts in operation in the transformed Hungarian companies, the management in medium-size Hungarian companies remains basically the same, operating according to traditional authoritarian management methods, due to an entrenched resistance to change.

Opinions are different as to what kind of management practice is followed by the large number of multinational companies, which are present in Hungary partly as a consequence of privatization since the early 1990s. Some of them are implementing the most up-to-date management culture, while others are importing their traditional culture.

The knowledge and application of the MBTI and other contemporary management models (e.g. Hersey's Situational Leadership or Thomas Kilman's conflict-management model) is limited to an easily identifiable circle of companies. Some experts think the good companies will become even better because they are using modern management methods, while those with traditionally Thinking top managers do not regard these approaches as useful for themselves and their companies—this disregard melts down their competitive advantage. Therefore, availability of information, benchmarking and other ways of generating knowledge are becoming increasingly important missions for organizations like the Hungarian Organization Development Society.

Consultants, professors, teachers and researchers at universities, having access to the management literature in English, and having connections to the business world, are making this knowledge available. They can help with diagnostic and management development models, and can also work as consultants, disseminating knowledge of the models to the business world. A large number of different tests, models and self-evaluations are used in the companies, and because it is hard to find information about these in Hungarian, it is often the case that nobody knows about the original author or resource. So while the models and management development tools are gaining ground, their authors are quite often left in the shade of anonymity.

Such methods which can be used instantly and bring immediate results are used the most widely. One such example is project planning and management. A market leader in this field is Szinergia Kft. (Synergy Ltd.), which aims at reaching results and success at their partners by involving all the collaborating parties. They provide consulting and training for organizations in order to reach a more effective project planning and realization culture.

At the same time, a lot of efforts are made for strengthening the behavioral science based organization development. As we have mentioned earlier, Concordia was one of the pioneers in this field. A significant and successful series of pilot development programs was initiated also by the Share-Participation Foundation to adapt an employee ownership, empowerment and involvement based organizational culture in Hungary. This work was supported by a grant of the US Agency for International Development (USAID).

Management development methods can also be spread through the meetings of the workers of different organizations when they can exchange their different experiences. Major initiatives were made to invite leaders of successful American companies to come to Hungary to help the organization in its further development. The New York based Financial Services Volunteers Corps (FSVC) helped to arrange such visits, too. Another possibility is that Hungarian company managers visit successful foreign companies to gain a close look at their success. The Share-Participation Foundation — besides the previously mentioned other method — organized tours for about sixty Hungarian managers to highly successful, participative American employee owned companies.

Learning and experimenting is going on. In 1998, a training program started for development of 100 change management experts with the support of the British Know How Fund. In the first phase, twenty people were trained in English with the participation of British consultants. In the second phase, the first twenty Hungarian consultants trained eighty others in Hungarian language. Half of the participants were selected from small- and medium-size companies and nonprofit organizations, while the other half were independent consultants. Concordia developed another program for training external and internal organization development consultants. The International Business School at the Budapest University of Economics run also such programs, and there is an independent initiative for training the trainers.

Some professionals are trained abroad, which would hardly be possible without the support of foreign institutions. As an example, the Gestalt Institute in Cleveland also gives scholarships to some Hungarian participants to take part in the International Organization and System Development program.

In Hungary, just like in other countries, a wide range of different methods and procedures for management are available. Some of these are in contradiction with each other, and some of them focus on short-term successes. Others seem useless

▼▼▼▼▼▼▼▼▼▼▼▼▼▼▼▼▼▼▼▼▼▼▼

in the short run, but promising and productive in the long run — some of them concentrate on processes, and others on people. As none have shown us the stone of wisdom, we can only be happy to see so much experimenting going on, which is typical of this part of the world. We also can hope that these experiments are taken cautiously, and that the people involved do matter the most in all of them.

ENDNOTES AND REFERENCES

[1] Without mentioning their names, I would like to thank all those who agreed that their names and thoughts be published. Special thanks to Ildikó Magyar, who shared the details of her exciting and symbolically important life with us. I would also like to thank János Lukács for his ideas and support. Ákos Riczmann was helping me a lot with gathering nation-wide data. The author takes all the responsibilities in connection with the contents and interpretation of this study.

[2] ilovey@concordia-od.hu

[3] Lövey, I. (1992). Characterisation of Hungarian managers with international test score comparisons. V*ezetéstudomány (Management Science)*, Issue No. 1–2. Budapest.

[4] jobbagym@mail.hupe.hu

[5] Jobbágy, M. and Takács, P. (1997, June–July). Az a közös bennünk, Hogy mások vagyunk [One thing is common in us, we are all different]. *Iskolakultúra* [School Culture].

[6] peari@egon.gyaloglo.hu

[7] andrea.domolky@nokia.com

[8] www.mik.hu

[9] To find out more information about the Share-Participation Foundation, contact them at www.rvaspf.hu

MACEDONIA

Cvetko Smilevski
Detra Centre, Skopje

EDITOR'S NOTES. Dr. Smilevski, Co-Founder of the Central and Eastern European Center for Applied Psychology (CEECAP), introduces us to Kiro Stevanovski, a successful Macedonian entrepreneur. We follow Mr. Stevanovski's story as the Republic of Macedonia makes the transformation from a controlled to a free economy.

Dr. Smilevski then acquaints the reader with the history of Macedonia including the creation of the Republic of Macedonia during the last decade. We also learn about the introduction of the MBTI to Macedonia. The MBTI spreads rapidly to neighboring countries across Southern Central Europe. It was the Macedonians who first shared the vision with Dr. Mary McCaulley of CAPT, and myself, for using the MBTI as a tool for opening dialogues with those of different ethnic origins across the region.

KIRO STEVANOVSKI

In the spring of 1992, a war was underway in the former Yugoslav territories. Economic liaisons between a large number of companies were disrupted one after another. One of the largest of these organisations, with factories and cooperatives throughout the region, was Crvena Zvezda Institutes. Crevna Zvezda Institutes is a large, vertically integrated car manufacturer. The company plant, "Heroj Toza Dragovic" (HTD), located in the lakeside resort town of Ohrid, was one constituent of the integrated system. HTD produces a number of spare car parts, mostly accessories. For example, the safety belts manufactured in the Ohrid plant were then completed with plastic lids produced in "Jugoplastika" plant located in Split, Croatia.

Because the war reached into Croatia, this cooperative stopped delivering half-finished goods for the Zastava system. After many months of procrastination, HTD Ohrid was still not able to find a solution for the completion of the safety belts. In a discussion on the participation of their cooperative for plastic products from Bitola, Kiro Stevanovski (ISTJ), the founder and owner of the Enigma Company, was asked if he could produce a solution for a new source of plastic lids for the safety belts. Mr. Stevanovski asked to see a sample of the desired product. After a cursory inspection, he said, "Come to my company tomorrow to see a prototype." The people present at the occasion could not believe him at first, but they went to Bitola anyway. After a day's and night's hard work, without access to the most appropriate manufacturing equipment, the first sample was produced. HTD immediately placed an order and Kiro Stevanovski then produced a whole series. A difficult consequence from the war was overcome, and another success entered the entrepreneur/leader Stevanovski's record — another satisfied client and another market opportunity created for the development of his company.

The entrepreneur Stevanovski has the best combination of three very important leadership factors:

- entrepreneurial tradition in his family,
- systematic technical education,
- hard work and persistence.

His grandfather, Krste, got into and developed a business with flourmills very fast in the Prilep area, even before World War II. After the war, his mills and a part of his agricultural property were nationalized. However, once legal grounds were established, he rented some of his mills from the state and then, working within the frames of the legislation concerning private business, spread the business to the larger town of Bitola.

Krste's son, Kiro Stevanovski's father, Aleksandar, took on the family entrepreneurial tradition. Aleksandar undertook reconstruction and improvement of machinery, independent production of chicken incubators and farming chickens. He was among the first in Macedonia to become involved with production of TV antennas, electric heaters and other consumer goods. These were all activities in addition to his teaching practical work in the area of metals.

Kiro Stevanovski observed his father's work from early age, and after he had become a high school student, he began to work with his father on electricity installations and repair and maintenance of machinery. This left a deep mark on him — love for technology, innovation and self-realization. The desire to work and earn from every opportunity the market offers led Kiro Stevanovski, from as early as sixteen years of age, to work all over Macedonia with a combine where, together with his father during summer recesses, he harvested barley and wheat in Pelagonija, then rice in the Kocani area, and finally sunflower back in Pelagonija. It goes without saying that Kiro and his father maintained the first, and then the second and the third, combine themselves. Kiro Stevanovski says, "The basis of everything I have earned as experience and capital lies in the twenty years of work with combines — one of the hardest jobs."

After graduating from high school, Stevanovski acquired a University diploma from the Faculty of Mechanical Engineering and started working as a high school teacher. After a year's work, he abandoned teaching and found a job in the Bitola Feed Mill as the Head of the Vehicle Department (1980–1983). He then moved on to Avtoremont-Bitola, a company for maintenance of cars (1983–1989). In both of these companies he made several innovations and improvements to the operations, which enabled him to become an assistant on motor vehicle maintenance in the Technical School in Bitola as an additional engagement.

▼▼▼▼▼▼▼▼▼▼▼▼▼▼▼▼▼▼▼▼▼▼

The first incentives for starting up his own business, which would emphasize his technical knowledge in machinery maintenance, evolved in the mid-1980s, when small businesses started to develop rapidly in Slovenia. There, Mr. Stevanovski and his colleague, Volkanovski from Kavadarci, learned that the production of plastic products could develop into a good business. In 1997 their wishes came true — they entered the plastics business by buying second-hand machinery from Slovenia.

At the very beginning they faced the main problem of most entrepreneurial ventures — they invested all their money into the machinery, so they did not have anything left for the production of some very expensive tools for vacuumed plastics. Nothing else remained but to make the tools. Another, even greater problem followed immediately — in the existing society, the large, government owned companies, which were the only ones in a need of their products, were reluctant to work with private suppliers. So, they were clearly very satisfied when they started to work on plastic packaging for "Jadran" from Negotino. They signed their names on the first notes they earned and have kept them as a trophy.

After two years working together as one firm, the two partners decided to create separate companies. In that period it was not possible to create private companies, so in 1987, the company, Enigma, was founded as an independent proprietary store with a basic activity of manufacturing plastic materials and employing up to ten persons, pertinent to the law. With the process of democratization of the country and the opening of the legal possibilities for private initiative brought by the Law on Companies, it was possible to engage in a more rapid development of the company.

This period matched Stevanovski's inability to fulfill his managerial and entrepreneurial capability and ambitions in the company he worked for. As most people with an entrepreneurial spirit do, he decided to abandon the safe state job and to take up the risk of private work. The private store was transformed into Enigma — a fully liable, private company for production, trade, services and export-import, a family company owned by the Stevanovskis.

The basic activity of the company was offering products and services that were imported from the former Yugoslav republics, mostly from Slovenia:

- polyethylene foils, bags for packaging food and industrial products, hoses, protection tapes, belt protectors, etc.,
- vacuumed PVC and polysterol packaging,
- package print.

The need for collection of debts through compensation, as well as procurement of raw materials and spare parts, conditioned the development of wholesale and retail trade as a secondary activity. Their most recent activity has been transportation of goods in their own vehicles. The main clients of Enigma are candy, confection and food factories, the knitted fabrics industry and retail trade.

The development of Enigma has been followed by a number of difficulties that other new companies face as well, and has been augmented by the consequences of the various wars that occurred during the break up of the former Yugoslav republics.

In the beginning, it was very hard to cover the overhead costs. The premises were far from the communication lines and were inadequate. The purchase of spare parts and raw materials required extra efforts. The insolvency of the whole economy made the collection of claims very difficult, so trade had to be developed, besides the basic activity — production.

The persistence and expert knowledge created an opportunity to overcome the limitations, and the business year of 1992 ended successfully in every aspect: administrative space was leased to be used for production as well as adequate offices, and investments were made in freighters and other equipment.

There are always new challenges for entrepreneurs. The completion of the production of plastic goods created further financial conditions for the development of the company in new areas: new machinery for broadening the scope and quality of the existing production, increasing the number of vehicles, opening warehouses, joint investment with foreign capital in deficient products. Responding to the needs of the market and the clients is the basic orientation of Kiro Stevanovski and his company.

In 1998, the entrepreneur Stevanovski managed to obtain an investment credit of 600,000 DM (German Deutch Marks) for the purpose of buying his own premises where Enigma is now situated and from where they offer complete

▼▼▼▼▼▼▼▼▼▼▼▼▼▼▼▼▼▼▼▼▼

production spectrum of plastic products. However, Stevanovski's ambitions haven't stopped here. Only 50 percent of the space is engaged in a current production program. The remaining portion awaits favorable conditions, including partner investments in a new program, most probably the production of paper packaging as a part of the broader environmental program in the Republic of Macedonia.

MACEDONIA

The Republic of Macedonia is a small country located in the south central region of Europe. Our neighbors include Yugoslavia to the north, Albania to the west, Bulgaria to the East and Greece to the south. The Republic of Macedonia officially declared its independence from the Yugoslav Federation on September 8, 1991, following a referendum on Macedonian independence. The capital of Macedonia is Skopje, with a population of 545,228 inhabitants in 1994. At that time 59 percent of Macedonians lived in urban areas, 40.2 percent in rural settings; 50.1 percent male and 49 percent female; 24.9 percent were below fourteen years of age, 66.5 percent were from fifteen to sixty-five years of age and 8.6 percent were over sixty-five. The official language is Macedonian, written in the Cyrillic alphabet. The main religions are Eastern Orthodox Christianity and Islam.

In 1996, the GDP was 3.1 billion U.S. dollars, actual growth being 0.75 percent; per capita GDP was 1581 U.S. dollars. At the time, 789,081 people were economically active: 17.72 percent in agriculture; 28.92 percent in industry; 45.30 percent in the service sector; and 8.06 percent in other branches of the economy. The national currency is the denar, which has a floating exchange rate.

The Republic of Macedonia has a parliamentary system of government. An assembly of 120 deputies is elected for a term of four years in national elections. A President is elected for a five-year term by free and fair national Presidential elections. The President can serve only two terms. Executive power is vested in the Government. The key political parties are: the Macedonian Social-Democratic League; the VMRO-Democratic Party for National Unity of Macedonians; the Liberal-Democratic Party; the Party for Democratic Prosperity; the Democratic Alternative; the Socialist Party; and the Democratic Party of Albanians. Following administrative reforms in 1996, there are now 123 units of self-government in Macedonia, replacing the previous system of thirty-four municipalities.

Some fundamental changes in the political, legislative and economic spheres have taken place as a consequence of abandoning the old system and the disintegration of the former Yugoslav Federation. The establishment of a new socio-economic system in a relatively short period of time was very important in terms of the adoption of new values (democracy and a market economy). Democracy meant coming closer to the European Union (EU), mostly in the creation of legislation compatible with EU standards, and also the acceptance of Macedonia as a member of the international community.

Apart from the positive outcomes of political democratisation and market orientation, the Republic of Macedonia faces serious problems. Situated in the centre of the turbulent Balkans, it has experienced negative consequences from the UN embargo imposed on Serbia due to its aggression in Bosnia and Herzegovina and more recently due to events in Kosovo. The economy has declined significantly following the loss of markets in the former Yugoslav republics. There was also a serious blow dealt to the Macedonian economy by the blockade imposed by Greece as a result of an earlier disagreement about the name of the republic; the problem has since been resolved. Even at the beginning of the new millennium, however, stagnation is evident in Macedonian economic development.

In addition to negative trends in the economy and the general instability in the region, Macedonia is also coping with political problems with its resident ethnic Albanians. Increasing tension between ethnic Macedonians and ethnic Albanians is a serious factor of internal destabilization. We struggle with our goal of being a multicultural society surviving in a region with a long history of ethnic intolerance.

Although the country faces many difficulties, there are reforms in the process of finalisation. There is genuine consensus, accepted by the key political players, with regard to the strategic targets to be achieved by the Republic of Macedonia, such as the market economy, democracy and membership of the EU and NATO. However, there is still little agreement about the details and the ways of achieving these targets. Political views differ considerably on these key changes that are to take place.

Similar to Mr. Stevanovski's family tradition, the beginnings of entrepreneurship in Macedonia should be sought between the two World Wars (Sexton et al, 1993:173–281), if we disregard general retail trade, which is dated much earlier.

▼▼▼▼▼▼▼▼▼▼▼▼▼▼▼▼▼▼▼▼▼

The correlation between entrepreneurial leadership and economic emigration is typical for the development of entrepreneurial leadership amongst entrepreneurs in Macedonia, regardless of their ethnicity (Macedonians, Albanians, Vlavs etc.). In the beginning of the 20th century, a number of Macedonian emigrants who left the country to work in the European countries (Serbia, Romania, Bulgaria) or USA returned with their savings and undertook certain entrepreneurial ventures in their place of birth, in Macedonia. However, the development of the economy did not provide enough work for everybody, so many men able to work left the country again, and some of them started to develop their entrepreneurial ventures abroad.

In light of this emigration, construction ventures — which do not require substantial financial resources — and the development of businesses dealing with food (bakeries and catering) emerged as the predominant areas of activity in the developed centres of the neighboring countries (Belgrade, Sofia, Bucharest, Prague, Gratz, etc.). Personal or family savings were the basic recourses of financing for most entrepreneurs of Albanian ethnic background coming from Macedonia. These entrepreneurs' main competitive advantage was that they provided human resources from Macedonia.

The so-established entrepreneurial tradition in Macedonia after the Second World War was slackened, but not completely terminated. The process of nationalization in the new Yugoslavia significantly restricted the further development of entrepreneurial leadership. In the area of private initiative, the law limited the number of employees an entrepreneur could hire, while entrepreneurial leadership in the newly formed state owned companies was ideologically limited by centralized planning. The channel of economic migration in this period was reduced by the employment opportunity, accelerated industrialization and the strict regulations for obtaining an emigration license.

Entrepreneurial leadership manages to find a space for action even under those circumstances: renting nationalized capacities, building internal entrepreneurial migration in the other Republics of the former SFRY, erecting buildings and finishing off construction work, as well as developing the food industry and catering facilities. After the failure of the economic reform in Yugoslavia in the mid-1960s, successful corporate entrepreneurial ventures emerged at the beginning of the 1970s, paralleling the efforts for liberalization of the political system. These ventures were an effort to transfer the western entrepreneurship into an environment where companies have already gained their autonomy through the system of self-government. However, parallel to the clash of the Communist party with liberalism as a political movement, the processes of entrepreneurial leadership in the companies were suspended drastically and sanctioned as ideologically unacceptable "techno-management" that neglects workers' rights.

In the mid-1980s, the development of entrepreneurial private companies, cooperatives of the large government companies, began. Large government companies opened to the small cooperatives in order to increase regular supply, which in big systems can be slow.

ENTREPRENEURIAL LEADERSHIP AS A PREREQUISITE FOR SUCCESSFUL TRANSITION

Entrepreneurial leadership is a product of the market economy. Therefore, the transition from central planning towards a market economy can be seen as a development of entrepreneurial leadership through entrepreneurial leadership. This synergy includes a much broader understanding of the terms entrepreneurship, entrepreneur and entrepreneurial leadership with regard to their historical and traditional identification with the fulfillment of private initiative in the economy.

Recognition of business opportunities in a certain situation and undertaking the risk of turning them into reality through an entrepreneurial venture are probably the two least disputed features of entrepreneurship and entrepreneurial leadership amongst academics. Entrepreneurial leadership is determined by the two macro-variables of any leadership: the entrepreneur's personality and the situation in which she or he acts. For managers at different levels, this situation is created through the work task and the personal characteristics of their subordinates and superiors.

For entrepreneurs, especially in the early period of development of the business, the situation is reflected in the external surrounding, specifically, the market and its opportunities. This feature of entrepreneurship, the fact that a lot of it is determined by a particular situation, is probably the main reason for the different types and forms of entrepreneurial leadership, as well as for the different definitions of this phenomenon by certain authors (Sexton et al. 1993, 5–6).

▼▼▼▼▼▼▼▼▼▼▼▼▼▼▼▼▼▼▼▼▼▼▼▼

Considering transition as a macro-phenomenon with different significant changes (social, political, personal, etc.), for the purpose of our thesis we can consider entrepreneurial leadership in the Republic of Macedonia through the following three types:

- start-up entrepreneurial leadership,
- corporate transformational entrepreneurial leadership,
- nonprofit entrepreneurial leadership.

The start-up entrepreneurial leadership is most easily recognizable in the period of transition. Its basic characteristic, the right to start a private company in order to compete in the market where the opportunities lie, was used by many, some of whom disregarded the fact that they would also need resources: from personal traits and competence, to financial and other resources. The legalization of private ownership and the promotion of private initiative resulted in a mass creation of new, private companies, which were expected to provide entrepreneurial leadership for a number of individuals. This expectation was only met to some extent: a huge number of new, private companies were registered, a portion of which never began to operate, and the remaining portion of which ceased to operate in their first year. In most cases, the unfulfilled entrepreneurs stated the lack of financial resources needed for the initial period of work as the main reason for the failure. The analysis of the successful private companies, although conducted on a small sample, emphasizes the significance of financial resources, but the main element in resolving this problem, and later in the process of growth and survival of a company, was the personal features of entrepreneurial leadership.

One of the misconceptions about entrepreneurship in transitional countries, especially in the Republic of Macedonia, is the setting of a date of emergence during the period of change to a new social and political system. This misconception arises from emphasizing ownership of resources (Sexton et al. 1993, 9) over the recognition of opportunities and their utilization.

Entrepreneurship and entrepreneurial leadership in the transitional context of the Republic of Macedonia are treated from two dominant viewpoints: theoretical and conceptual (Kralev 1994), and economic-the contribution and significance of entrepreneurship in the economic development (Pejkovski 1997, Popovska 1993,

Fiti 1994). The empirical research of the entrepreneurial leadership phenomenon and the entrepreneur as the carrier of entrepreneurial ventures is relatively modest.

THE MBTI IN MACEDONIA

The potential for the use of the MBTI in Macedonia first came to my attention in 1994. I met with Dr. Donald Sexton, then of The Ohio State University, and Dr. Charles Ginn of the University of Cincinnati. Drs. Ginn and Sexton had utilized the MBTI with Inc. 500 CEOs/founders and other samples of leaders. We agreed to introduce the MBTI to Macedonia during a psychological conference that focused on psychology and scheduled the transition to be held in Kurchevo, Macedonia in October 1994.

However, rather than focus solely on the MBTI in Macedonia, Dr. Ginn contacted Consulting Psychologists Press, the USA publisher of the MBTI, and determined that no one was currently working with the MBTI throughout Central Europe. Dr. Ginn and I became partners in a bold academic entrepreneurial undertaking and co-founded the Central and Eastern European Center for Applied Psychology (CEECAP).

CEECAP would serve as a consortium for introducing the MBTI and related applied psychological instruments across Central Europe. CEECAP also served as the impetus for the development of this book on leadership.

The first serious research on entrepreneurial leadership in Macedonia using the MBTI was conducted by Dr. Milan Kochankovski (1996), who investigated the profile of the Macedonian managers. The research included 320 Macedonian managers from different types of companies. This effort was the foundation of Dr. Kochankovski's dissertation, which was the first MBTI based dissertation from Central Europe.

In 1997, a pilot research on the professional development of an entrepreneur was conducted (Gorcevski 1997); it dealt with the educational aspects of the development of entrepreneurial leadership in Macedonia. In our attempts to undertake more sound research of this phenomenon, we have used the JPI/PRF-E questionnaire developed by Professor Douglas Jacksons, which determines the profile of an entrepreneur. The results gained from the sample of thirty small business founders and owners were not enough to clearly show the profile of the Macedonian manager, but were still indicative of certain characteristics. Twenty out of thirty entrepreneurs exhibit energetic behavior as their main trait. However, the second most often found trait (in eighteen entrepreneurs) was avoidance of risks, which is a result of decades of forced passive behavior. The sense for change was in the third place, which was found in fifteen entrepreneurs. Other traits were found not to be significant.

The team of professors, practitioners and students who are focused on psychological type and the constructive use of differences will build upon the solid foundation established by Dr. Kochankovski and his colleagues. In the years ahead, the Republic of Macedonia will play a central role in introducing the MBTI across Central Europe.

BIBLIOGRAPHY

Adizes, I. (1995). Adizes Metodolo{ki prira~nik, Skopje

Danilov, V. i dr.(1997). Prira~nik za pretpriema~i po~etnici. Agencija na Republika Makedonija za transformacija na pretprijatijata so op{testven kapital: Skopje.

Borcevski, B. (1997). Profesionalniot razvoj na pretpriema~ot (specijalisti~ki trud). Univerzitet Sv. Kiril i Metodij: Skopje.

Janev, M. (1994). Prisposobenosta na pretprijatijata za uspe{na transformacija, vo: MANU zbornik: Ekonomska tranzicija. MANU: Skopje.

Kocankovski, M. (1996): Kadrolo{kiot profil na makedonskiot menaxer (doktorska disertacija). Univerzitet "Sv. Kiril i Metodij": Skopje.

Kochankovski, M. (1997, April). Personality types of managers in Macedonia: Entering a period of transition in the Republic of Macedonia. *Proceedings: Myers-Briggs Type Indicator & Leadership*, pp.101-107. Washington, D.C.

Kralev, T. (1994). Menaxmentot i pretpriemni{tvoto vo uslovi na preobrazba na ekonomskiot sistem, vo: MANU zbornik: Ekonomska tranzicija. MANU: Skopje.

Novaevski, D.(1995). Pretpriema~ki duh, vo: ZBORNIK, Ekonomski fakultet: Skopje.

Pejkovski, J. (1997). Pretpriemni{tvoto i razvojot. NIP Ekopres, MagnaSken: Skopje.

Popovska, Z. i dr.(1993) Zbornik: Menaxerstvo i pretpriemni{tvo. CESI, Ekononmski fakultet: Skopje.

Sekston I. (1993). Pretpriema{tvo: kreativnost i razvoj: iskustva od SAD i Makedonija. Centar za kadrovski i informatgi~ki uslugi "DETRA": Skopje.

Smilevski, C. (red.) (1994). Sovremenei pristapi vo menaxmentot: zbornik na avtorski trudovi i prilozi. Univerzitet "Sv. Kiril i Metodij" Skopje i Univerzitet na Nebraska, Linkoln, SAD: Skopje.

Smilevski, C. (1997, April). Personality dimensions and organizational transition. *Proceedings: Myers-Briggs Type Indicator & Leadership*, pp. 279–287. Washington, D.C.

Fiti, T. i dr. (1994). Pretpriemni{tvo i pretpriemni~ki menaxment. Ekonomski fakultet, Skopje. *** (1994) "100+100" najuspe{ni pretprijatija vo R. Makedonija. PIP "Argumenti": Skopje.

In this bibliography we have included texts on entrepreneurship and entrepreneurial leadership published in Macedonia and texts pertaining to this topic published in other languages.

NEW ZEALAND

John Bathurst
Michael Cash

EDITOR'S NOTES. Dr. John Bathhurst and Mr. Michael Cash provide a fascinating profile of Karroll Brent-Edmonson, a native Maori entrepreneur. We learn about the political environment and economic conditions in New Zealand as Brent-Edmonson incorporates her personal values into her business operations.

The authors review literature on leadership as it relates to New Zealand. A review of the introduction and applications of the Myers-Briggs Type Indicator in New Zealand is also provided.

KARROLL BRENT-EDMONDSON

New Zealand experienced radical change in 1984. The Conservative government in power unexpectedly lost a snap election to a "New Right" regime.
"Rogernomics," a new concept advocating a free-market economy, similar to
Thatcherism and Reaganomics, was embraced with vigour. The social costs of this
concept's implementation were high, particularly among the minority Polynesians
— Maori and Pacific Islanders — and consequently in the city areas where Polynesian
groups lived, such as South Auckland.

Against this background of radical economic and social change, K.T. Footwear
emerged. Led by Karroll Brent-Edmondson, a Maori woman, this small business
embraced Maori values of community and family as part of its core business
concept.

Karroll's early years were miserable, being abused in early childhood in her
own home, as well as in a foster home. At age nine, she became a ward of the
state. At age sixteen, she felt the need to establish her identity and do something
worthwhile with her life. Two years later she left for Australia.

Living in Brisbane, she set up a halfway house for battered children, a soup
kitchen for expatriate Maoris, and did kitchen work in a nursing home, marrying
an Australian in the process. She also discovered she had a talent for sales, setting
a sales record for one company she worked for.

Karroll moved back to New Zealand in 1990. In 1991 she decided it was time
she did something for the people of her community. She started a business that
aimed not only to create work for the jobless, but also benefit the hungry children
she saw walking to school in ill-fitting shoes.

Karroll wanted to manufacture shoes for these children, but also wanted the
factory to be profitable so she could do other things to help the children. She also
wanted to be able to provide jobs for long-term unemployed Maori and Pacific
Island people from local communities in South Auckland.

She relates her ambition:

> *I had this fantasy to start this factory. I thought women can do
> anything — I thought women were out there in shoe manufacturing. I
> was wrong. No one had a factory they had created out of nothing.*

Women have never played a large role in shoe manufacturing — except as labourers, or in partnership with men. It's a tough industry.

However, the industry itself resisted Karroll's entry. She recalls:

I thought I was paying for first grade leather, but I was paying top dollar for seconds and thirds. I was sold a machine that blew up. We were called names, the Walkout school shoe was called a joke, but we've showed them.

Karroll found people who genuinely wanted to help. Inside the industry, Bostik Glue and the United Shoe Manufacturing Company gave technical advice. Legal, banking, management and accounting advice was offered, and support came from local authority, politicians and key people from key businesses, notably Stephen Tindall, owner of The Warehouse chain of discounted goods. The chain was to be her major retail outlet.

The Auckland based K.T. Footwear exported to Australia in the early 1990s. However, Karroll decided to concentrate on fully developing opportunities in the domestic market and later withdrew from the export market. Karroll is again investigating opportunities in the Australian market and aims to re-establish a presence there shortly.

K.T. Footwear specializes in producing low cost leather shoes for children. Most are retailed through The Warehouse and Farmers chains of stores, though the company is planning to retail directly to schools in Australia.

Karroll says her road to success hasn't been easy. The early days were a real struggle and the company almost went broke. But she persisted, acquiring a business partner, learning from the experience of others and utilizing experts to help turn her vision into a serious and profitable business venture. She has particular praise for the Bank of New Zealand and Coopers and Lybrand: "They proved to me that the big organizations do have faith in the little businesses and can provide the support and skills necessary to make your business succeed."

Karroll sees herself as an example of cooperation between the workplace and the community. As well as creating jobs for the unemployed and producing decent, affordable shoes for children, the business also provides around 300 free school lunches per week for needy children in South Auckland. Everyone pitches in to

▼▼▼▼▼▼▼▼▼▼▼▼▼▼▼▼▼▼▼▼▼

help to make substantial meals, not just the chicken soup style of meal offered by other social agencies. She relates, "When we started the lunches we got angry and had to speak out, to stop people dumping on the Government or Social Welfare, saying it is their role to do something."

There are no labels on K.T. Footwear's shoes and they have no packaging, partly because Karroll was initially too busy to think about such cosmetics and, when she did, she couldn't see the point of the extra cost involved.

Karroll points out that outsiders mistake Maori business or management as *whanau* (family):

> *They believe it has no structure, that people get paid under the table. That's not true of course, there's huge awareness of the need to get it right. The biggest favour Maori people in business can do is to encourage each other and go on courses and learn more.*

The company's success and Karroll Brent-Edmondson's commitment to sharing the benefits with the community have resulted in many accolades. In 1995, Karroll was voted Maori Business Woman of the Year and received the Te Mana Wahine Trophy for overall excellence in business management. Prior to that, she was voted New Zealander of the Year in 1993 by readers of the national weekend newspaper, the Sunday News. Other awards for K.T. Footwear have included Small Business of the Year, Business Development Quality Award from the Business Development Board, runner-up for the National Employer of People with Disabilities, and the Kiwi Award of Excellence from the Bank of New Zealand.

Karroll's community involvement extends to supporting women's sporting achievements, as patron of the Woman's Rugby League Association. She is also a member of the Retail and Wholesalers Industry Training Organization and a representative on the Ministry of Maori Development's committee to develop an Asian Maori Economic Strategy. In early 1996 she was invited to the United States as a guest of the government to study community-based enterprises there.

Karroll is justifiably proud of her achievements:

> *We, and by that I mean all that work at our company, have built a strong and profitable Maori company that has retained uniquely Maori features in its overall operations. In that regard, we hope that we are*

*setting a business model that other Maori can use. In addition to
making a profit we can bring some real benefits to the community
around us.*

Brent-Edmondson says while the domestic market is great, expanding into
exports will ensure long-term jobs for her team of workers and ongoing benefits
to the community.

NEW ZEALAND

New Zealand lies in the southwest Pacific Ocean and consists of two main
islands and a number of smaller islands comprising a total land area of 270,534
square kilometres. New Zealand has jurisdiction over the territories of Tokelau and
the Ross Dependency (Antarctica) and special relationships with the Cook Islands
and Niue, whose residents have New Zealand citizenship. There have also historically been close ties with Western Samoa.

New Zealand has been culturally and ethnically connected to Polynesia for at
least 1000 years and up to 200 years ago was solely Polynesian. Currently about 80
percent of the total population of about 3.4 million is of European origin, mainly
from the British Isles, but with significant numbers from parts of Western and
Central Europe. Indigenous Maori make up about 13 percent of the overall population, and Pacific Islanders about 5 percent.

About 85 percent of these people live in urban areas with populations being
concentrated in the northern parts of both islands, particularly in the Auckland
region, which comprises 26 percent of the overall population. Maori were originally in rural areas but most have migrated to the cities. In 1945 around 75 percent of Maori lived in rural areas, while in the 1990s over 80 percent live in urban
areas. The Pacific Island populations are concentrated mainly in Auckland and
Wellington; there are significant net migration gains from Polynesia.

Many refugees from around the world have settled in New Zealand over the
last century. These include Poles and Jews from the time of the Second World War,
Hungarians from the 1956 uprising, Indo-Chinese from the conflicts in that area,
and, more recently, refugees from Chile, Russia, Eastern Europe, Africa and Assyria.

New Zealand is a sovereign nation, recognizing the monarch, Queen Elizabeth

▼▼▼▼▼▼▼▼▼▼▼▼▼▼▼▼▼▼▼▼▼▼

II. The Queen has formal executive power exercised by the monarch's appointed representative, the Governor-General. The Governor-General's main function is to arrange for the leader of the majority party, or coalition of parties, in Parliament to form a government, thus becoming Prime Minister.

The Governor-General's assent is required before bills passed by Parliament can become law. By convention, the Governor-General is required to follow the advice of ministers, although in extraordinary circumstances he or she can reject advice if he or she believes that a government is acting unconstitutionally. The monarch appoints a Governor-General, on the Prime Minister's recommendation, for a term of usually five years.

Although the constitution is monarchical in form, it operates democratically, and the Government cannot act effectively without Parliament's approval. Parliament has to be assembled regularly to hold the Government to account. Parliament is elected by a form of proportional representation known as a Mixed Member Proportional (MMP) system. Voters have two votes, one for a candidate to represent their electorate, and the other for the party the voter wants to see represented in Parliament. The second vote determines the number of seats each party is allocated in Parliament.

There are 120 members of Parliament: sixty-four electorate members and fifty-six appointed from party lists. Five seats are allocated to Maori who register on the Maori electoral roll, although Maori can also stand for election in any electorate if they choose not to be on the Maori roll. The party which gets the majority of the votes — or, if no one party gets a majority, a coalition of parties to make up a majority — will be asked by the Governor-General to form a government.

The relationships between Maori and other races is defined by the Treaty of Waitangi, signed in 1840, which guaranteed Maori governorship of their treasures and possessions, their lands, fisheries and forests through partnership with the Europeans. Unfortunately this has been observed more in the breach by alienation of their lands and possessions by confiscation or other dubious means, which has given rise to deep-seated resentment. Resolution of these resentments is currently a high priority of Government.

With the arrival of Europeans in the early 19th century, New Zealand entered the global trading arena, commencing as a colonial farm exporting to the United Kingdom and in return becoming a ready-made market for British industrial goods.

New Zealand's geographical isolation protected its economy from competition from other countries in this time.

State intervention in the areas of import substitution, markets, investments and regulating and controlling production occurred during the 1930s depression and the Second World War. These policies turned into a structural weakness as they relied on a narrow commodity base and a small internal market, coupled with trade and balance of payments problems exacerbated by highly protected overseas markets. This structural weakness was fully exposed with the entry of the United Kingdom into the European Community in the early 1960s, and the subsequent loss of markets. This resulted in the primary focus of the economic planners turning inwards, to internal markets.

During the 1980s, the economic focus was overturned and the economy reformed through deregulation. Change was fundamental and swift, with huge and painful effects. Any residue of colonialism was purged, removing the import substitution framework and reconnecting to the global economy, thus allowing offshore investment and development within New Zealand and allowing New Zealand capital to invest overseas.

The public service was virtually dismantled, firstly by the formation of State Owned Enterprises, which were in turn sold to private interests, attracting both New Zealand and offshore purchasers. This led to huge reductions in state employment, with large numbers of workers being laid off. Core government services were divided into three categories:

• policy making departments;
• funding departments;
• provider departments, financed by the funding departments
  though competitive processes.

Health and educational services, for example, were placed in a competitive market. There was a consequential decline in standards in these areas that were unable to gain sufficient funding due to their perceived inability to be economically efficient. High levels of unemployment, long waiting lists for surgery in hospitals, and an inability to properly staff schools with teachers were some natural consequences of the economic restructuring.

LEADERSHIP RESEARCH IN NEW ZEALAND

The case of K.T. Footwear and its remarkable entrepreneurial leader/founder shares many features typical of entrepreneurs across New Zealand and, perhaps, throughout the world:

- disadvantaged beginnings, used as a spur to later success;
- involvement in many attempts before succeeding;
- willingness to enter fields they know little about;
- obtaining overseas or other cultural experience;
- being given a rough ride by the incumbent players;
- having to learn quickly from damaging experiences;
- being prepared to improvise and innovate to reach the marketplace;
- being unwilling to give in when others might do so;
- using a mentor or champion to help support their enterprise;
- being skilled in using both formal and informal networks;
- having a missionary zeal for their business and products.

However, some features of this case are typically, perhaps uniquely, Maori. We suggest that these features are closer to those of other indigenous peoples than to mainstream business ventures. These three key features, evident in this instance, include:

- disrespect for the system;
- a new/old way of seeing people;
- a different concept of business strategy.

DISRESPECT FOR THE SYSTEM

What we call "the system" is often the greatest barrier to entrepreneurial success. Entrepreneurs with little business experience are baffled and confused by a bewildering array of forms, statutes and impositions (many quite costly) demanded by government officials, bankers, lawyers and industry associations. A healthy disrespect for the system grows up wherever the system has been systematically used to keep people from sharing in the good things the system seems to deliver effortlessly to those who fall within its bias.

New Zealand's Restructuring Reforms of the 1980s and early 1990s brought productivity and competitiveness gains to the country's economy and personal gains for those supporting their rather harsh economic and social thrust. The pain, so went the myth, had to be experienced first. Only later would the gain be felt by all (the "trickle down" theory).

However, the negative impacts of the restructuring process (hailed overseas as "the New Zealand Experiment"), fell more heavily on some sectors of society — the economically deprived, women and Pacific Islanders and Maori. Maori statistics on unemployment, health status (particularly death rate) and on virtually every other key social indicator run well outside the comparable figures for non-Maori people. It is not surprising, therefore, that Maori have consistently sought ways to undermine the system they see as working against them.

This does not always mean fighting the system. Rather, as the case shows, it means using the system where it supports the enterprise (using a mentor, the supportive bank, the entrepreneurial discount store), and going around, behind or over it (employing the unemployed and the disabled, for example) when it is becoming too great a barrier.

This flexibility may be the direct consequence of a healthy disrespect for the system. This disrespect may explain the rather mystifying rise of Maori women entrepreneurs in the 1980s and 1990s, of which Brent-Edmondson was a forerunner. Facing a double disadvantage (as women, and as Maori), the fear of the system that holds back so many entrepreneurs has given way to a determination to score off the system. Innovation is unlocked in this process.

The flexibility in marketing in different locales (avoiding the standard marketing channels of footwear chains for direct selling through schools and through discount stores), and total absence of brand identification, in defiance of marketing theory, point to a different approach to the way business is run.

The reason why the entrepreneur/leader in this case was "too busy" to devise brand identification was because her focus was elsewhere, as was that of the anonymous craftsman working on the detail (even that which could not be seen) of the medieval cathedral. We see and subsequently get around to giving attention to what culturally is important to us.

A NEW/OLD WAY OF SEEING PEOPLE

The growth of unemployment as a consequence of restructuring, downsizing, redundancies and the closure of many local agencies in rural areas (post-offices, for example) has impacted the Maori community disproportionately, with the pre-dominantly Maori extreme North (Hokianga) having unemployment rates above 70 percent.

In working-class multicultural South Auckland, where Brent-Edmondson began her enterprise, double figure unemployment was the norm during this period. In particular, the number of long-term unemployed (those out of work for up to two years) grew steadily in this locality, breeding a kind of despair. It was this group that Brent-Edmondson targeted for her workforce. Maori values put people first, allowing her to "not see" the shame and stigma attached to long-term unemployment (unemployed people being portrayed as shiftless layabouts "bludging" on the taxpayer).

Moreover, she appreciated that this very group, precisely because of their experience of long-term unemployment, brought positive values to the work force which were priceless — a willingness to work, a readiness to accept the improvised system needed for a start-up enterprise, loyalty (which cut the costs of re-employment and retraining in a notoriously mobile industry), and an appreciation of the effects of hardship on others.

The staff working on preparing lunches for local schools (as distinct from paying caterers to do so), can therefore be seen best as a form of what Maori call koha (inadequately translated as "donation"): returning some of the gift you have received to those less fortunate.

To European eyes, koha may be seen as contributing to an invisible and informal system of sharing the goods of life (if you can't give, you can't expect to receive) — a system that confronts the very consumerism the Reform process was designed to feed. As is paralleled in many European self-help communities of interest (e.g. Alcoholics Anonymous), actively helping others in a related difficulty keeps alive the realisation of the value sought and received. The process is seen as an ongoing one.

Thus, the contribution to others feeds an awareness of the current blessing received. One is employed not simply for oneself, but also for others. This older myth confronts the inherent selfishness of the Reform myth, reshaping business values in the process.

The Maori have a saying:

Uia mai koe ki ahau
He aha te meu nui a te ao
Maku e kii atu

He Tanagata
He Tanagata
He Tanagata

You ask me
What is the most important thing
In this world

It is the People
It is the People
It is the People

A DIFFERENT CONCEPT OF BUSINESS STRATEGY:

What all this points to is a different concept of business strategy, one that is culturally based (*tikanga* Maori). The alternative system exemplified here is one that embodies a different generic concept of the fundamental purpose of business — its very *raison-d'etre*. Here the vision is community-tied, not so much as duty or payoff, but as something taken for granted.

Karroll Brent-Edmonson's puzzled question is culturally based: "If we can't manage to put a percentage of our profits back into the community, what are we doing it for?" Her puzzlement demonstrates how deep this value, borrowed from the *Marae* (Meeting House), and the *whanau* (family), is for her.

What is puzzling for European observers of this case (the community commitment as a normal part of everyday business life) is, in reverse, equally puzzling to those with Maori culturally based values — how can it be otherwise? The mainstream business concept of helping others in a very noticeable sponsorship way (showing or wearing the sponsor's label), sponsorship as a form of advertising (even showing in the advertising budget) with the competition for "trendy" or high profile charity is light years from this strategic principle.

▼▼▼▼▼▼▼▼▼▼▼▼▼▼▼▼▼▼▼▼▼▼▼

Even the more closely related concept of "socially responsible" business does not go as far. It emphasises being aware of social responsibilities along the way, but does not alter the reason for being in business.

Karroll's story reflects the early findings of research undertaken by Wayne Taurima and Michael Cash that suggests that culturally based Maori businesses tend to reflect in their fundamental values and systems, cultural concepts such as te reo (Maori language), *whanau* (family), *wairau* (spirituality), *koha* (giving), *kaupapa* (community business or strategy) and *aroha* (love).

The strange case of entrepreneur Brent-Edmonson, is better understood by non-Maori in terms of the re-conceptualisation of business strategy and purpose than standard business concepts. Though the case highlights innovation as seen in the business strategy and practice of one of the cultural partners (Maori) of the bicultural nexus of New Zealand society, we suggest that where there is evidence of genuine innovation among non-Maori (*pakeha*) entrepreneurs, a similar phe-nomenon occurs a culturally biased disregard for standard (i.e. overseas) theory and practice, a more engaging way of dealing with the workforce, and a more far-reaching and challenging concept of what business is for.

Local models may be far more instructive to New Zealand entrepreneurs than borrowed ones. The Maori identify with their mountain. So, we suggest, should our innovators.

THE USE OF THE MBTI IN NEW ZEALAND

The MBTI came to New Zealand in the 1980s for use primarily in the reli-gious education ventures of the Roman Catholic Church. Personal development and spiritual formation were the predominant uses for a number of years up until the formation of the New Zealand Association for Psychological Type (NZAPT) in 1990. This association was affiliated with the Association for Psychological Type in the United States of America (APT) and became accredited to offer the APT's Qualifying Training Program.

As the pool of qualified administrators increased, so did the use of the MBTI. Schools, community colleges and voluntary organisations all benefited from the insights gained through personal discovery of personality type. The enthusiasm gen-erated from these groups started to infect the corporate world and the MBTI found its way into areas such as career development, team building and conflict resolution. A number of organizations established their own databases and gained useful insights into the dynamics of their operations.

Our implementation team voiced concerns about the applicability of an instrument developed in another culture. Numerous items on the American version of the MBTI were found to be subject to cultural differences. For example, the American version does not account for variations in the meanings of common words. In order to rectify this incongruity, we worked with the problematic word and phrase pairs, completed an item re-weighting and produced revised scoring keys.

Research on the MBTI and its use continues in several institutions. The validity of the instrument in a culture different from its culture of origin is the focus of a number of projects. Workplace demands and other pressures of the administration setting can lead to the misidentification of a person's type and it is important to understand the effect these pressures are having. Projects looking at the administration environment are well underway and it is hoped to be able to quantify these effects and point towards methods of minimizing their influence in the identification of a person's type.

Choosing an optimum career is a major task for most young people as well as many older people. Using a large database which links personality type to chosen occupations, considerable effort is being made to advise people of possible successful career paths. This is proving to be popular and helpful in career planning for both younger and older people.

In New Zealand, the MBTI is in popular use and is proving helpful in the lives of many of its citizens. It looks likely it will continue to be used and developed for a long time.

BIBLIOGRAPHY

Le Heron, R. & Pawson, E. (1996). *Changing places: New Zealand in the nineties*. Auckland: Longman Paul.

Mazany, P. (1995). T*eamthink — Team New Zealand: The "Black Magic" of management behind the 1995 America's Cup success*. Auckland: VisionPlus Developments.

McLennan, R. (1995). *People and enterprises: Organisational behaviour in New Zealand*. Marrickville: Harcourt Brace.

Poulin, B. (1993). *Strategy: five roles of effectiveness*. Hamilton: Department of Strategic Management and Leadership, University of Waikato.

Rabey, G. P. (1997). *Workplace leadership: moving into management today*. Palmerston North: Dunmore Press.

MAGAZINE ARTICLES

From the heart. *Her Business*, September/October 1996, pp. 5–7.

Karrol Brent-Edmonson and KT Footwear. *Management*, October 1997, p. 50.

The birth of K.T. Footwear. *Te Maori News*, February 1992, 1 (1), p. 12.

Making waves in the footwear business. *Te Maori News*, September 1994, 3 (18), p. 10.

NORTHERN CYPRUS

David Gary Tucker
Eastern Mediterranean University

EDITOR'S NOTES. Dr. Tucker introduces us to President Rauf Denktash, The Northern Cyprus Head of State. We explore President Denktash's leadership approach as he guides his people through a most difficult period of history for those of different ethnic origins on the island of Cyprus.

Dr. Tucker then provides us with a brief history and economic model of Northern Cyprus. We learn about the introduction of the Myers-Briggs Type Indicator to N. Cyprus and of other initiatives designed to integrate N. Cyprus into the international community.

Dr. Tucker's efforts with the MBTI in Northern Cyprus, along with efforts by Eduardo Cassus and his colleagues in Greece with a Greek version of the MBTI, provides an exciting potential to eventually conduct type workshops on the island that include representatives of both the Greek and Turkish communities.

▼▼▼▼▼▼▼▼▼▼▼▼▼▼▼▼▼▼▼▼▼▼

The act of profiling a living leader can be comparable to being a theatre critic who leaves a play after the first act. Time, events and the scribes of history can have a way of conspiring to make a leader look either good or bad. Memories fade, half-truths become complete truths or falsehoods, and myths are born and perpetuated. Cultures and societies also have a way of rewriting history to have it meet contemporary needs.

Recent American history provides two relevant examples. Shortly after his untimely death, words such as great, extraordinary, charismatic and courageous were used to describe United States President John F. Kennedy. Thirty-plus years later, his presidency has been described as almost mediocre. Kennedy's presidency is now most remembered for the Bay of Pigs and the Cuban missile crisis — two extremes in leadership.

During his four years as President of the United States, Jimmy Carter was described by some as unemotional, hands on, caught up in the minutiae and unimpressive. Now, almost twenty years later, he is considered a great ex-President, and words like "intelligence," "integrity" and "superb statesman" are often used to describe him.

Therefore, to write about a living leader, one who is still center stage, is to welcome disagreement and criticism from every quarter — especially from those who have already written about the leader in question. This factor was a consideration in the profile of Rauf Denktash.

RAUF DENKTASH

Rauf Denktash is many things to many people. Who and what he is depends upon one's perspective. To some Greek Cypriots, he is a traitor and a terrorist. To many Turkish Cypriots, Denktash is a hero, while to his Turkish Cypriot political rivals he is an old man, out of touch, a person whose time on the world stage has come and gone. As President of the Turkish Republic of Northern Cyprus, he has been the voice of the Turkish Cypriot community to the outside world for over thirty-five years.

Educated as a lawyer, he might have had an impressive career outside of Cyprus, but inspired by the leadership of Dr. Fazil KuÁuk (Vice President, Republic of Cyprus, under the 1960 constitution), he elected to follow in his footsteps. For all of his presumed faults, the author believes President Denktash is the embodiment of a servant leader as envisioned by Robert Greenleaf.

Denktash's importance to the Turkish community on Cyprus cannot be over stressed. After the 1963 Christmas War on Cyprus, the United Nations committed a peacekeeping force to the island. On the same day as the first UN troops arrived (March 26, 1964), Rauf Denktash was declared persona non grata by the Republic of Cyprus.

It was also ironic that when Denktash returned from exile four years later, he arrived, not discredited, but to lead the Turkish Cypriot delegation to peace talks which the Greeks had at last adopted.

Many leaders make one crucial mistake — they do not know when to step down and let someone else assume the leadership role. After so many years in the job, they become ineffective, lose their creativity, become unwilling to accept change and jealously guard the status quo. Their perception is that only they can do the job, therefore they assume they are indispensable. Not true! It is like the fist in the bucket of water; it, too, can seem indispensable to the bucket. But, if the fist is pulled out, the water quickly replaces the space it formerly occupied.

While interviewing President Denktash for this chapter (March 2, 1998), I found he continually used a football (soccer) analogy: both sides play by the same rules — the field must be level. From his perspective, the United Nations and the European Union, acting as umpires, have both overlooked the rulebook. In Denktash's words, "They are not playing by the rules." Rules are very important to President Denktash.

President Denktash is a politician and statesman, and so may have to act in concert with the exigencies of a situation. Statesmen, leaders, need room to manoeuvre, to assemble forces and press home the initiative. His behaviors may be dictated by the situation. We have all witnessed politicians and statesmen weave and dance to the current tune and need to understand that those behaviors go with the position. Having said that, it is important to understand that President Denktash's most important values are his word, his honour, justice, service to the larger community and staying on task. He has an inherent ability to persevere in the face of nearly overwhelming obstacles and he is dependable almost to a fault.

▼▼▼▼▼▼▼▼▼▼▼▼▼▼▼▼▼▼▼▼▼

President Denktash agreed with his MBTI reported type of ISTJ. He felt very comfortable with the tough minded TJ approach to making decisions, preferring to focus on the relevant facts involved with a decision and seeking objectivity in his decision making.

The public persona of President Denktash would suggest that he energizes from the presence of others. However, he agrees that his preference is for Introversion and that he will seek periods of solitude to re-energize his internal batteries.

NORTHERN CYPRUS

The Turkish Republic of Northern Cyprus (TRNC) is a very small country, both in land mass (approximately 1100 square miles) and population, with less than 200,000 citizens. The small scale lends itself to a neighbourly, hospitable and friendly environment. For example, it is not at all uncommon for President Denktash to attend weddings, funerals and other family milestones of his people. On the other hand, the small size creates a situation in which everyone seems to know everyone else's business.

The TRNC is a mix of old, the very old — with ruins dating back before the time of Christ — and the modern. Today, homes are built with solar panels flat to the roofline and water heaters hidden under the eaves.

Since the division of the island in 1974, many would say that time has stood still, but that is not entirely true. While progress is slow in infrastructure improvements on roads, water treatment and sewerage, telephone and electrical systems, and new economy technologies, such as wireless cell phones, are increasingly evident.

Power outages are not as frequent, nor as long, as they were back in 1994-1995. Bottled water is still a necessity, as in many places the local water is not suitable for drinking. Medical care is elementary, so individuals with hard-to-treat conditions or serious injuries are evacuated to more advanced countries for treatment. In emergency situations, coordination is effected with the UN to the most appropriate medical facility.

In a country where the minimum wage is $220 per month, the automobile of choice is the Mercedes-Benz, followed by the BMW. However, during 1997–99, it appears that four-wheel drive vehicles are gradually becoming more popular.

Our taxi drivers hold firm to the belief that the fastest way to "B" from "A" is a straight line. If that means going against traffic, driving on the wrong side of the road, or driving the wrong way down a one-way street — then so be it!

The TRNC is predominately Muslim. Mosques dot the countryside calling the faithful to prayer. Some go, many do not.

Crime is at a minimum in the TRNC and there are few crimes of violence and passion. It is not uncommon to see people out at the wee hours of the morning, returning from discos and pubs, and no one fears for their physical safety. However, traffic accidents and fatalities are all too common on both sides of the island.

The official language is a distinctly Cypriot form of Turkish. However, the use of English is common, on the rise and taught in all of the better schools. The language of instruction at most universities is English.

Geographically, Northern Cyprus is comprised of plains, mountains and beaches. While there are communal beaches shared by many, one can always find a stretch of beach totally devoid of other humans. The mountains offer a variety of trails for hiking, mountain biking or just walking. There are many places to go to just enjoy the "quiet," get back to nature and reflect on life.

Northern Cyprus lacks the hustle and bustle of other countries, the frenzied rush to get things done now, and the need to be always on the move. In many ways it is calm and soothing. It is a country that is becoming modern, but has remained unspoiled by modernization.

By its very location, Cyprus has been influenced over the centuries by the multitude of armies, navies, traders and refugees moving either east or west. Countries and civilizations which have left their mark on Cyprus include Egypt, Persia, Syria, Greece, Turkey, the Phoenicians, the Romans, Christian Byzantium, the Crusaders from Western Europe, the Lusignans from France, the Venetians, the Ottoman Turks, and, lastly, the British. In fact, the British still view Cyprus as a large aircraft carrier at anchor and maintain forces in two British Sovereign Bases. All who came exploited the island and its inhabitants.

▼▼▼▼▼▼▼▼▼▼▼▼▼▼▼▼▼▼▼▼▼

Under British rule since 1878, the island became a British Crown Colony in 1925 until independence was won in 1960. That independence was hard won by a Greek Cypriot organization known as EOKA. Both sides in Cyprus still have strong links to the United Kingdom.

Since 1974, many political initiatives to reconcile the divided Cyprus have been advanced by the United Nations, the European Union, the United Kingdom, the United States and even Russia. All have met with stalemates by one side or the other. The UN peacekeeping force has been here for thirty-five years now and appears to have no plans to leave any time soon. In 1983, the Turkish Cypriot community declared the island the Turkish Republic of Northern Cyprus.

THE ECONOMY

The following economic indicators provide an overview of the TRNC economy:

- The largest "industry" in the TRNC is the public sector or government offices. Public service" is an oxymoron. A primary reason for obtaining a position in the public sector is to ensure job security. Service to the larger community is not a major consideration in job selection.

- A large portion of the service industry is now in education. There are six universities operating in the TRNC, which have been sanctioned by YOK (the Turkish accreditation body). Eastern Mediterranean University in Famagusta is the largest, with 11,000 students and over 600 staff and faculty. When Cyprus International University, the newest university, was opened in Nicosia in 1997, it started with over 800 students.

- Education is primarily accomplished using a rote memorisation model. While universities are attempting to break away from this model, it is difficult, and students who are asked to be innovative or creative in their thinking risk failure. The basic education has not prepared them to syn-thesize, integrate and analyse data, and then make decisions based on the data. Many students still search for the "one" correct answer. Students feel frustrated when asked to voice their opinion because they believe their opinion will be "wrong."

- University graduates faced with few job options look for work elsewhere. Many attempt to find work in Turkey or the United Kingdom. While there are no accurate figures on the amount of "brain drain," the number of individuals thought to be leaving the TRNC is significant.

- The economic embargoes, initiated primarily by Greece and the Greek Cypriot community in southern Cyprus, have impacted the TRNC. For example, the TRNC is forbidden to export citrus products to the EU. With official recognition of the TRNC withheld by all countries except Turkey, the economic experience is fraught with frustration.

- Tourism is a sizeable industry and could be much larger once the Cyprus problem is resolved.

- Inflation is a continual problem. In 1993, one US ($) dollar equaled 10,500 Turkish Lira (TL), or one million TL was almost one hundred dollars. Today, with that same one million TL, I can barely purchase a six-pack of Coca-Cola.

THE MBTI IN THE TRNC

To the best of my knowledge, the MBTI is currently being used only at the Eastern Mediterranean University in my advanced business classes. I have used the Indicator in both graduate and undergraduate organizational behavior and human resources management classes for the last five years. I also use the FIRO-B in the MBA organizational behavior class.

At this point, we have only preliminary results for the use of the MBTI in Northern Cyprus. We have reservations about the use of the English language MBTI, as English is either a second or third language for our students. In the fall of 1998, a Turkish translation of the MBTI was introduced to students in the MBA program. It is anticipated that the Turkish MBTI will be used in other classes validate the translation.

DEVELOPMENT OF A RESEARCH CENTER

It is hoped that the current MBTI and FIRO-B research and use will evolve into a Leadership and Executive Development Center, sponsored by the Faculty of

▼▼▼▼▼▼▼▼▼▼▼▼▼▼▼▼▼▼▼▼▼▼

Business and Economics, Eastern Mediterranean University. The author would initially staff the center, with administrative and research assistance provided on a day-to-day basis by an MBA research assistant.

Any extensive consulting using the MBTI will have to be predicated on the availability of native language translations of the MBTI. Individuals providing feedback will have to be paired with a native language speaker to ensure that the recipient better understands his or her feedback. Emphasis will be on one-to-one feedback; therefore, it will require that others be qualified in the interpretation and use of the MBTI. More research will have to be accomplished to ensure that existing MBTI base sample profiles and behaviors apply in the Turkish Republic of Northern Cyprus. The question of a "national type" begs to be answered.

OTHER INITIATIVES

Project ICONS. During Spring Semester 1999, a pilot project ICONS (International Communication and Stimulation) course is being offered in conjunction with the University of Cincinnati. Students from different universities are paired based on their MBTI type and use Internet skills to communicate and negotiate global issues in this University of Maryland based program. If successful, the course will be adopted as a permanent part of the curriculum.

New Course. Using the MBTI and FIRO-B in graduate organizational behavior classes has proved so successful, it is anticipated that a first-year, student development course will get off the ground in the near future. In addition to the MBTI and the FIRO-B the Strong-Campbell Inventory will also be used. Other psychometric instruments may also be added. Conceivably, this course might be offered in conjunction with the EMU Psychological Counseling Center on Campus.

Leadership Development. With adequate support, it is conceivable that a series of MBTI/FIRO-B workshops could be developed and the Leadership and Executive Development Research Center staff could go on the road. Workshops would be provided to governmental ministries, school buildings, small industries and agro-industries.

MBTI Urdu Translation (Pakistan). Working with Pakistani MBA graduates from EMU, it might be possible to introduce the Urdu translation of the MBTI into

Pakistan. Initially working with colleges and university populations, the MBTI workshops could then be introduced to businesses and industries in the larger cities of Pakistan.

United Nations. Numerous vehicles and initiatives have been introduced to foster working relations among Greek and Turkish Cypriot communities. The MBTI might prove to be a useful instrument in facilitating an understanding between the two groups.

REFERENCES

Denktash, R. *Amnesia a key element in the Cyprus problem.*
www.pubinfo.gov.nc.tr/denktas1.htm, (p.2). (Note: the president's name is normally spelt with an "s" but "sh" when it is Anglicised).

Isachsen, O. & Berens, L. (1991). *Working together: A personality centered approach to management.* Coronado, CA: New World Management Press, p. 52.

Pope, N. & Pope, H. (1998). *Turkey unveiled: A history of modern Turkey* (p. 109). Woodstock, NY: Overlook Press.

Moran, M. (Ed.). (1997). *Rauf Denktash at the United Nations* (pp. x-xv). Huntington, UK: Eothen Press.

Rossidou, M. and Tinos, I. (1991, July-August). The first Attila was wearing Foustanella. *International Socialism*, p. 2.

Tucker, D.G. (1998, March 2). Personal interview with President Denktash.

SOUTH AFRICA

Jan van Rooyen
Jopie van Rooyen & partners

EDITOR'S NOTES. This chapter covers two remarkable
entrepreneurial leaders, Joan and Yusuf, both of whom have
elected to be identified by their first names only. In Joan, the
readers observe an executive facing and finding her place in a
patriarchal business world that has historically closed its doors
to women. In Yusuf, we find a leader advocating and implementing African philosophy and culture into an arena dominated by white males. Both leaders exemplify extraordinary
strength and determination in the face of adversity, and are
illustrative of the changing cultural and entrepreneurial paradigms in South Africa.

Dr. van Rooyen also examines the history of South Africa, and
explores the volatile issue of apartheid and its repercussive
effects. She looks at the tenuous current economic conditions
and many of the socio-cultural factors relevant to leadership
applications, and details the history and development of the
MBTI in South Africa.

JOAN'S JOURNEY FROM
INTRAPRENEUR TO ENTREPRENEUR

Joan considered her recently announced appointment with her customary rational approach. She was to become the first female to be appointed a member of the executive team in the Human Resources division of a large corporation. As she was also only the second female member of senior management in an organisation with more than 40,000 employees, she realised that her male colleagues, ten years her senior on average, would be watching her progress critically.

The department which Joan was appointed to manage was created to facilitate the transformation of the corporation from a highly bureaucratic monopoly to a more customer and performance oriented organisation. This meant that she would be advising the company executive on culture change strategies as well as such processes as quality improvement, teamwork and a new performance management system that was to be implemented throughout the organisation.

A complicating factor in her work was that, although her team would be located in one place, they would be working throughout the country in all the major urban and some rural centres. Accordingly, Joan realised that the three major focus areas of her department could not be worked on individually, as achieving the overall objective would require cross-functional involvement.

Joan reviewed the factors that led to her appointment. From a young age, she was always an individual with a strong personal drive for what she believed in, understanding that you could only achieve your objectives through hard work. This belief in hard work was what drove her to achieve her own high standards. She could not remember having ever accepted defeat, even when faced by what others would claim to be insurmountable odds. Joan's personal standards and her drive often isolated her from others, but this just resulted in her becoming even more committed to achieving her objectives.

Her personal drive had helped her to obtain a degree in Clinical Psychology when, financially speaking, it seemed to be impossible that she would be able to attend university. She had accepted part-time jobs and achieved academic results that allowed qualified her for bursaries. After graduating, Joan accepted positions in various organisations, working her way up through the ranks, ultimately to the position on the Human Resources executive team. She was certain that no one who knew her would ever be able to say that she got things she did not deserve. One of her colleagues once noted: "She never stops working, she even reads academic books when she is on holiday. I don't know when last she read a novel."

Joan understood that the future success of her department would depend on her ability to build a strong team out of what could only be termed a group of individualists who she had no real hand in selecting. The team members were also quite varied in both their levels of personal development and their experience in the specific field of organisational change that would be required for the task ahead. The geographical spread of the organisation's offices would also mean that her team would have to operate individually, away from the head office, for extended periods of time. She finally concluded that she had to create a team of experts she could trust and who could work on their own for the good of the group.

After having discussions with each member of her team, she reviewed their abilities and developmental needs. The first discussion she held with the team was focused less on what needed to be achieved than how each member of the team saw themselves fitting in with the other members. Joan's overall impression from the discussions was that the majority of the team members had the ability to understand the future developments, but also had a strong interest in possible personal development opportunities that might result from their work with the team.

Although willing and hard working, these people were also highly critical of management and one another; they would not accept another member unless they believed the person to be competent. Joan realised that to lead them, she would have to work on building relationships around competence and mutual benefit. Fortunately, some team members had worked together in the past, and so had already commenced the development of these relationships.

Joan's natural leadership style was one of personal involvement and caring about both the personal and work related problems experienced by each team member. With her belief in the potential of people, she understood that you had to recognise the abilities of each member and find ways to help them to extend themselves beyond what they might have thought possible. She realised that each individual had a particular contribution to make to the team and that her role would be to help them believe in themselves and build on their individual

▼▼▼▼▼▼▼▼▼▼▼▼▼▼▼▼▼▼▼▼▼▼

strengths. In doing so, she would need to assist all members of the team in their understanding of the overall objectives they were working towards, and to help them realise that their individual success would depend on a collective effort. She would, however, have to be careful that she did not create an impression of undue interference.

The approach that Joan adopted was to set up a management team and guide them through regular meetings where the latest organisational developments were discussed, with Joan facilitating and everyone having his or her say in prioritising focus areas. These meetings were followed up by monthly feedback sessions away from the office for the whole department, usually scheduled for a full day. At these sessions, which were compulsory, progress reports were given by relevant team members. Although a full day was set out for the feedback sessions, they usually only lasted until lunchtime; for the rest of the day, Joan arranged some relaxation and socialising sessions.

Over the next five years, Joan's personal involvement with each team member resulted in the development of friendships. These friendships, her example of hard work and her never-ending drive for continuous improvement became the standards against which individual team members started measuring their own performance. After setting herself up as the performance standard, she was then able to focus on guiding her team in the right direction by actively seeking development opportunities to assist each team member in achieving both their personal and organisational objectives.

Joan believed in never taking personal credit for the team's achievements and often recognised the successes of the team in ways that were contrary to company policy. An example of this was when, unknown to the team members, she personally paid a large part of the expense of a full day of celebration at a well-known South African resort. Through Joan's caring for each person and the team members' understanding that she was always available to discuss problems, the team grew in strength and developed into a closely-knit group of specialists. Their success is illustrated by the fact that, after departmental objectives were met successfully, all the members obtained senior positions in other departments and organisations.

This department was disbanded twelve years ago. Following its closing down, Joan and three members of her original team started their own consultancy businesses. Their businesses, due to differing interests, each have their own areas of specialisation within the broad field of organisation development. Given the nature of the field of operation, however, they are for all intents and purposes in competition with one another. But the friendships that developed whilst working for Joan have remained as strong as ever.

Five years ago, Joan's clients, and the sizes of the projects they offered, started becoming too big for her to manage on her own and she started thinking about expansion. Joan decided to phone her old colleagues with an offer to start working together again. Given the increased size and number of contracts, as well as the entrepreneurial leadership of Joan (although she does not see herself as the leader), the network of businesses have since expanded to include three new members.

For the past four years these seven businesses have been operating as a network of equals, with no written contracts or agreements governing their interactions. All it takes is one phone call from any of the members, asking them to check diaries and commitments, and the team will start working together on a project. One thing that has remained to this day is a commitment to the sharing of knowledge and ideas relevant to the current and future needs of the members. The sharing of knowledge and experience does not stop with the team, but has recently extended to their customer base, where customers now share their experiences with other existing and future customers through conferences.

As was the case when working in the bureaucratic organisation, Joan has become an entrepreneur that people look up to and respect for her competence, honesty and caring.

SOUTH AFRICA

Entrepreneurial flair and leadership in South Africa can be found in all walks of life and in all aspects of the economy. It is as diverse as the hawker on the street corner selling handmade wire sculptures, or the person teaching others to grow vegetables in community gardens, or billion-Rand mergers and acquisitions being negotiated with international financial backing.

Some established organisations with long track records are also implementing processes aimed at developing new cultures that would facilitate entrepreneurial and intrapreneurial skills among their staff. In other organisations, people who always believed that they were employed for life are accepting voluntary retrenchment packages and taking personal responsibility for their own economic survival.

These examples cover only a small fraction of the entrepreneurial foci that have started emerging in the so-called New South Africa. This short overview of recent changes will attempt to help the reader understand the atmosphere of entrepreneurial leadership that is developing in a rapidly transforming country, amidst some hindrances.

The body of this text will attempt to set out the background, and through case studies, will attempt to indicate some different perspectives on the entrepreneurial dynamics of the country. In the text, attention will also be given to some influences of past governmental policies on current thinking and employment reform processes currently being implemented by both government and organised business.

To understand recent developments in South Africa, some major changes will be discussed under the headings of Politico/Legal changes, Socio/Cultural influences and Economic developments. Lastly, attention will be turned to changes influencing entrepreneurship in the country. These developments will be discussed from the perspective of entrepreneurs and intrapreneurs in government and private industry and also from the perspective of individuals.

HISTORICAL BACKGROUND

One of the best-known words in the international political arena is apartheid. There can be no doubt that the implementation of the policy of apartheid resulted in numerous social injustices and economic imbalances in South Africa. However, it does not fall within the scope of this chapter to review these injustices or to debate how they could be corrected. In any case, given the complex nature of the country, it is also impossible for one person with a few pages of notes to create a comprehensive understanding of the situation for the reader, let alone attempt to provide a solution.

In addition to all the social injustices that accompanied the policy of apartheid, four major factors influenced businesses in the country. The first three factors, directly attributable to this policy, were that the majority of South Africans were prohibited from owning property or businesses, they were denied meaningful education opportunities, and certain jobs were reserved exclusively for a privileged minority. These three factors effectively excluded the majority of South Africans from participating and sharing in the benefits of mainstream business.

A fourth factor was that years of international sanctions imposed on the country after extensive lobbying by people who were worst affected by apartheid resulted in businesses becoming somewhat myopic. The majority of businesses developed a narrow focus, both internal to the company and within the borders of South Africa.

These businesses also developed labour intensive processes due to the low cost of labour as compared to the difficulties of obtaining the latest technology and even some international business developments that were not available to South African businesses. With the exception of some large organisations, contact was, to a large extent, lost with international business developments and trends. It was as if the systems theory of organisations did not apply to influences from across the borders.

In February 1990, Mr. F.W. de Klerk, then President of South Africa, delivered a speech in the South African Parliament that started a visible chain reaction of changes in the country. Often this date is seen as the date when apartheid was officially ended, although a review of some changes in the country prior to this speech shows that small cracks had already started in apartheid policies during the late 1970s (e.g. the change in the Labour Relations Act of 1979, whereby black employees were, for the first time, allowed to legally set up and manage trade unions). Given the situation in the country, and the atrocities that took place, however, the changes could be compared to trying to stop a flood with a single sandbag.

De Klerk's speech in February 1990 should therefore be seen as the date that the starting gun in the race to equality was fired and the face of the country started changing radically in accordance. These changes, albeit largely political at the time, also affected the socio-cultural, economic and technological aspects of South Africa and will continue to have an effect on South African business and society well into the next millennium. The extent of the change was such that the foundations on which basic personal (and some religious) beliefs were built were removed. This resulted in large numbers of people starting to question some of

▼▼▼▼▼▼▼▼▼▼▼▼▼▼▼▼▼▼▼▼▼

their deepest held cultural beliefs. There was a move from the belief that it is us against them, a belief which rejects diversity, to the concept of all of us in a rainbow nation, embracing diversity.

The changes announced affected the basic beliefs about society and the value systems of all the different South African cultures. The ways these diverse beliefs and values were, and still are, affected by the De Klerk speech were quite varied, however. There can be little debate that the changes can be classified as revolutionary.

Millions of people around the world followed the release of Nelson Mandela from prison, the initial discussions between all relevant groupings and the first stages of democratisation, culminating in the first democratic election in South Africa. Since the lifting of sanctions and the release of Mandela, who became the first President of the new South Africa, the country is returning to the global economy and the accompanying competition.

February 1990 also saw the disbanding by the government of a number of political groupings and democratic organisations. Some of the internationally better-known political groupings whose banning orders were lifted were the African National Congress (ANC), South African Communist Party (SACP) and the Pan Africanist Congress (PAC). Since the disbanding of these and other organisations, numerous alliances were forged and numerous discussions began.

Two major discussion forums created were Convention for a Democratic South Africa (CODESA) and National Economic Development and Labour Council (NEDLAC). CODESA discussions focussed on the transition of the country to a democracy and the compilation of an interim constitution; NEDLAC focussed on talks between government, organised labour and organised business. After four years of preparation and discussions, the first ever democratic election in South Africa took place on 27 April 1994. This resulted in the election of the new government — the alliance of the ANC, SACP and Congress of South Africa Trade Unions (COSATU) under the banner of the ANC.

Since the start of the move to a democracy and the subsequent election, various new laws and policies have been set out. Two documents and one law are directly relevant to the topic at hand and were aimed at setting out the road ahead. The first document — chronologically — is known as the Reconstruction and

Development Program (RDP),[1] and the second a macro-economic strategy entitled Growth, Employment and Redistribution (GEAR).[2] The law is the revised Labour Relations Act of 1996,[3] as agreed to by the participants in NEDLAC. This highlighted numerous factors which, when implemented, would influence the development and emergence of intrapreneurs. A short overview of the documents will give a better understanding of their potential influences. It will be noted that referral is often made to possible influences of laws and documents. The reason for this is that democracy in the country is only a few years old; the predominant thought processes according to which people and organisations operate do not change overnight.

The RDP served as the election platform for the current government and was described as *"An integrated program, based on the people, that provides peace and security for all and builds the nation, links reconstruction and development and deepens democracy."*[4] The RDP set out five key programs that the government wanted to achieve. These programs, with extracts from their objectives, are:

• Meeting Basic Needs
This would be achieved through empowerment that gives the poor control over their lives and increases their ability to mobilise sufficient development resources, including from the democratic government where necessary.[5]

• Developing Human Resources
It is a process in which the citizens of a nation acquire and develop the knowledge and skill necessary for occupational tasks and for other social, cultural, intellectual and political roles that are part and parcel of a vibrant democratic society.[6]

• Building the Economy
Critical programs in this area include urban and rural development, industrial strategy, providing support for small and micro enterprises (including small-scale farming), job creation and land reform.[7]

• Democratising the State and Society
Democracy requires that all South Africans have access to power and the right to exercise their power. This will ensure that all people will be able to participate in the process of reconstructing our country.[8]

• Implementing the RDP

This requires a strategic approach that combines public and private sector funding, taking into account the sequence and timing of funding sources and programs.[9]

One underlying belief, continually highlighted throughout the document, is that as there is democracy in the political scenario, the economy also has to become democratised. According to the RDP, democratising the workplace requires both people development and the growth of the economy. The democratisation process has been identified as a priority of government and government departments. Based on this document, the concept of Affirmative Action is strongly supported as a process aimed at correcting past undemocratic appointments and promotions within organisations.

There is no doubt that the majority of the South African population was denied certain basic rights, regarding aspects such as education and employment, in the apartheid period. The concept of discrimination on any base has been outlawed in the constitution of the country, but allows for a process of Affirmative Action aimed at the correction of past wrongs. The practical ramifications of the implementation of Affirmative Action can, however, be found in the fact that the majority (approximately 80 percent) must now be affirmed into fewer available positions which were, and in the majority of cases still are, occupied by the minority.

The major result is that increasing numbers of people, with long track records and experience, are losing what they perceived as career prospects. In practice, the constitution thus indicates that people who have been appointed in positions as a result of previous government policies, and who can be broadly classified as white males, may be discriminated against. It is often in this area that a large percentage of the entrepreneurs are found, as they believe that their futures and career paths in the formal economy are disappearing.

The second document, published in 1996, is a macro-economic strategy setting out processes and objectives aimed at developing:[10]

• a competitive fast-growing economy which creates sufficient jobs for all work seekers;
• a redistribution of income and opportunities in favour of the poor;
• a society in which sound health, education and other services are available to all;

• an environment in which homes are secure and places of work are productive.

Reviewing the RDP and the GEAR documents it will be noted that the GEAR strategy is a document which turns the RDP objective of economic growth into more tangible targets and strategies.

With regard to entrepreneurs, the GEAR strategy indicates, *"the promotion of small, medium and micro enterprises (SMMEs) is a key element in the Government's strategy for employment creation and income generation."*[11] The promotion of such SMMEs are largely under the control of the Governmental Department of Trade and Industry.

Based on the GEAR objective of developing SMMEs two new, wholly government owned organisations were created to assist in their start up provided such SMMEs operate primarily within the country. The first of these is an organisation called KHULA Enterprise Finance with the mission to *"ensure improved availability of loan and equity capital to SMMEs by offering in a sustainable manner Loans, Guarantees and Seed Funds to Retail Financial Intermediaries (RFIs) in need of capital and capacity."*[12]

KHULA itself does not supply funding directly to SMMEs, but operates through retail financial intermediaries, similar to loan companies. These intermediaries, with the support of KHULA, fund organisations with a projected annual turnover of no greater than ten million South African Rand (R10m). Funding of organisations does, however, depend on compliance to both qualitative and quantitative (turnover) criteria. Some of the aspects they consider in granting loans are the potential for self-sufficiency, the involvement in the manufacturing industry and balancing historical inequalities in the country.

At the end of its first year of existence KHULA had approved:[13]

• loans to seven RFI's to the value of R28.3m of which at least 65 percent would be provided to women,
• R29.2 m in business loans which comprise bridging finance or revolving credits for RFIs and
• R6.1 m in seek loans, meaning that KHULA helps legally constituted RFI's in obtaining start-up capital.

In addition, the board of KHULA had reviewed 167 guarantee applications and mobilised R42m in bank funds. In the credit guarantee scheme, KHULA provides

▼▼▼▼▼▼▼▼▼▼▼▼▼▼▼▼▼▼▼▼▼▼▼

banks with appropriate guarantees, to a maximum of 80 percent, on behalf of approved RFIs requiring additional funds for SMMEs.

The second organisation that was registered is NTSIKA Enterprise Promotion Agency, created to provide non-financial assistance. The assistance they provide is access to information, advice, markets, appropriate technology and training. The mission of the agency is "to render an efficient and effective promotion and support service to small, medium and micro enterprises through a broad range of intermediaries to contribute towards equitable economic growth in South Africa."[14] NTSIKA aims to achieve its mission by providing a variety of products and services to SMMEs through five divisions, namely:

- Management and Entrepreneurial Division
- Targeted Assistance Division
- Business Development Services Division
- Marketing and Linkages Division
- Policy, Research and Information Division

On reviewing the RDP and GEAR documents, including the two organisations established, it becomes clear that a high priority has been placed on the development of SMMEs, specifically in manufacturing. It also becomes clear that a number of processes have been set in place for the development of such organisations. Given the historical perspective it is also understandable that the major focus is on assisting the development of entrepreneurs from previously disadvantaged communities.

Labour-Employer relationships have historically been markedly antagonistic. Given the political situation in the country, the unions with predominantly black membership naturally became one of the forces involved in lobbying for political change in South Africa. It stands to reason that union membership, specifically among the disadvantaged population, became strongly linked to political aspirations, and membership numbers grew every year.

After 1990, numerous negotiations began to assist in the transformation of South Africa to a democratic nation. One of the areas of negotiation was the formation of NEDLAC (National Economic Development and Labour Council). Here, representatives from business and labour negotiate "national agreements" which may eventually become laws governing the workplace. The Labour Relations Act of

1996 was the first law that was negotiated on this forum. In this law the most influential factor regarding changes in employee involvement is the degree of worker participation in the running of the business. One of the purposes of the bill was "to promote employee participation in decision-making through the establishment of workplace forums." This document is also largely aimed at governing the relationship between employers and employees.

The Act stipulates that unions could request the formation of workplace forums where representatives of management and workers would discuss a number of work related issues. It is indicated that once established, "a workplace forum is entitled to be consulted by the employer about proposals relating to any of the following matters:

- restructuring the workplace, including the introduction of new technology and new work methods;
- changes in the organisation of work;
- partial or total plant closures;
- mergers and transfers of ownership, in so far as they have an impact on the employees;
- the dismissal of employees for reasons based on operational requirements;
- job grading;
- forming the criteria for merit increases or the payment of discretionary bonuses;
- education and training;
- product development plans; and
- export promotion."[15]

It should be noted that the workplace forum is different from the usual union management negotiation forums in that, once created at the request of the union, all employees — including middle management and non-union members — would be represented in the discussions with the executive management grouping. As will be seen from the socio-cultural discussion, these workplace forums could experience initial problems, specifically as a result of the skills and educational levels in the country.

It should also be remembered that, as is the case internationally, unions in South Africa have more socialistic objectives than the capitalistic objectives of the

▼▼▼▼▼▼▼▼▼▼▼▼▼▼▼▼▼▼▼▼▼▼▼

owners of business. From a political perspective, it is clear that there is a strong drive for employee involvement and participation in the growth of the economy. Participation is aimed at facilitating the development of leaders as both entrepreneurs and intrapreneurs — people who contribute to the running of the company for which they work and thereby are allowed to participate in creating wealth. We will study one such leader, Yusuf, later in this chapter.

THE ECONOMY

Reviewing the politico-legal drive for greater participation in and democratisation of the workplace is only one part of the picture affecting the emergence of entrepreneurs. The economy itself also has a strong influence on the emergence of entrepreneurs.

From a government perspective, the development of the national economy has been identified as a priority, as it is believed it will materially affect future political and social changes in South Africa. It should be remembered that by using the RDP as an election platform, the current government promised their followers a better life for all. Initially, this better life was promised within a time frame of five years, but given a number of factors, this time frame has since become more open-ended.

In order to help in understanding economic developments in the country, a summary of changes in some indicators of the South African economic performance are set out in the following table.

TABLE 1 ECONOMIC INDICATORS		
INDICATOR	Period	Average Percent Change[i]
Gross Domestic Product (GDP)	1982–1996	1.16 percent pa
Government debt increase as percent of GDP	1990–1996	2.92 percent pa
Consumer Price Increase (CPI)	1989–1996	8.01 percent pa
Labour Cost per unit	1996 vs. 1989	2.2 percent
Labour Productivity	1989–1996	1.94 percent pa
Employment in formal sector	1996 vs. 1989	-7 percent

Note: Figures indicate average percentage change over the indicated period

South Africa experienced an economic downturn during the late 1980s as a result of the years of sanctions, the pending changes locally and world economic influences. This downturn lasted four years, finally ending in the second quarter of 1993. It is apparent that from the second half of 1996, the recovery had lost some of its momentum and the economy was again starting to slow down. Considering the slowing of the economy and a 7 percent reduction in available positions — 392,000 since 1990 in the formal sector — it is clear that if the downturn continues, a large number of entrepreneurs could shortly be experiencing financial problems without the option of returning to formal employment.

One objective of the government, as set out in their GEAR policy, is a 4.2 percent average annual growth in the GDP for the period 1996 to 2000. However, the average annual growth in GDP for the period indicated in Table 1 matched or exceeded the GEAR objective on only two occasions. The highest percentage increase in the GDP since 1982 was in 1984, when it reached 5.1 percent, while an increase of 4.2 percent was achieved in 1988. Taking growth in real GDP for South Africa back even further, the average annual growth for the period 1956 to 1992, was 3.29 percent.[16]

▼▼▼▼▼▼▼▼▼▼▼▼▼▼▼▼▼▼▼▼▼▼▼▼

In comparing the 1.16 percent growth in the GDP during the past fifteen years with the 2.9 percent annual increase of government debt as a percentage of the GDP over the last six years, it becomes clear that government expenditure will soon have to start slowing down. A further indication of the need to reduce government spending can be found when considering that government debt, as a percentage of the GDP, increased by 17.2 percent between 1990 and 1997. This does not bode well for organisations such as KHULA and NTSIKA, or the entrepreneurs that are expecting government to supply them with start-up funding.

The lifting of sanctions brought the realisation that the majority of South African businesses were not competitive in the global market. One clear indication is labour cost per unit compared to labour productivity. It will be noted here that although productivity improved during the indicated time (Table 1), labour cost per unit increased even more. Because of the sanctions, South African consumers often did not have a large selection of products or manufacturers to choose from and increases in South African production costs were largely passed on to the consumer. Frequently, this was done with only a limited effort to reduce the costs. The Production Price Index (PPI) for locally manufactured goods increased by an average of 7.2 per year for the period 1989 to 1996.[17]

With the lifting of sanctions and the signing of the General Agreement on Tariffs and Trade (GATT) by the South African Government, some organisations have attempted to streamline their operation and reduce costs. Large numbers of organisations have started implementing various processes — the one most often followed is a reduction in staff numbers. Based on the economic indicators, this strategy has not yet been totally successful.

The changes implemented by organisations have, however, been complicated by the adversarial relationship in existence between labour and organised business. Labour was (and, with its involvement in government, still is) strongly aligned to furthering their socio-political objectives in the workplace.

Considering the extent of the changes in employment during the 1990s, remember, as mentioned previously, that positions in the formal non-agricultural sector employment opportunities were reduced by 392,000.[18] The GEAR strategy, discussed earlier, set out proposals for the creation of an average of 270,000 jobs per year over the same period. There has actually been an increase in number of employees in central government from a 1990 base of 100 to a figure of 105.4 in 1996.

One of the major reasons for the increase in the number of positions in public authorities is that the South African constitution has changed the number of provinces (each with their own provincial government) from the previous four to nine. A second reason can be found in the policies of democratising the government and attempting to have governmental organisations reflect the demographics of the country. The need for government to reduce spending will also affect the possibility of achieving the stated objective of democratising the state if they continue attempting to do it through increasing staff numbers. This means that this avenue to formal employment will soon be unavailable as well.

An interesting aspect is the change in employment figures for public business enterprises. These semi-governmental business enterprises showed a decrease of more than 25 percent in their employment figures during the period 1989 to 1996. This is by far the highest percentage decrease of any grouping. Two of the major reasons for this reduction in staff numbers are the reduction in their subsidies from government and their preparation for possible privatisation. The result is that these organisations have had to refocus their business. In a number of cases, some have actually started competing with companies they used to supply with research data, while others have actually either stopped delivering certain services or reduced the service to such a level that it is no longer effective. These changes have actually opened the door for a number of entrepreneurs.

Unemployment is a point of great debate and is conservatively estimated at 35 percent of the South African economically active population. The greatest majority of unemployed people are also under the age of twenty-five. It should be noted that the unemployment figure is based on employment in the formal sector. South Africa has a fast growing informal sector, as alluded to earlier, and which will again be discussed in more depth later. Comparing the proposed increase in number of jobs indicated in the GEAR strategy to the growth in the economically active population, it can be noted that, even if attained, it will not be sufficient to ensure a meaningful decrease in unemployment figures. The economically active population increased on average by 2.8 percent per year over the past decade. In short, fewer jobs are becoming available for the increasing number of people seeking formal

▼▼▼▼▼▼▼▼▼▼▼▼▼▼▼▼▼▼▼▼▼▼▼

employment. Indications were that by 1990 only 7.5 percent of new work seekers could expect to find employment in the formal sector.[19]

A saving grace for the country is the number of entrepreneurs that are starting to appear in various sectors of the economy. Although a large number of the emerging entrepreneurs are classified in the informal sector, in the private sector the number of people employed in service industries have increased from a base of 100 in 1990 to 104.3 in 1996. Although this sector comprises only a small portion of the economy, it is increasing.

SOCIO-CULTURAL DIMENSIONS

In the previous sections it was noted that the development of human resources is seen as a critical objective of the government. Demographic statistics show that South Africa has eleven official languages and more than twenty major ethnic cultures. In 1996 the population, distributed largely around five metropolitan areas, stood at 37.9 million, comprised of:[20]

- Whites, 12 percent
- Coloured, 8.5 percent
- Asians, 2.5 percent
- Blacks, 77 percent

Of these 37.9 million people, 55 percent are urbanised. To complicate matters further, 54 percent are under the age of twenty-five and 18 percent of adults are illiterate. Add to that the fact that the economically active population is growing at 2.8 percent annually and it becomes clear that even a growth of 270,000 jobs a year, as envisaged in the GEAR strategy, will not result in all unemployed South Africans being able to find formal employment.

A further factor to consider is that the majority of South Africans were not allowed meaningful education; only limited numbers were able to complete their schooling, let alone progress to tertiary education, as limitations were placed on universities regarding the numbers of "non-whites" allowed. These aspects have influenced and increased structural unemployment where the skills people have to offer do not necessarily match the skills required by organised businesses.

The situation in South Africa is also influenced by the country having the best developed infrastructure in southern Africa and so large numbers of people cross the border from neighbouring countries – often illegally – in search of employment.

With the recent political changes, a strong call has emerged from certain quarters that business should change from what is called Eurocentric management philosophies and principles to Afrocentric management – the implementation of African cultural heritage in the workplace. This is usually linked to Ubuntu, an Afrocentric concept that finds one of its biggest advocates in a South African management consultant called Lovemore Mbigi. One of the major reasons for the call to Afrocentric management is an accusation that the application of western management principles have not benefited or developed the population.

Mbigi notes:[21]

> *If we are going to build a competitive developed nation, competitive institutions as well as organisations, the unmistakable collective solidarity in African life should find its expression in our modern forms of business entrepreneurship, business organisations and management.*

Implementation of Ubuntu in organisations is described as an all-embracing process of accepting the best from all cultures and incorporating such into the heritage of African culture.

At its deepest level, Ubuntu means the implementation of a brotherhood among all South Africans and can best be translated as "I am because we are." This brotherhood can also be linked to the basic religious principle of caring for one's neighbour and forming caring communities. Based on this caring, Ronnie Lessem[22] indicates, "the African perspective is therefore communal rather than individual." Lessem goes further, equating this communal perspective to the Jungian idea of the Feeling preference.

When Ubuntu is implemented, Mbigi and Maree[23] indicate, "*loyalty and conformity become prized values for every member of the group.*" It cannot be argued that the loyalty aspect would be prized by most organisations. In terms of the conformity, some debate can be held as to its feasibility in a changing work world, and the increasing need for entrepreneurs. The views regarding Ubuntu and its implementation should also be considered in the light of significant MBTI type preferences found in South African populations, as will be discussed later.

At face value, the implementation of Ubuntu sounds feasible as the accepted way of doing business in South Africa. Mbigi does, however, caution that Ubuntu can be hijacked and trivialised. In discussions with a number of black managers, he found they interpreted Ubuntu to mean "that you should care for your kind." This approach is actually contrary to the deepest meaning of the Ubuntu philosophy: inclusion. The minute it becomes differentially exclusive, it is no longer Ubuntu. The exclusivity being proposed by some managers under the banner of Ubuntu is actually leading to increased tensions and uncertainty among certain groups regarding their futures in organised business.

With all the differences that exist in the country, one common thread among the peoples in South Africa is that they have all lived in strongly patriarchal societies. The patriarchal dominance varies in that some believe that a wife is bought and thereby becomes the property of the husband, by him paying *lobola* to the parents of his future wife. Others believe that the role of the wife is to support her husband, who has the sole, or at least the major, responsibility as breadwinner. The changes announced in 1990 affected this belief in that all South Africans are now theoretically equal.

This patriarchal culture has influenced organisations in that very few employed females are at senior management levels, and often those who were appointed in such positions were never really accepted as equals by all their male colleagues. In some cultures, a female manager was never accepted as a person being allowed to hold a position of seniority over a male, and often males would not listen to instructions from that manager.

In a recent publication, Mr. Cyril Ramaphosa, former general secretary of the ruling African National Congress and deputy chairman of New Africa Investments Ltd (NAIL), was quoted as describing the white male culture that exists in businesses as "nauseating,"[24] and that "this culture will not be acceptable in the type of South Africa we live in."

Whether this statement was aimed purely at white males or simply at male dominance is not clear, but statements such as these are frequently made by prominent black leaders, usually resulting in increasing the tension felt by people placed in managerial positions. Such comments are also seldom accompanied by clarification of what should be implemented in its place, as patriarchal dominance does not only exist among whites but in the majority of cultures.

Now that we have reviewed the historic, economic and socio-political context for conducting business within South Africa, let us follow the story of a contemporary South African entrepreneur.

YUSUF'S ROLE IN SOUTH AFRICA'S CHANGING BUSINESS CULTURE

From his luxurious office on the forty-seventh floor, Yusuf reviews the reasons for starting his security business. Believing in the potential of people and his country, he reflects that there are four major obstacles to a successful transition of the country. These obstacles are exclusivity, lack of leadership, lack of knowledge and continued high levels of crime.

With the recent political changes, the struggle has changed from being political to economic. Based on his perception that there is a belief amongst some South Africans that "people of African stock are not capable of building anything sustainable from nothing," he feels that it is important for him to make a statement that would help the struggle.

Following the end of the political struggle, he decided to utilise the knowledge he had gained and started off as a consultant on South Africa to various international organisations. This did not satisfy him and he reviewed his abilities and the needs of the country. He could, like many of his ex-comrades, enter politics, but this would not make the statement that he believed had to be made. He calculates that we as humans live for less that one million hours and should thus make every minute count. There is just no time to waste or for trying to take short cuts to achieving what needs to be done.

With his consulting income, which he felt was too irregular, he decided to start a security company. This would satisfy his personal needs, build on his strengths and at the same time, make a contribution to building the South Africa he believed possible, the South Africa for which he originally joined the struggle.

Yusuf realised that the building of this South Africa would not be achieved by waiting for international finance, but only when people realise that it is up to them to build the country. This realisation would, however, only come through the investment of time and effort in the development of people and the continued sharing of information.

Yusuf started training his new recruits, using available personal funds. The training he implemented, and is still implementing, was not aimed at skill building alone, but at sharpening the abilities of people that are "born security personnel." Training has always been important to him, for his preference is to work with independent, autonomous people that are linked to a common objective. Yusuf believes that people should have the ability to think every situation through, identify what must be achieved and then plan how to achieve the objective. He wants to empower his staff to be able to overcome problems they might face, for as they progress in life, they will meet enemies who will be neutralised by the imparting of knowledge. In this way, each member of his organisation will be able to guide others. By doing this, Yusuf will be helping people believe in themselves and others.

When turning his mind to the day-to-day running of the business and interaction with staff Yusuf realises that it is based on his deeply held religious beliefs. His religion and the philosophy, "the more money you make, the more humble you must become, and the higher you climb, the more sensitive you should be," have become his guidelines for running the business. Based on this humility and sensitivity he recognises his own insignificance in the universe and sees himself as a servant of all the people of South Africa.

This view of himself has led him to make an effort to remain in touch with people at the grassroots level. Having built his multimillion Rand business with only his personal finances, it often happens that people from his hometown believe he has achieved the pinnacle of success. When visiting them and, according to custom, arranging a feast, they usually place him at the table for honoured guests. Believing that he has not yet achieved the success he is capable of, he accepts this in his normal, quiet-spoken way, but at the first opportunity, he will be found eating with the people shunned by those honoured guests.

Applying the same approach to his business, Yusuf reflects on the times he can be found in the back of the van travelling with the lowest-level staff members employed by his company. Here, dressed in the same uniform as them, he finds that he can have honest and frank discussions about both personal and work related problems experienced by his people.

These work related problems are also discussed at his quarterly reorientation meetings with his supervisors, aimed at improving the workplace. At all the meetings and discussions he has with his staff, anyone can say what they want about any other person or work process.

TYPE IN SOUTH AFRICA

In research conducted on the MBTI in South Africa,[25] Johanna de Beer found that, when compared to available USA data, a South African sample of 6,452 subjects more often chose Extraversion (E), Thinking (T) and Judging (J) (p > 0.01). There does not, however, seem to be any statistically significant difference in the preference for Sensing (S) or Intuition (N) between South African and USA data. The South African data also show higher incidences of ET, ST, NT, EJ, SJ, NJ and TJ than in the USA base sample (p > 0.01).

With regard to whole types, de Beer also found that 43.12 percent of the total South African sample preferred ESTJ (23.22 percent) and ISTJ (19.9 percent). When reviewing the distribution of type across different cultural groupings within the country, it was found that the indigenous cultures had an even higher incidence of ST preference than their white counterparts. The predominant xSTJ type could have some influence on the type of entrepreneurial developments in the country.

It is also interesting that type preferences in a sample of 200 unemployed South Africans came out as almost exclusively xSTJ. Considering the high occurrence of xSTJ in the South African population, some projections could be made regarding the impact on entrepreneurship and the entrepreneurial ventures that would be embarked on. The increasing number of franchises being started could be related at some level to the personal type preferences in the country.

Theoretically, those who prefer Judging usually seek control and order in their lives and find ambiguity uncomfortable. As indicated throughout this chapter, the changes in the country since 1990 are filled with ambiguity and could result in increasing personal uncertainty and a feeling of losing control. Analysing the population further, it is found that there is a statistically significant higher incidence of preference for Perceiving among females than among males in South Africa. A concern here is that the Perceiving attitude, in which the South African base is significantly lower than that found in the USA data, is often associated with entrepreneurship. Considering this in the light of a patriarchal society, the possibility of the numbers of Perceiving oriented female entrepreneurs emerging is debatable. Given the country's political changes, it is interesting that there is a higher incidence of Perceiving among Caucasian South Africans than among other indigenous groups, suggesting that the people who feel they are being denied future employment in formal business exhibit a higher tolerance for ambiguity than other South African ethnic groups.

The high incidence of Judging among people who have recently obtained political control could, however, be a cause for concern if such leaders seek excessive control, structure and regulations. Should the government implement strong controls and attempt to regulate entrepreneurs, entrepreneurial spirit could be inhibited. Added to this is the interpretation of the philosophy of Ubuntu as discussed earlier, where the underlying philosophy seems more based on the Perceiving but is often implemented from a Judging perspective.

When comparing the findings regarding national type tables to research on organisations,[26] it is found that, in a sample of 137, the most preferred MBTI profile across all levels of management was xSTJ. This finding is in line with the national data discussed earlier.

Reviewing the data by level of management it was found that there was a higher frequency of NT types among the executive management grouping when compared to any other management grouping. This leaning towards Intuition and Thinking, although slight, became clearer when using continuous data on mean strength of preference. Utilising this same process, it was found that middle management remained with an xSTJ preference. Senior and executive management showed that although their highest whole type frequency was ISTJ the collective mean preference, calculated through continuous data, was for Extraversion. In addition to the E-I difference the executive management team also showed a continuous data mean preference for Intuition. This slight shift toward Intuition could indicate that among executive managers there may be a stronger focus on identifying tendencies, associations, patterns and possibilities.

When comparing the findings of personal type preferences to results on organisational type, as obtained with the SETA, some possible contradictions are found. One interesting factor is that managers in businesses staffed and run by whites perceive the company type as predominantly ESTJ whereas managers in businesses in the same industry, but staffed and run predominantly by blacks, see their business as predominantly ESFJ. Caution, however, must be taken in generalising the T-F difference, as further investigation will be required to determine the true understanding of the identified preference for Feeling. This preference for Feeling seems, at face value, to support the theory of Lessem, but during discussions with managers regarding the Feeling function, it seems to be centred more around a feeling of belonging than around organisational empathy. It does, however, remain that the established organisations surveyed were perceived by their management employees as having a predominantly ESxJ culture.

Discussions with a number of executive management groups on possible culture changes within their organisation indicated that they also perceived their organisations as predominantly SJ. It was found, however, that the majority of these groups, wishing to adapt to the international competitiveness and changes in the country, perceive the ideal culture for their organisation as being more entrepreneurial and as being predominantly NP.

This finding was compared with research among a small sample of twenty-one entrepreneurial consultancy firms. Among the entrepreneurs, the most frequent personal type preference was for xNTP. Utilising SETA, it was determined that the perception of the culture of their organisation was significantly ENxP. It should be noted, however, that entrepreneurs with franchise type businesses showed a higher xSTJ personal preference. The preference for NP among those entrepreneurs creating something from nothing seems to support literature on entrepreneurship. Although use has been made of small samples, there also seems to be an indication that large, established organisations see the formation of a perceived ENxP organisational type as the one required for future survival in South Africa.

Research has recently been completed on a questionnaire developed and statistically validated in South Africa called the OCTA$^{©}$ — an acronym for Organization Character Type Assessment. This is an integrated questionnaire determining employee perception of organizational character in terms of cultural dimensions, cultural styles and cultural type.

In line with previously mentioned assessments, results obtained with the OCTA$^{©}$ indicate that employees of entrepreneurial concerns perceive their companies to be functioning as ENFP. This matches a perception of the required culture for South African organizations. As the organization's staff complement increases, the culture becomes more J in character, whilst initially still having an NF character. Once the number of employees exceeds 100, a shift in culture takes place, becoming first ESTJ, then INTJ, and finally, organizations with more than 1000 employees are seen by their employees as having a predominantly ISTJ culture. These changes are represented as follows.

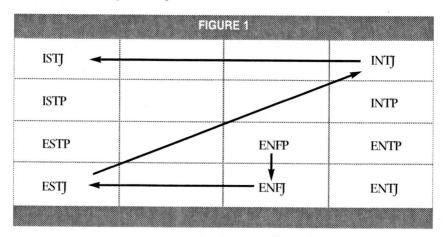

FIGURE 1

During the years of sanctions (which started with an arms embargo in 1977), a large amount of creativity was utilised to find ways of overcoming them. Creativity was also displayed in the development of various processes and industries aimed at satisfying societal and governmental needs. Some industries were developed in an attempt for the country to become self-sufficient, with others aimed at preventing possible future problems. The armaments industry and the conversion from coal to fuel created two of these industries.

As mentioned earlier, one problem that resulted from the years of sanctions is that South African businesses developed a certain degree of myopia regarding markets and customer service. Furthermore, due to the availability of relatively cheap labour and the frequent inability to obtain international technology, South African businesses opted for labour intensive processes, resulting in large numbers of organisations becoming overstaffed in comparison to their international competitors.

To overcome some of their cost and productivity problems, organisations are implementing numerous changes. In a recent survey among a randomly selected cross-section of South African organisations[27] (seventy in number), it was determined that during the past two years:

- 43.4 percent embarked on re-engineering;
- 71.7 percent restructured;
- 39.6 percent downsized;
- 20.8 percent have been involved with mergers or acquisitions;
- 37.7 percent embarked on Quality improvement processes;
- 41.5 percent started implementing team based structures.

A review of the number of changes in each of the organisations found that they implemented an average of two changes (1.93) in the past two years, with the majority of these processes resulting in a reduction of employee numbers. In attempting to determine the success of the changes it will be noted that on the whole, these organisations all indicated an improvement in their short-term financial situation. Considering the country as a whole, as reflected in the National Labour productivity figures, it has been found that productivity increased nominally from a base of 100 in 1990 to 108.3 in March 1997. This 8.3 percent productivity improvement should, however, be reviewed against a backdrop of a 7.5 percent reduction in positions of formal employment. One labour consultancy indicated on national news that their estimates show there has been a net loss of one million jobs in the formal sector over a period of ten years (1990s).

The drive to become competitive through processes such as mechanisation, re-engineering and reduction in employee numbers, whilst having to show concerted efforts towards democratising the workplace, have resulted in numerous organisational strategies that affect the need for entrepreneurship.

One of the two most frequent methods that organisations use to reduce their numbers of employees is offering voluntary retrenchment and early retirement packages. This in itself is nothing new, as many organisations offer such packages. In the South African scenario, where there is the need to correct past wrongs and where businesses are required to reflect the demographics of the country, businesses are offering more and more middle managers a mentorship position. Acceptance of such a position means that the person will, for a particular period of time (usually two years), mentor an Affirmative Action candidate to take over his

▼▼▼▼▼▼▼▼▼▼▼▼▼▼▼▼▼▼▼▼▼▼▼

or her position, after which the contract terminates. This method is aimed at ensuring that there is a transfer of skills whilst implementing Affirmative Action. Given the predominance of STJ preferences in South Africa, it is possible that this process is being accepted by the employees due to their loyalty to the organisation and a personal need for stability.

One of the results of this process is that more and more consultancy firms are focusing on mentorship. Affirmative Action and training are being started on almost a daily basis. A large number of the people who accepted the mentorship process are now selling their experience as consultants on the implementation of mentorship programmes. An indication of the increased number of these intrapreneurs is the constant increase in the number of Closed Corporations (a maximum of eight members) that have been registered in the country since 1993.

The increase in the number of small businesses selling mentorship skills and processes is causing an oversupply of service providers, resulting in a decrease in predictability of the future, thereby perhaps adding additional stress to the significantly high proportion of people with STJ preferences. This in turn has opened more opportunities for new businesses, as an increasing number of entrepreneurs are turning to stress management consultants and psychologists for help.

A second approach adopted by larger, mostly quasi-governmental organisations is that employees are allowed to operate their own private businesses whilst remaining employed with the organisation. These organisations usually have policies governing such practices that stipulate such private businesses do not either interfere or compete with the company. From a purely business perspective, this seems illogical. The thought behind allowing such private organisations is twofold. On the one hand, the country needs an increased number of businesses to help improve economic growth and employment opportunities. These organisations feel that they are making an investment in the future of the country. On the other hand, the thought process is that once the entrepreneurial business grows, the entrepreneur will resign from the organisation and create a position for a previously disadvantaged person. This in turn will assist with the government's objective of democratising the state and society.

However, in discussions with managers in established organisations, it becomes clear that the majority of respondents see the CEO as the only person carrying the entrepreneurial responsibility for organisations. This does not seem to be unique to South Africa and seems to compare well with international research.[28] Among the organisations surveyed, it is seldom that the transformational leadership function is perceived as extending to the top team of the company, let alone the employees.

The major reason for this perception that exists among managers and employees is cited as the large number of rules, regulations and policies that govern the workplace. It is interesting to note that, during the research, three people indicated that they had lost their jobs as a result of making suggestions on how the company could be improved. Two of these people are actually taking their companies to court for wrongful dismissal or, as it is called in South Africa, Unfair Labour Practices.

When considering the changes in the country, the need for continued formal employment, and the bureaucracy in organisations, it seems as if South African people have adopted a philosophy of keeping their heads down and doing only that which will not rock the boat. Employees do not want to be seen as questioning the status quo, for they believe they could then be seen as troublemakers. Executive teams initiate the majority of organisational changes, an example being the implementation of team based structures. Further, one of the latest change processes implemented by organisations is the formation of self-directed work teams. Within these teams, employees are given the freedom to act (within certain parameters) and achieve objectives they have set for themselves. In addition to the teams having to set their own objectives and clarify their own processes, the remuneration that the team obtains is linked to their own performance.

What has happened in a number of organisations is that successful teams have started becoming more intrapreneurial, to the benefit of those organisations. In some instances, it has even happened that a few of the more successful teams have begun considering the possibility of starting their own businesses and offering their services to their employers on a supplier basis.

From an entrepreneurial leadership perspective, implementing this process in organisations requires a leap into the unknown by the CEO. Based on the organisational history and culture, it requires that the CEO believes implicitly in the potential of her or his employees and, based on implementing this belief, is

▼▼▼▼▼▼▼▼▼▼▼▼▼▼▼▼▼▼▼▼▼▼

prepared to risk losing everything. What has started as a small group of companies has turned into a large group of organisations, all implementing team-based structures. It should be noted that a large percentage of organisations implementing these structures are actually stopping short of full employee empowerment and still maintaining strong, directing control at the executive level.

CONCLUSION

This chapter has attempted to indicate the extent of the most extreme change process South Africa has ever experienced, focusing on organisations and entrepreneurship. Politically, these changes are influencing all aspects of society. On the socio-cultural front, the country is busily attempting to develop a South African culture, without eliminating the rich cultural diversity that already exists. These changes are being attempted in an economy that is unable to ensure employment for all its citizens and is experiencing a decrease in the international demand for its mineral reserves. Based on these changes, the government is attempting, through KUHLA and NTSIKA, to develop a culture of small businesses specifically in manufacturing.

When adding the changes in employment patterns experienced throughout the world to this situation, it makes sense to say that the majority of citizens are either punch drunk from all the changes or, due to past processes, not experienced in fending for themselves on the economic front. From a change perspective, the majority of South Africans are currently in a state of uncertainty. They know and understand why things should change, but they have not yet identified how things should change. The low levels of literacy and accompanying low business knowledge further exacerbate this uncertainty. Fortunately, increasing numbers of organisations are embarking on skills enhancement processes for their employees, implemented both voluntarily and as a consequence of legislation.

This review of change in South Africa could create a picture of doom and despair within the reader. It has been agreed that large numbers of "previously advantaged" people are leaving the country, forming part of what is termed the "brain drain." There are even cynical car bumper stickers that ask the last person leaving the country to please switch off the lights. The people leaving are often professionally qualified, with a tertiary education and a relatively strong financial situation. Others in the country have developed a perception that the standards in the country are declining. Add to this the frequently published articles regarding high levels of crime and the reader could easily develop the perception that South Africa should be written off.

There is an Afrikaans saying, "n Boer maak `n plan," which means that South African people, by applying their minds, overcome obstacles and come up with new solutions to problems even when faced by almost impossible odds. In English, the saying is "necessity is the mother of invention." People in South Africa are slowly awakening to the realisation that the future of the country, and their own future, is their responsibility. Historically, the population has shown that they can overcome obstacles; the latest demonstration of their ability to rebound can be seen from the different examples set out in the case studies. These case studies highlight just a few examples of the hundreds of people and organisations that have started developing the entrepreneurial spirit in themselves and their employees.

A more visible change in entrepreneurship is the increasing number of morning markets. At these markets, which usually operate over weekends, it is not unusual to see up to 500 stalls where people sell things they have made: anything from hand-made shoes to musical instruments, food, toys and clothing. It is also no longer unusual to come across one of these entrepreneurs who has resigned from formal employment, now spending five days manufacturing goods to sell at the morning market during the weekend. It is also not uncommon to find that some of these stallholders earn more over weekends than they do from the position they held in a large company.

From a socio-political perspective, it is also encouraging to see people from different backgrounds looking after one another's stalls and joining in the understanding that people should create their own economic future. These markets and the home manufacturing industries, however, are not included in the South African GDP; often the people running their stalls are included in the unemployment figures.

One problem that still exists is that a large number of entrepreneurs do not seem to be focusing strongly enough on innovation of South African products and are becoming more involved in buying into so-called franchise opportunities. The problem with this is not the increasing number of franchised organisations but that

▼▼▼▼▼▼▼▼▼▼▼▼▼▼▼▼▼▼▼▼▼

often these businesses do not contribute to making South Africa competitive in the international economic market. A new magazine has recently been published in South Africa that focuses specifically on small businesses and franchise opportunities, and is created to help meet the increasing demand for employment and the immediate focus on franchise, which also seems to suit the needs of the large SJ preference found in the country.

These developments indicate some of the changes among the small entrepreneurs. No document, however, will be complete without recognising that several large businesses have taken the lead by entering the international arena. One such example would be the gold mining companies that have moved into Europe and also commenced operations in East Africa. A second example is a well-known chain of food stores that have started setting up outlets throughout Africa. There are also other companies that have diversified by setting up production plants in, amongst other places, Southeast Asia.

It can thus be seen that, although on the surface not much has been happening in the country, there is a strong driving force pushing people and businesses into developing their entrepreneurial abilities. Be it through adaptive or innovative creativity, South Africa is slowly turning its back on the past and returning to the entrepreneurial society often referred to in its history.

In South Africa, two waves of entrepreneurial change seem to be taking place at the same time. On the one front, previously disadvantaged people are moving into corporate employment. These corporations are also attempting to change the way they have been working towards one that is competitive on international markets, whilst also creating a feeling of belonging. The second wave is the increasing number of people previously employed in such organisations now moving into an entrepreneurial sphere. A large number of these people are buying franchises whilst an ever-increasing number are moving into the knowledge and service industries.

TYPE BASED RESEARCH

Given the short period of time that type has been used in South Africa, it is understandable that only a limited number of specifically South African information on type and the MBTI has been published. Various research projects and presentations have, however, been produced. Included below are some of the titles of English publications and research on type, and some publications and research that has been done in Afrikaans.[29]

MBTI RESEARCH REFERENCES

Alves, V. (1997). *Discriminating the performance of salespeople on the basis of behaviour, values and personality using the Style Analysis Instrument, the Personality Interests and Values Instrument and the Myers-Briggs Type Indicator.* Unpublished Masters Study. University of Witwatersrand, Faculty of Arts: Johannesburg.

Bayne, R. (1990, March). A new direction for the Myers-Briggs Type Indicator. *Personnel Management,* 48-51.

De Beer, J. (1998), South African Myers-Briggs Type Distribution: A Comparative Study. *Unpublished Doctorate Study: Faculty of Arts,* Rand Afrikaans University, Johannesburg.

Dugmore, P. (1988a), Myers-Briggs and strategic planning. *Paratus,* 39 (1), 54-55.

Dugmore, P. (1988b), Myers-Briggs and strategic planning. *Paratus,* 39 (2), 46-47.

Dugmore, P. (1989), Two Myers-Briggs problem solving patters. *Paratus,* 40 (1), 48-51.

Frazer, M. (1994). *A South African validation of the Myers-Briggs Type Indicator.* Unpublished Masters Degree, Rand Afrikaans University: Johannesburg.

Hinckley, M. (1996). *A marriage enrichment program based on the Myers-Briggs Type Indicator.* Unpublished Master of Arts Study. Rand Afrikaans University: Johannesburg.

Van Rooyen, J.H.P. (1997). *Organisational character and managerial team type.* Unpublished research report for the degree in Masters of Business Administration. University of the Witwatersrand: Johannesburg.

▼▼▼▼▼▼▼▼▼▼▼▼▼▼▼▼▼▼▼▼▼▼▼▼▼

Van Rooyen, J.H.P. *Technical manual to the organsiation character type assessment*. Unpublished Documentation. Jopie van Rooyen and Partners: Johannesburg.

Fourth International Type Users' Conference. Sandton, South Africa.

ENDNOTES

[1] *The Reconstruction and Development Program (RDP): A Policy Framework.* African National Congress. Johannesburg, South Africa. (1994).

[2] *Growth, Employment and Redistribution (GEAR): A Macro-Economic Strategy.* 1996

[3] *Labour Relations Bill,* Republic of South Africa; ISBN 0 621 16576 X

[4] *RDP* page 7

[5] *RDP* page 15

[6] *RDP* page 60

[7] *RDP* page 81

[8] *RDP* page 120

[9] *RDP* page 138

[10] *GEAR* strategy page 1

[11] *GEAR* strategy page 13

[12] Khula Enterprise Finance Ltd. 1997. Annual Report.

[13] Khula.1997. Annual Report, p. 13.

[14] NTSIKA Documentation

[15] *Labour Relations Bill,* p. 98.

[16] 1995 South African Statistics.

[17] *South African Reserve Bank Quarterly Bulletin.* September 1997.

[18] South African Reserve Bank *1997 Annual Economic Report,* p.12.

[19] Government reports on small business. Supplement to *Success SA,* Winter 1997

[20] *SA* 97-98, South Africa at a Glance

[21] Mbigi L. (1997); *Ubuntu; The African dream in management* (p. 3). Pretoria: Sigma Press.

[22] Christie, P., Lessem, R. & Mbigi, L. (1994). *African management: Philosophies, concepts and applications* (p. 35). Knowledge Resources.

[23] Mbigi, L., Maree, J. (1995) *Ubuntu: The spirit of African Transformation Management.* Pretoria: Sigma Press.

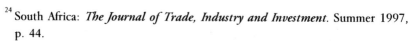

[24] South Africa: *The Journal of Trade, Industry and Investment.* Summer 1997, p. 44.

[25] De Beer. Unpublished Doctoral Thesis. Rand Afrikaans University. (1998).

[26] JHP van Rooyen, unpublished MBA Research Report, University of the Witwatersrand 1997.

[27] JHP van Rooyen; unpublished research

[28] *MBTI applications: A decade of research on the Myers-Briggs Type Indicator.*

[29] For a more comprehensive list of research, presentations and publications it is advised that readers visit the web site at www.vanrooyen.co.za

PUBLICATIONS ON AFRICAN LEADERSHIP

Adonisi, M. (1993). *African management — The career in community.* Pretoria: African Management, Sigma Press.

Christie, P., Lessem, R. & Mbigi, L. (Eds). (1994). *African management philosophies, concepts and applications.* Johannesburg: Knowledge Resources (Pty) Ltd.

Koopmans, A. (1993). *Trans-cultural Management: In search of pragmatic humanism.* Pretoria: African Management, Sigma Press.

Lessem, R. (1993). *Four worlds — The South African businesssphere.* Pretoria: African Management, Sigma Press.

Mbigi, L. & Maree, J. (1995). UBUNTU: *The spirit of African transformation management.* Randburg: Knowledge Resources (Pty) Ltd.

Mbigi, L. (1997). UBUNTU: *The African dream in management.* Randburg: Knowledge Resources (Pty) Ltd.

Steyn, M.E. & Motshabi K.B. (1996). *Cultural synergy in South Africa.* Randburg: Knowledge Resources (Pty) Ltd.

TURKEY

Bob Schemel
Middle East Technical University

EDITOR'S NOTES Dr. Robert Schemel profiles the most famous of all 20th Century Turkish leaders, Mustafa Kamal Atatürk, affectionately referred to as simply Atatürk.

Atatürk transformed Turkey into an advanced modern industrialized nation within an amazingly short time span. He epitomizes this book's focus on transformational leadership.

Dr. Schemel next provides a summary of Turkish history along with a demographic profile of the country. We then meet Çağlayan Arkan, a modern Turkish entrepreneur whose ingenuity and ambition turned a struggling business into a successful enterprise. We examine the facets and dynamics of leader/team relationships through a centrality/marginality model, and though Dr. Schemel has approached typology with Arkan, the MBTI is still in its early stages in Turkey. The author has summarized efforts to develop the Turkish MBTI in his concluding paragraphs.

▼▼▼▼▼▼▼▼▼▼▼▼▼▼▼▼▼▼▼▼▼▼▼

MUSTAFA KAMAL ATATÜRK

Modern Turkey, like all nations of the world, has been formed by a variety of forces. But an overwhelming majority of Turks agree that the greatest single force for change in the modern history of their nation was a man of modest origins but spectacular achievements — Mustafa Kamal Atatürk.

Atatürk was a genius of military strategy and tactics. He rallied the Turkish nation to preserve its identity and independence when European powers stood poised to destroy it. Once he achieved this, he set his then feudalistic society on the course of social, political and economic modernization. He attained great success, but not complete success. The conditions of modern Turkey reflect, in part, how Atatürk succeeded and how he fell short.

Atatürk's leadership was born in the brutality of war. His skill as a military leader first showed itself in World War I, when as a new commander in the Ottoman army, he rallied his forces to halt the British advance into Eastern Turkey. Then, at what the Turks call the Battle of Çnakalle, and what the West calls the Battle of Gallipolli, he stopped the British-led attempt to invade Turkey through the Dardanelles Straits.

But the ultimate defeat of the Ottoman Empire and its allies occurred when large sections of Turkey were subjected to foreign occupation.

With the army backing him, Atatürk combined guerrilla tactics, strategic retreats and major attacks until the foreign powers returned home. Turkey was reunited, with most Turks giving full credit to Atatürk.

Atatürk understood his power and used it to mold the nation as he thought best. At times he worked with specially convened congresses, at times with regular sessions of parliament and at times he simply issued decrees. Turkey declared independence from Ottoman rule, then the monarchy was eliminated and Turkey was declared a republic. Turkey abolished the Caliphate — the spiritual office that headed most of Islam — which had been invested in the person of the sultan. (The equivalent in the West would be the abolition of the papacy.) This was followed by measures that officially transformed Turkey from a center of Islamic orthodoxy to a secular state. For example, Atatürk established laws to Westernize men and women's dress.

One of the most impressive changes imposed by Atatürk was the conversion from the Arabic to the Latin alphabet. Atatürk called in his advisors who determined that it would take a full decade to make such an all-encompassing change. Atatürk responded by giving them six months. On street corners, on buses and trains, in offices and factories, the Latin alphabet was taught. In six months Turkey was on the Latin alphabet.

This measure, combined with the creation of thousands of schools and a massive adult literacy campaign, increased the literacy rate from less than 10 percent to over 30 percent within a few short years. A civil legal system suffrage was adapted, molded on those used by a number of European nations, and universal adult suffrage was established. Women were accorded civil rights and measures were adapted that went a long way in recognizing women as the legal equals of men.

Atatürk's achievements in the development of the Turkish economy were no less impressive. The government supported industrialization and agricultural development. Atatürk promoted state investment in industrial projects only as long as private investment was not attractive. Once private investors showed interest, Atatürk believed the state should sell its interest in an industry or a project. By this policy, he achieved an economic growth of about 6 percent with no government defect or deflation — an actual increase in the value of the national currency.

But Atatürk's measures met opposition — particularly his moves to Westernize and secularize Turkish society. Opposition was most ardent from a number of Islamic sects. While exact calculations are difficult, certainly their members numbered in the hundreds of thousands and possibly in the millions. Sheiks or holy men usually headed these groups. Each had developed different spiritual, often highly mystical, traditions. They maintained their different religious codes and sacred writings, their different religious centers, holy places, prophets and places of pilgrimage. They were united in their allegiance to the Koran and to the Prophet Mohammed, and in their desire to see Turkey governed by their understanding of the Koran's law.

These sects and their leaders saw secularization as an evil they were obliged to combat. Atatürk had many sect leaders arrested as rebels. Any sect or sect leader that offered further resistance faced military action and charges of treason. Atatürk allied with Islamic clergy willing to support his secularization drive. Prayers in mosques and the Koran itself were no longer to be in Arabic, but in Turkish.

Despite resistance among significant segments of the society, Atatürk's secularization efforts continued at a rapid pace. In addition, his industrialization efforts brought basic, necessary industries to the country. At the time of his death in 1938, Turkey was well on its way to assuming its place among the modern, secular, industrialized and economically robust nations of the world.

ATATÜRK'S LEADERSHIP PROFILE

However, in the generations that have followed, Turkey still has not fully achieved this goal. Why? There are, of course, a number of reasons, but as I have focused so far on Mustafa Kamel Atatürk and the transformations he brought Turkish society, it is perhaps fitting to examine Atatürk's leadership in searching for reasons that Turkey is less developed than much of the West. Atatürk's leadership style had its limitations. And, in part, it is those limitations that may have destined his nation to fall short, so far, of what Atatürk himself so passionately wanted — a modern, secular, industrialized and economically strong Turkey.

Perhaps the two most striking things about Atatürk's leadership style are his determination and his authoritarianism. Atatürk pressed his vision tirelessly. He was determined that his vision for the secularization and modernization of Turkey be made reality. This was not a matter open to debate. He resisted those who challenged this, insisting that Turkey change in the way he saw fit. He retained final control of the Turkish government throughout his lifetime.

Today, those who defend his actions in this regard remark that Atatürk's vision, in the context of his times, required an authoritarian style. How else could a feudalistic society — one whose prevailing ideology and structure had basically been unchanged in the last 1000 years — be moved into the modern age? How could a fully participative style achieve modernization and secularization when there were so many pockets of opposition? This question makes the fundamental point that, indeed, no other style of leadership could have brought such basic reforms to the Turkish society of the 1920s and 1930s. But what is the legacy when the central figure in the modern history of a nation is an authoritarian leader? Authoritarianism gains credibility.

And how do more modern views of leadership, emphasizing participation, establish themselves in such an environment? They must produce convincing results. They must produce the kind of results that Atatürk and those who joined his struggle sought to achieve for Turkey — a modern, industrialized, democratic society, an economic power that bows to the will of no rich nation and achieves a high living standard for the bulk of its people.

TURKEY

THE PROMISE OF BUSINESS GROWTH

Turkey is a large, multi-facted society that is assimilating into the global village. While I have no intention of exploring the topic of leadership from a purely economic perspective, I shall address leadership with a focus on economic participation in the global economy.

Turkey is blessed with a central location, sitting at a crossroads between Europe, the Middle East, the Ukraine and Russia, the Caucuses, Central Asia and South Asia. Turkey is taking advantage of the opening of markets, which followed the collapse of Stalinism in Eastern Europe and the former Soviet nations. Trade with these nations has increased in the tens of billions of dollars. Textiles has been a major beneficiary. In the dollar value of business, Turkish construction firms are second only to Russian construction firms within the nations of the former Soviet Union. However, the Russian economic crisis has hit Turkish exports and Turkish businesses in the former Soviet Republics and Eastern Europe. The rapid growth in Turkish business in this region suffered a setback, though it does seem to be recovering.

Privatization of government-owned industry proceeds slowly. By some estimates, over half the workforce is employed directly or indirectly by the government. However, privatization has not been rapid due to ongoing political and legal obstacles. While the Asian crisis hit Turkey hard, economic growth has returned; though it is difficult to measure in exact terms, some rank Turkey as one of the ten most rapidly growing economies. Economic growth is hard to measure because there are no records for approximately 30 to 50 percent of all economic activity (according to many estimates). Why? Most explanations point to the wide

▼▼▼▼▼▼▼▼▼▼▼▼▼▼▼▼▼▼▼▼▼▼▼

perception of corruption among politicians and leading businesses, leading to an "everyone does it, so I'm a fool if I don't" mentality.

POLITICAL PROBLEMS

The promise of Turkey's business future faces three potential political dangers. The first two concern national politics, and the third concerns international politics.

The first problem is national political instability. In the late 1970s Turkey was enduring massive civil strife that was, in fact, a low-level civil war. In 1980, the military took control of the government in a coup and established its own sense of order. Military rule continued for several years. After civilian government was reestablished, a large array of political parties emerged. A number of political parties share fundamentally similar ideologies, yet retain their distinct organisations.

The power of personality to unite or divide political parties is often as compelling a force as it is an ideology. The large number of political parties has resulted in a lack of support from the voting majority for any one party. The power of personality often results in short-lived coalition governments, which are based on the ability of party leaders to get along with one another and strike deals to provide jobs for supporters. The similarities of ideology often appear to be of lesser importance. This has produced ideologically diverse coalitions, with very different parties often working as coalition partners, while two or more parties that are ideologically similar will often find themselves on different sides of the in-government/out-of-government divide.

Another factor is that the military remains a major force in Turkish politics and is given a constitutional role in government. The Turkish constitution gives the heads of the various branches of the military seats on the National Security Council, together with leading civilian government officials. This body is officially empowered to oversee matters relating to the security of the Republic. The National Security Council reviews implementation of laws and policies and submits recommendations to the Council of Ministers. Whether its recommendations are, at least at times, directives to government agencies and offices is a matter of interpretation. The military also enjoys wide popular support.

Many Turks view government as widely corrupt and place more trust in the integrity of the military. The military thus wields unofficial as well as official influence in political affairs. The military exercised its official and unofficial political power after the 1995 elections.

The military takes a strong stand against Islamic Fundamentalism and for a secular government as espoused by Atatürk. The major Fundamentalist political expression had been the Refah Party (which can be roughly translated as the Welfare Party). In the 1995 election Refah received about 21 percent of the vote. The secular vote, on the other hand — over 70 percent of the total — was fragmented and divided among several parties. Thus Refah's showing placed it narrowly ahead of all other major political parties. The leaders of the secular parties were not able to unite in opposition to Refah. It took several months for a coalition government to be formed — the longest time to form a coalition government after an election for any parliamentary system anywhere since World War II.

In early 1996, Refah emerged to head a new coalition government. For the first time since Atatürk's transformation of Turkey, a group whose members openly opposed secular government and called for the imposition of Koranic law, headed the government. Within a few months, Refah policies were under attack by secular forces — with the military leading the charge. A number of military officers were openly critical of government policies and government officials.

In February of 1997, led by its military members, the National Security Council asserted the separation of government and religion. This was, in fact, an ultimatum that government policy and action comply with the principle of secularization. Tension between the military and Refah continued, and the military was able to pressure the Refah Prime Minister to leave office. A new, short-lived coalition took control of government, soon followed by another coalition formed with the implicit understanding that new elections would be held within several months. Since then, Turkey's highest court, the Constitutional Court, ordered the Refah Party abolished on the grounds that it was a threat to democracy and secular government. The party has reemerged under the name *Fazilet*, or the *Virtue Party*.

New elections were held in April of 1999. There was a major shift in voting patterns. Two nationalist parties emerged as the biggest vote-getters. One was the Democratic Left Party, a leftist nationalist party, while the other was the *National Action Party*, a rightest nationalist party. These two parties were able to put aside differences and stop bickering over charges that the rightest nationalists worked with a death squad before the 1980 coup. They formed a coalition to head a new government, and the Fundamentalist party fell to third place among voters.

Why the shift? It is likely that the electorate was influenced in part by the military's earlier stand against Fundamentalism. But another major factor was one of the most important legal and political developments in Turkey this decade — the capture of the leader of the *Kurdish Workers Party* (PKK), Abdullah Öcalan.

For some time Öcalan had been openly living in Syria. The Turkish government held him responsible for the large scale terrorist campaign waged by the PKK throughout Turkey, but primarily conducted in the predominantly Kurdish Southeast. In late 1998 Turkey began to threaten war with Syria if the country continued to offer Öcalan refuge. Syria finally expelled Öcalan, who resurfaced in Rome.

What happened next shocked Turkey. Italy appeared poised to offer Öcalan refuge on the grounds that the Italian constitution forbade extradition of criminals to any country with a death penalty. Many European governments offered Italy statements of explicit or implicit support. Turkey's general popular mood was one of indignation and anger. The Italian government's position was viewed as a disregard of the tens of thousands of casualities produced by the PKK's violence and disregard of Turkey's national integrity. Of all the Western powers, only the United States took a strong position, calling for Öcalan's return to Turkey for trial. In this climate, Turkish nationalist sentiment grew, and the two leading nationalist parties benefited in the April 1999 elections.*

The Öcalan saga has a deeper impact than the electorate's increased support for the nationalists. It brings to focus another problem facing Turkish business. This is the charge against Turkey's human rights record. Most charges about violations of human rights concern action by security forces against the PKK, but there are charges about government activity against other groups as well, some of which claim to be non-violent.

---

*After several weeks the Italian government expelled Öcalan, who then went undercover. Öcalan was discovered in Kenya by American intelligence, which informed Turkey of his whereabouts. Turkish security forces captured Öcalan and returned him to Turkey. Öcalan was tried and sentenced to death. But parliament's approval is needed for death sentences. And the government has agreed to delay requesting parliament's approval of Öcalan's execution until the European Court of Human Rights hears the case. At the time of this writing it remains to be seen whether Öcalan will be the first person executed in Turkey since 1984.

The Turkish government complicates the human rights problem with vague laws. For example, the law prohibits any expression that could endanger the "national unity." Several journalists, academics and authors have been incarcerated for violating it; there have also been libel cases for "insulting the army" by criticizing its actions. The good news is that the record may be improving due to public pressure, but the feeling of intimidation is still widespread among many intellectuals and social critics.

However, Öcalan's capture will ultimately require that Turkey either execute Öcalan or commute his death sentence and imprison him for life. If the death sentence is commuted, there may be a renewed PKK terrorist campaign to free him. If Öcalan is executed, there may be a terrorist campaign to avenge his death. Already, less than a dozen terrorist attacks since Öcalan's capture have created an extreme crisis in the tourist industry. A few well-publicized terrorist attacks have virtually dried up an $8 billion a year industry. A renewed terrorist campaign could lead to further crackdowns and charges of human rights violations. A sharp downturn in the tourist industry could lead to a slowing of economic growth, and possibly result in a number of social problems.

These issues involving internal matters are critical factors in Turkish business, not only because terrorism hurts industries such as tourism, but also because Turkey wants membership in the European Union. Turkey has attained a Customs Union with the EU and has recently been promised eventual full membership. The government wants full membership, but there are barriers because of Europeans' views of Turkish political affairs. European Union concerns continue to focus on the role of Islamic Fundamentalist parties, the role of the military in politics, Turkey's human rights record and the need for unpopular economic reforms that will be very difficult in an environment where the rule is political instability. Many Turks often say that these issues are only disguises for European racism. Yet Turkey's future membership in the European Union remains in doubt as long as Europeans offer objections for which Turkey has no convincing answer.

Another problem is on the international scene, specifically Turkey's relations with its neighbors, Greece and the Greek portion of Cyprus. Turkey and Greece have had difficult relations for centuries. Today's disputes concern conflicting territorial claims, differences over the right of passage through shipping lanes in the Aegean Sea and the status of Cyprus.

▼▼▼▼▼▼▼▼▼▼▼▼▼▼▼▼▼▼▼▼▼▼

A bright spot in Turkish-Greek relations was provided in 1999 during the aftermath of the tragic earthquakes in both countries. Turkish and Greek rescue teams worked side by side at the site of collapsed buildings in Turkey and in Greece. People of both nationalities were moved by this show of common humanity. While a Turkish rescue team was risking its life in the rubble of a collapsed building to save a young Greek boy, one Greek TV journalist remarked, "What can you call this? This is love." Politicians from both nations have found this groundswell of feeling impossible to ignore, and are making cautious steps toward greater reconciliation. The fruits of these political developments have not yet withstood the test of time.

INABILITY TO LOWER HIGH INFLATION

Another potential problem for Turkish progress is the persistently highest inflation rates in the world. Real inflation, higher than the official figures (as is the case for most countries), has been as high as 100 percent a year in recent years. Inflation and its consequent high interest rates are a drag on business. Loans are expensive. High interest rates also draw capital into high yielding financial investments and away from capital investments in basic industry. Thus, modernization of production facilities is often difficult. All attempts to lower inflation have failed so far.

A RESILIENT ECONOMY, A RESILIENT PEOPLE AND THE HOPE OF THE NEXT GENERATION

Despite political problems and high inflation, Turkey's leadership in the world of commerce is impressive. None of Turkey's problems have been big enough to stop it from achieving one of the most rapidly growing economies in the world. And a younger generation is now coming to power in a better-educated and more democratic nation and world. As one high ranking government official remarked to me a while ago, "You must remember that parliamentary government is only seventy-five years old in this country. I knew more about how to make democracy work than my father did. My son will do a better job at making democracy work than me."

Most members of the new generation are fully aware of Turkey's problems. They also have great energy and are aware of Turkey's promise. They insist that when they have their turn at the reins of power, they will build on their nation's ancient heritage and its modern achievements. Business is one of the forums where the new generation is demonstrating its ability to build the dream of a modern and prosperous Turkey, that understands the power of openness, education, equity and a refined participative process. With this understanding, Turkey will be able to unite and empower its citizens to achieve their potential. One member of the new generation is Çağlayan Arkan.

ENTREPRENEURIAL LEADERSHIP IN TURKEY

Çağlayan (Cha-la-yan) Arkan is an outstanding example of a Turkish entrepreneurial leader. I have talked to a number of people who have worked with him and know him. They all agree that Çağlayan is a superb example of an effective leader. Much of this chapter will focus on the work of Çağlayan when he was with a previous company — Nashuatec (later named Kopiteknik).

As of January 1, 2000, Çağlayan is President and General Manager of Siemens Business Services (SBS) Turkey, a global e-business solutions and services provider. Çağlayan's goal is to make SBS Turkey the industry leader in Turkey by 2004. SBS Turkey has 490 employees with roughly 70 million US dollars in annual business. SBS Turkey, a two-year-old organisation, was created after the worldwide merger of Siemens Nixdorf and SBS. SBS Turkey came to host Siemens Nixdorf Turkey, a fifteen-year-old organisation. These two companies were merged in Turkey into one company, effective October 1, 1999. Çağlayan sees his challenges as:

- Transitioning these two companies into one organisation;
- Transforming this organisation into "*THE* services and solutions provider" from a product-oriented, internally focused culture;
- Making SBS Turkey "the employer of choice for employees and the business partner of choice for customers";
- Transforming this organisation from a company where the best people are leaving to a company where the best people in Turkey want to work and grow in their careers;

▼▼▼▼▼▼▼▼▼▼▼▼▼▼▼▼▼▼▼▼▼▼

- Transforming this organisation from a company whose customers are unhappy to a company that excels in delighting its clients;
- Winning new business that strategically positions SBS in the Internet/Telecommunications and Utilities markets as the service provide/outsourcing company;
- Creating a consultancy culture and processes that will move SBS to fulfill its vision;
- Delivering short-term financial results while achieving all these goals.

We will examine Çağlayan's entrepreneurial achievements before he took his present position. This story illustrates how the development and application of good theory can help entrepreneurs in designing and refining their organisations.

Most of the less industrialized world is not as rich as the industrial world. Our lack of resources shows in many ways, including a lesser ability to support larger university faculties and vast library collections. So, we usually import research and theory — primarily from the United States, Europe or Japan. This can present two problems. One is that while there do indeed seem to be universal truths about people, management, entrepreneurship and organisations, there are also differences between regions, nations and cultures of the world. Some research and theory developed in one culture may need modification, or may not apply at all to another culture. Only work within the culture itself can tell us whether this is true. Secondly, we in the less industrialized world have our own contributions to make to world thinking. Our different conditions can help us to develop different ideas and to investigate different issues. If our situation is different, so, too, is our potential contribution.

ÇAĞLAYAN ARKAN

Çağlayan began his professional life when he was twenty-two years old after graduating in 1983 with a degree in industrial engineering from one of the leading universities in Turkey. For about one year, Çağlayan worked as a salesman with Teko Fax, which was at that time the distributor for Panasonic fax machines in Turkey. After his first year as a salesman, Çağlayanwas promoted to Sales Manager in the Ankara region, a position he would hold for two-and-a-half years. Çağlayan remembers:

We would always double all of our sales quotas — our thirty day quotas, our sixty day quotas, our ninety day quotas. At first, we could not deliver the machines we sold. We simply would keep running out of inventory. There were, when I started as Sales Manager, 184 fax machines in all of Turkey. When I left my position as Sales Manager, there were 7,000 fax machines in Turkey. We — our team — sold thousands of them. We sold between 4,000 and 5,000 machines in Ankara between 1985 and 1987. Many of our leading competitors sold only a few hundred machines a year.

With such a record of success, you might think that Çağlayan would have a guaranteed future in Teko Fax, and that his rise to the top of the organisation would be assured. But it was not to be. Çağlayan recalls:

There were a number of problems with the organisation. Sales people would not get their commissions on time. I was able to solve some of them, but many problems continued and I simply could not solve them all or bring about significant organisational changes. So I felt I had to leave since I couldn't create a better environment.

Çağlayan made a sales visit to the General Manager of one of the largest photocopy machine distributors in Turkey — Nashuatec. (The business usually refers to itself as "office automation.") Nashuatec was headed by a General Manager in the Central Office and composed of regional offices in three of Turkey's largest business centers: the cities of Istanbul, Izmir and Ankara. Çağlayan was offered a position with the company — General Manager for the Ankara region — and he accepted. At that time, there were about 400 Nashuatec photocopy machines in the Ankara region, and most of the revenue was generated from servicing and selling machines.

Ankara operations were in trouble. Customers were dissatisfied with service and delivery time, and many were questioning product quality due to poor service. The day after he assumed his new position, most of Çağlayan's technical service staff suddenly left Nashuatec and formed their own company. They offered customers maintenance and repair service, and generic maintenance and replacement parts at significantly reduced prices. Çağlayan quickly countered by

▼▼▼▼▼▼▼▼▼▼▼▼▼▼▼▼▼▼▼▼▼▼

contacting customers. He listened to their concerns and spelled out to them the steps he would take to address past problems. His quick action enabled him to keep most customers. Nevertheless, Çağlayan estimates that the service company these technicians formed was able to take away about 20 percent of Nashuatec's total service business in the Ankara region.

REFINING ORGANISATIONAL SYSTEMS

Çağlayan set about to change Nashuatec Ankara's culture:

> I wanted to become a company that was customer and employee focused. These were two stakeholder groups I took very seriously. As a result, people in the market began to believe that we do things differently than the rest. When I came to Nashuatec we were viewed as doing things in the same way as our competitors. [In time we became viewed] as doing things differently. One of the reasons we were different was that we performed regular customer surveys. What our customers would tell us would impact our performance management system. We would devise our company, departmental and employee performance objectives to reflect our customers' concerns. What our customers told us they wanted would become company objectives, departmental objectives and individual objectives.

MY EARLY WORK WITH ÇAĞLAYAN

I met Çağlayan about seven years ago, within a few months of coming to Turkey. Çağlayan wanted to help his organisation to improve. As is true for many managers who want "organisational improvement," Çağlayan was not fully certain what this might look like.

Our work would involve the participation of the whole organisation. I suggested that what Çağlayan do first is bring his top managers together and devise a draft mission statement for the Kopiteknik Ankara (the organisation's name had changed from Nashuatec). I suggested that as a follow-up, the managers and employees of individual departments meet to review the draft mission statement, suggest any possible revisions and draft their own departmental mission statements.

These departmental mission statements would be written to be consistent with the organisation's mission statement, but would also reflect the unique work, functions and purposes of the individual departments.

We first conducted a number of group dynamics exercises. As a part of this we reviewed Jung's theory of personality and its implications for group work — particularly focusing on the various contributions that different types of people tend to want to make when working in groups. After this discussion on how individuals and groups operate, the group set about writing a mission statement for the Ankara region. I suggested we do so using a stakeholder approach, which involved identifying those groups affected by the work of the Ankara Region, then deciding how it adds value to the lives of these groups. Groups that Çağlayan and his top managers identified included customers, employees, owners (shareholders), suppliers, other competitors, the community of the region, the nation and the global human community. The mission statement was drafted and, with few alterations, was accepted by the company employees.

After devising the mission statement, the managers in the Ankara office devised a set of operating principles. These were derived from the mission statement, but provided a more concrete description of the actions the company would standardize in order to meet the goals put forth in the mission statement. As with the mission statement itself, a participative process finalized the operating principles — managers discussed them with the people in their groups, who suggested some changes.

Once the mission statement and the operating principles were in place, Çağlayan and his managers defined job dimensions consistent with the mission and operating principles. A list of job dimensions would apply to most jobs in the organisation, but a few would apply to some positions and not to others. Employees in the different departments gave input and every job dimension was defined in concrete terms. This set specific standards for each employee.

There were four sets of criteria used to evaluate employee performance: 1) the *mission statement*; 2) the *operating principles*; 3) the *job dimensions*; and 4) *additional assignments* or *additional goals* for individual employees as needed. These criteria were one of the bases for a new merit pay system. The merit increases of

▼▼▼▼▼▼▼▼▼▼▼▼▼▼▼▼▼▼▼▼▼▼

each employee could then depend, in part, on how well they met their goals. Managers were not the only source of feedback on performance. For example, every time a technician made a visit, there were guidelines to be followed. These guidelines were given to a customer at the end of the visit in the form of a survey in which the technician could be evaluated on each of the items. The survey form could be immediately completed, placed in an envelope and sealed, and either mailed (the envelope was stamped), given to the technician for presentation to her or his manager or faxed directly to Çağlayan if there appeared to be any problem, Çağlayan himself would contact the customer and discuss it. The feedback from these surveys was used as information about an employee's performance.

Other factors in the size of merit pay increases (besides an employee's performance) were company performance and inflation. Çağlayan wanted individual, team and company-wide effort. Kopiteknik, like most other organisations, next faced the challenge of developing incentive systems that encouraged high performance on all three of these levels. In achieving this, one must always take culture into account. Culture influences all levels of organisational performance – individual, group and between group. Like any culture, Turkish culture presents some unique challenges when aiming for improved performance at these three levels.

THEORIZING AND APPLYING TO SYSTEMS

CULTURE AND COLLECTIVISM

Every culture has idiosyncrasies – things about it that you don't see in other cultures, qualities that set it apart from all others. Sometimes these distinguishing qualities may be a bit hard to see.

Before I came to Turkey I worked in the management training department of a major pharmaceutical company. In this capacity, I had the opportunity to work with some of the leading management consultants in the United States. One was David Cambell from the Center for Creative Leadership. Several times I saw David use an exercise he called "Towers." The exercise would work this way. People were divided into teams of five to six. Everyone in the workshop would give a certain amount of money – usually a few dollars – to a "kitty." The company would match this total sum, and this amount became the prize. Each group would be given some raw materials — straws and tape — and told they had about forty-five minutes to build a tower.

The team that built the best tower would win the prize. The best tower would be determined by voting — each team casting one vote. The team whose tower received the most votes would be declared the winner. What would immediately happen was that a number of the members of each team would begin to design and construct their team's tower. But then within five to ten minutes, a few of the members of a few of the teams would realize that it was not the quality of the tower that determined the winner — it was the number of votes a team could get. A number of teams' members would then begin negotiating with other teams for votes, attempting to put together a majority coalition. These coalitions would agree to equally share the prize among all members. A minority of teams would refuse to join in a coalition. The majority coalitions would, predictably, win the prize and divide the money.

People's attitudes would be shaped by whether or not their team was in the coalition, and those whose teams did not join a coalition defended their actions and criticized others on grounds of integrity. Their criticism usually ran something like this: "They [teams that joined the coalition] weren't playing fair — they sold their votes. We voted for the tower [usually their team's own tower] that we sincerely thought was the best." Coalition members would defend their integrity by answering that they played by the rules. They would argue that their intentions were worthy. They wanted the majority to share the prize. They would usually point out (if it were actually so, as was usually the case) that they were open to letting any, in fact all, teams join the coalition. They argued that they didn't try to exclude anyone from sharing in the prize. They would accuse those teams who refused to join the majority coalition of being selfish — of refusing to want to share the prize equally with everyone. The debriefing of this exercise would raise issues of ethics, integrity, team cooperation and organisational coalitions.

David Cambell would relate that he and his colleagues at the Center for Creative Leadership had run this exercise (about eight years ago at that time) on about 400 occasions in several different countries. With only one exception, the pattern was always the same. Soon after the start of the exercise, most teams would begin negotiations and form coalitions, and these majority coalitions would win the

▼▼▼▼▼▼▼▼▼▼▼▼▼▼▼▼▼▼▼▼▼▼

prize. The only exception involved high school students in the Netherlands. In this one case, the students looked at the towers built by the different teams, then came to agreement on which tower was indeed "the best." That team was awarded the prize. But of course, even in this case there was a winning team.

I first ran this exercise in Turkey with undergraduate students at my university. Students each contributed about one dollar to the kitty and I dug into my pockets and matched the total. I was surprised at the results. No coalitions were formed. No team looked at other teams' towers to evaluate them in any way. There was no winning team. Each team voted for itself. I wasn't sure how to evaluate this result, except to express my surprise that to my knowledge this was the first time in over several hundred runnings of this exercise that no team had won.

My students didn't quite believe me. They were convinced that I "knew" that each team would vote for itself, and so my contribution to the kitty was certain to be returned. I could only insist that this was contrary to my experience — there had always been a winner when this exercise had been run. These results were the same about 80 percent of the time I ran this exercise with my students. There would be no winner. When there was a winner it was never because there was a majority coalition. I had to accept pluralities, since no team ever received more than two votes — its own vote and the vote of one other team with which it had agreed to split the prize.

Some of my students suggested that the size of the kitty might make a difference — that if the prize were larger, more teams would have made coalitions. But when I conducted this exercise in business organisations, the organisation's contribution and the contributions of the participants would often result in kitties of several hundred dollars. Yet the results would be similar. There would be a winner only about 20 percent of the time, and winners never would receive more than a total of two votes.

How could this stark difference between the behavior of Turkish teams and the teams of other cultures be explained? I talked to a number of Turkish managers and academicians, and asked them how they explained this difference. The academicians included an anthropologist, several psychologists and several organisational scholars. The managers worked in a variety of industries. Everyone had a similar explanation. The explanation had to do with a particular form of collectivism that has evolved in Turkey.

Sometimes we are inclined to define terms such as collectivism and individualism in general ways — as if each of these two phenomena possessed only a monolithic form. A common description of collectivism is a concern for group needs over individual needs. It is common to define individualism as a concern for the individual over group needs. But we make a mistake if we forget that each of these concepts contains many dimensions: intellectual, emotional, behavioral, normative, etc. (Smith & Bond 1994). We also need to remember that, in what may seem to be similar situations within different collectivist and individualistic societies, the sets of rules for governing individual and group behavior may be quite different.

An example may be that when comparing two different collectivist societies or individualistic societies we observe that the norms for group inclusion and exclusion often change (see Schneider & Barsacs 1997. Schein 1994).

THE PRIMARY REFERENCE GROUP

The form of collectivism that has evolved in Turkey, as my academic colleagues explained, places an extreme emphasis on the small group. In such a case, we might call the small group the *primary reference group*. Our primary reference group is a group we feel a part of, or identify with in a given situation. This sense of identity and belonging defines our place in a larger social order. If loyalty to this primary reference group is extremely high and our primary reference group is a small group, it can mean that our small group might have difficulties in coming to agreements with other groups. This might be especially true when such agreements require us to place our group's product as second to another group's product in some way.

This may explain why Turkish teams find it more difficult to reach agreements with one another even when it may be in a group's material interest to do so, as in the case of the "Towers" exercise. In the hundreds of runnings of the exercise outside of Turkey, the teams that "won" did so precisely because most teams agreed to vote *for another team's tower*. In these runnings, a minority of teams often do refuse to join the majority and (usually) vote for themselves. This can occur, I suggest, because winning in these societies is defined in a different way than it is in Turkey.

How can we explain these events, except to say that in these cases, loyalty to the small group means something very different in some countries than it does in

Turkey? In other countries where the exercise has been conducted, the primary reference group for winning teams may, at the start of the exercise, be the small team, but as the exercise proceeds and agreements are made between teams, the primary reference group becomes the winning coalition. Loyalty can easily be shifted from the smaller team to the majority coalition.

Turkish managers I talked to about the "Towers" exercise would generally remark, "We have this problems all the time — small departments or work groups are unable to think beyond their own interests and come to working agreements with other groups." This makes the working of a modern organisation extremely difficult. Modern organisations are collections of smaller groups — each with its own function, schedule, specialization and interests. Different groups, at least from time to time, must come to working agreements and understand that not every group can attain everything it wants.

Sometimes we need to support the product of another group as more desirable than ours. Sometimes we need to put another group's scheduling requirements ahead of ours. In return, our group may tacitly or explicitly request some sort of recognition or eventual payback of the favor, or to share in possible rewards in some way. These kinds of understandings between groups allow for smoother workflow throughout the organisation. However, if it is difficult for someone in Group A, for example, to place another group's interests as primary even when it may be in Group A's interest to do so, such arrangements become more difficult or even impossible. Then other means, usually involving power and authority, must resolve disagreements between groups. We may see tactics such as:

- The more powerful group may simply insist that its interests be primary.
- Groups may appeal to higher authority to resolve disagreements.
- The group that "loses" may be slow to cooperate in implementing a decision.

These conditions might occur in any system where cooperation is difficult and disputes between groups are resolved on the basis of authority and power. Many managers tell me they see such problems time and again in Turkish organisations.

I told Çağlayan about my unexpected results when running the "Towers" exercise with students at the university as well as in organisations in Turkey. I discussed with him the explanations offered by my academic colleagues. He reacted much like other Turkish managers. "This is typical of Turkish organisations. We have a real problem getting different groups to cooperate." Indeed, I ran the exercise during a training program with Kopiteknik. Results were predictable: every group voted for itself. Çağlayan continued directing his attention to helping different departments and groups to better cooperate with one another.

LEVELS OF WORK PROCESS:
A HIERARCHY OF COMPLEXITY

As we have seen, Çağlayan promoted individual efforts and team efforts by beginning with company and department mission statements and then deriving job dimensions from them. But organisations need to do more than devise meaningful mission statements and set clear individual and group objectives. Organisations need to recognize that there is an additional layer of performance beyond individual and team efforts. There is a third layer of performance: inter-team performance. Methods need to be devised to measure and reward all three different types of performance:

1) *Individual performance*: when what the organisation needs can be best achieved by drawing primarily on the knowledge, competence and authority of an individual in the organization;
2) *Team performance*: when what the organisation needs can be best achieved by drawing primarily on cooperative effort with members of one's own team;
3) *Inter-team performance*: when what the organisation needs can be best achieved by drawing primarily on cooperative efforts between all or some of the members of two or more teams.

At each of these three levels, process issues are involved. Specific job dimensions and objectives are difficult to put in place in cases where processes can change from task to task. This is especially true when they can change in unpredictable ways. For example, the individual level may involve procedures for doing an actual task. It may also involve individual behaviors that foster the interpersonal communication and information flow necessary before, during and after the task is undertaken and conducted. At times these individual processes may need to change in unforeseen ways. This is why managers need to be flexible in their

application and interpretation of individual objectives, and why, during a performance period, individual objectives may need to change from time to time.

The problem of the changing nature of processes is more complex at the team
and inter-team levels. Many individual processes are also involved at the team level,
any of which may from time to time change in some unpredictable ways. In
addition, team performance is further complicated by the fact that there are many
interpersonal processes within teams — and sometimes, complex relationships
between team members — which also can change in unpredictable ways. The highest degree of complexity — because of the potential of changing processes — is the
inter-team level. Here, we have all the potential complexity that exists at the level
of individual and team performance, as well as the unpredictable changes that can
occur in relationships and the work processes between teams.

Thus, the problem of complexity, stemming from unpredictable changes
in processes at these three levels, is hierarchical in the sense that each higher
level includes the complexities of the immediately lower level and adds additional
dimensions of complexity.

The nature of the most complex level of work processes and inter-group
relations obliges us to rethink the meaning of the term *teamwork*. There are many
different kinds of teams and thus many different kinds of teamwork used in today's
organisations. Within the same organisation, a variety of team structures can be
employed — teams can be arranged by function or product, by level in the hierarchy, by geographic regions or according to size or type of customer. Teams can
be formed fully within the formal or informal structure. Teams may exist in a
matrix structure, with each member reporting to a number of different managers.
Teams can exist as parallel to the formal structure, as is often the case with special ad hoc or portfolio groups. Many employees are simultaneously members of
several different teams — particularly in organisations that use project groups, or
what Mintzberg (1979) calls ad hocracies. When we are members of several teams,
our individual membership in a particular team becomes more important or less
important as the situation changes and as the issues salient to a particular team
move more to the foreground or more to the background of a situation. With each
such change, different inter-team dynamics move more into play or less into play.
One obvious aspect of the complexity of inter-team dynamics is this fluidity.

CENTRALITY IN TEAM AND INTER-TEAM DYNAMICS

An additional complexity is that of *centrality*, which has implications for individual team members, team dynamics and inter-team dynamics. Often when teams operate, it is difficult to determine a strict boundary for the team. It is, however, common to disregard this fact. We ignore centrality when we think of teams as though they have exact boundaries, and when we think of teams as groups where each member is equally important and equally powerful in determining the course of events for the team. Organisations often make this mistake. Perhaps it is appealing to think that we can draw tight boundaries for a team. It may seem to make things simpler, more definite and easier to control. It is also appealing to assume that everyone on a team is equal to everyone else. In an age where democratic and participative management has wide appeal, there is a temptation to think that teams present an easy way to promote participation.

This may in fact be the case in a large number of situations. In many team situations, however, there are *central team members* and *peripheral* or *marginal team members*. Central team members tend to have higher status in the team, more influence and authority in strategic team decisions and often tend to be less involved in the routine logistics of implementation. Central team members usually gain more recognition and reward for team accomplishments. Peripheral or marginal team members tend to have less status in the team and less influence and authority in strategic team decisions. They usually play a larger role in the routine logistics of implementing decisions made by the central team members. Peripheral or marginal team members normally receive less recognition and less reward for their teamwork.

Some readers may notice a similarity to the concepts of in-group and out-group (Duchon, Graen & Taber 1986). The concepts of in-group and out-group explain that leaders and managers often treat certain people differently than others. The in-group is more favored, the out-group less favored. Teams, whether or not there is a single leader in the team, can do something comparable — this is something like what children often do when they come together to play a competitive sport, where one team competes against the other. Status in such situations is usually determined by a combination of athletic skill and popularity.

▼▼▼▼▼▼▼▼▼▼▼▼▼▼▼▼▼▼▼▼▼

Children often begin such a competition by the two highest status members of their group leading the selection of his or her team's members. Usually other higher status children are among the first selected as members of the competing teams, followed by children with a moderate level of status, with lower status children being the last selected. Once selected as a team member, a child may influence subsequent choices. Team leaders are ordinarily more influenced by the higher status children when making decisions about the play of the game. In fact, some of the lower status children may not even be allowed to actually play. The leader and the higher status children have a high degree of centrality. They are the core of the team. The lower status members are peripheral to the team — and may be team members in name only. This concept of team dynamics may be diagrammed as shown in Figure 1:

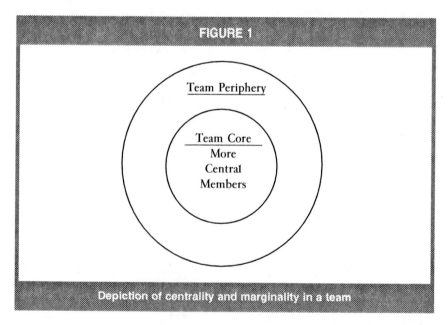

FIGURE 1

Team Periphery

Team Core
More
Central
Members

Depiction of centrality and marginality in a team

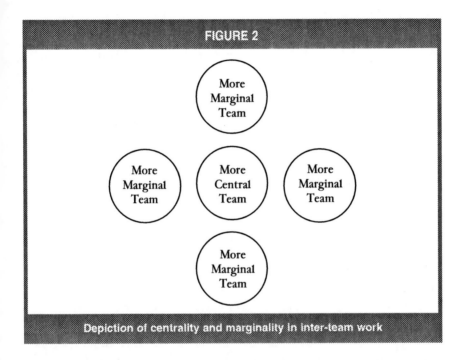

FIGURE 2

More
Marginal
Team

More
Marginal
Team

More
Central
Team

More
Marginal
Team

More
Marginal
Team

Depiction of centrality and marginality in inter-team work

Applying the concept of centrality to inter-team dynamics suggests that when a number of groups work together, some of the teams may be more central than others. We could expect that these central teams have greater power and status, have more immediate access to information, make more strategic decisions and tend to be less involved in the logistics of implementation. For more peripheral teams, the opposite is probably true. This concept of inter-team dynamics may be diagrammed as shown in Figure 2.

Centrality complicates inter-team processes. The teams that are central and the teams that are marginal can change in different situations. Even when the teams themselves are the same, the degrees of centrality or marginality can vary with the situation. Teams need to understand this, and to consider whether the degree of centrality/marginality is appropriate in a given situation. Marginality may indeed be appropriate in certain situations. A particular team may want to be marginal in certain situations while still performing vital functions in the work process.

ÇAĞLAYAN'S APPLICATION IN KOPITEKNIK

How Çağlayan changed the system for his technicians provides an example of how performance was linked to training and pay. Çağlayan implemented a performance-based pay system for his technicians. Their tasks were defined, and they were then paid base salary and commissions for the defined work tasks. One task was to show up for work cleanly shaved, washed and professionally dressed. Technicians started presenting a different image to the customer. They were trained in how to present themselves as problem solvers for customers and how to talk to customers in a friendly and persuasive manner.

Soon, however, technicians and other groups in the organisation began to remark that they were feeling outside of the central team in Kopiteknik. Technicians saw the central team as the Sales Department, because those representatives received commissions not only for selling machines to new customers, but also for selling service and maintenance contracts. Technicians often provided leads that resulted in the sale of new machines. In addition, the quality of service the technicians provided was an important factor in customers' decisions about whether to extend or renew service contracts.

Other groups were also feeling that Sales was a central team, and that they had been marginalized. One such group was the Customer Solution Center. The Customer Solution Center was Çağlayan's response to a customer problem. Çağlayan had conducted a number of customer surveys, which involved both "pen and paper" forms and a number of in-depth interviews. Many customers had indicated that they wanted easier access to a qualified (usually technical) person in Kopiteknik whenever they had a problem with a machine. Calls would come into a receptionist in Kopiteknik and usually be passed on to the Technical Department. But delays could occur in contacting the customer, and no single person or department had total responsibility for following up on a call from the time it came in to the final check on customer satisfaction with the quality of Kopiteknik service.

The Customer Solution Center was established to receive all customer calls. Each representative worked with a computer containing vital customer information — machine type, service record, spare parts purchased. Also, each representative was trained in understanding common minor problems and how they could be solved. If the Solution Center representative could not resolve a problem, the Technical Department was informed. A technician would usually call the customer that day, and the company visited at the latest the next day. Each Customer Solution Center representative was responsible for following up on a call he or she received about customer problems, and following up on the progress of Kopiteknik's response. In cases where Kopiteknik's response might take more time (for example in rare cases when a spare part might need to be ordered from Europe), the representatives were responsible for keeping the customer informed on progress.

Those working in the Customer Solution Center felt that they, too, were vital in the company. Yet they felt they were a marginal group. Much like the technicians, they wondered why sales people received commissions for selling new machines and service contracts, yet Solution Center representatives received no commission for their part in promoting Kopiteknik products and services. Çağlayan's solution was to create a structure where the Technical and Sales Departments and the Solution Center were combined and reported to the same manager. The Technical Department's name was changed to Support. Groups were divided by geographic region, not by function. Thus all three functions worked in the group and with the same customer base.

All team members received both individual rewards based on individual performance and team rewards based on team performance. While Çağlayan headed Kopiteknik, the company's business results continued to be excellent. Cooperation between functions became less of an issue, as they were joined together on the same team. Different regional teams also had incentive to cooperate, and they were rewarded with higher bonuses when the company as a whole increased its profits. Çağlayan told me, "The one question everyone is now asking their manager is, 'How can I increase my productivity?'"

ONE FINAL EXAMPLE OF EXCELLENCE —
THE HABITAT CONFERENCE

This discussion has focused a lot on theories and actions that give shape to systems. But we should not under-emphasize the importance of initiative, commitment to excellence, and imagination in Çağlayan's success as an entrepreneur and a leader.

The major project with which Çağlayan was involved during his time with Kopiteknik was the Habitat conference. This United Nations conference, held in Istanbul in 1996, drew tens of thousands of delegates from around the world. It was the second biggest summit of the century. Çağlayan says he "chased" the Habitat conference for two years, wanting to be its photocopy supplier. His main competitor was a large international office automation supplier. Çağlayan had already accumulated some experience in providing photocopies directly to businesses. Drawing on his experience, Çağlayan submitted to the Habitat conference a 200-page proposal detailing services, Kopiteknik's comparative advantage and pricing. The competitor's proposal was two pages.

Çağlayan was awarded the contract. Çağlayan lost several hundred thousand US dollars on the contract, but gained it back (and more) by refurbishing and quickly selling, at a 50 to 60 percent discount but with full warranties, the thirty-five high volume copiers he used during Habitat. This was more than double his normal annual sales for these machines. As a result of this activity he was also able to sell copying contracts totaling 10 million copies per year — these came from four new accounts, at the expense of competitors.

But more impressive to me is the activity that went on during the conference itself. As Çağlayan describes:

In Habitat we had a total of twenty-five photocopy machines each valued at about 20,000 US dollars. Two days before the Habitat Conference opened the fire system exploded and the sprinklers flooded our machines. We only had four spare, undamaged machines. Everyone was in panic. But I felt that the UN's and Turkey's reputations were at stake. We brought the wet parts from the damaged machines into a Conference Center meeting room. We brought dozens of hair dryers and lots of floodlights — and all the Kopiteknik technicians. We dried all the parts of the wet machines, one by one with the hair dryers and the floodlights. We did lose two of the machines, but saved the rest. Then we were ready.

In twelve days we made 6,500,000 copies. My technicians and I moved into dormitories at the Conference Center in case there were emergencies. This was not our responsibility. Our responsibility was,

according to our contract, to deliver the machines and to train opera-
tors. But I felt we needed to be there to respond to emergencies that
were sure to come up. And there were other emergencies. One night at
1:00 a.m. we sent our 275 machine operators home, along with our
technicians. Then a lady came in panic 'Fidel Castro is coming tomor-
row. We need 450,000 copies tonight!'

We phoned every Kopiteknik employee in the city with security clear-
ance. (We could have told Habitat to call the operators we had
trained. Instead we took initiative and quickly organized our work-
force.) We made 450,000 copies that night. Half the people [who
worked all night] had to work the next morning. Their dedication was
superb. The UN official from New York responsible for organizing the
Conference told me she had never seen service like this. She said that
it's typical for about half the photocopy machines at a conference to
be out of service.

CONCLUDING THOUGHTS

THE BEST STRATEGY

This final example shows that Çağlayan was able to lead his people to achieve spectacular results. He was in every way a leader and as well a member of his team. He joined them in drying out wet machine parts. He worked with them in making copies through the night. He saw solutions and worked to achieve them whether or not they were called for in the letter of his contracts and agreements. These are qualities that also contribute to making Çağlayan a superb entrepreneur.

Çağlayan also gives us an example of an entrepreneur who applies theory to practice and can design systems that encourage performance. He measures success in terms of contribution to customers, those he works with, company share-holders, his community, his country and his world. He is eager to learn new ideas that can help him in achieving success. His example tells us that you can learn to encourage thinking — your own and other's — and you can apply ideas that seem good and refine them through the participation of others — the participation of those who work for you and the participation of those who are your customers. You can learn how to help individuals to improve, but also understand the power

▼▼▼▼▼▼▼▼▼▼▼▼▼▼▼▼▼▼▼▼▼

of systematic change to transform individual behavior. When systems stay the same, so do most of the people who live and work in them. When systematic change is informed by sensible thinking and guided by good intent, it can achieve important successes.

THE MBTI IN TURKEY

In Turkey, a team of academics, professionals and graduate students is currently working on refining their Turkish translation of the MBTI. While this work is taking time, it continues to move at a steady pace. We are very hopeful about the work that can be done with the Turkish MBTI. Once the initial validation of the translation is completed, we plan to go into "high gear" in educating psychologists, counselors, teachers, families, managers and all those interested in applying the MBTI to their work and personal relations.

At present, our team does discuss Jung's theory in many areas of our work- from individual counseling to management consulting. We find that those with whom we work in Turkey consistently give us positive feedback on Jung's theory of types. We receive many requests from people wanting to complete the MBTI, but we lack a valid instrument and it is difficult to help people receive accurate feedback on their MBTI type. This deficiency will be corrected once our validation work with the Indicator is completed. We are excited about the work we will then be able to do in this rapidly developing nation of over 65 million people — more than half of them under the age of twenty-five. The future of the MBTI in Turkey looks promising indeed!

REFERENCES

Duchon, D., Graen, S. G. & Taber, T. D. (1986, February). Vertical dyad linkage: A longitudinal assessment of antecedents, measures and consequences. *Journal of Applied Psychology*, 56–60.

Luft, J. (1984). *Group Processes: An introduction to group dynamics*. Mountain View CA: Mayfield Publishing Company.

Mintzberg, H. (1979). *The structuring of organisations*. Englewood Cliffs, NJ: Prentice-Hall.

Schneider, S. C. & Barsacs, J. L. (1997). *Managing across cultures*. London: Prentice-Hall.

Schein, E. H. (1992). *Organisational culture and leadership* (2nd ed.). San Francisco: Jossey-Bass.

Smith, P. B. & Bond, M. H. (1994). *Social psychology across cultures: Analysis and perspectives*. London: Allyn and Bacon.

UNITED STATES OF AMERICA

Margaret Fields
Center for Applications of Psychological Type
James Short
University of Cincinnati

EDITOR'S NOTES. Margaret Fields (ABD) and Dr. James Short profile David Mueller, Founder and Chairman of the Board of Comair, Inc. Comair, a regional jet service, began as a dream and one dual engine prop plane. David and his father, Raymond Mueller, fueled the company's success, Raymond acting as President while David served as pilot, Executive Vice-President and luggage handler. In less than twenty years Comair grew to a fleet in excess of 100 jet aircraft, became a take over target and was acquired by Delta Airlines for a capitalized value in excess of two billion dollars.

Ms. Fields and Dr. Short next provide a brief history of the United States along with a summary of the development of the Myers-Briggs Type Indicator in the States. They intertwine the story of Comair as they review the MBTI and other leadership models.

DAVID MUELLER

The bond between parent and child remains strong through the life span. As we progress into young adulthood, venturing out to establish our own unique identity and our own lifestyle, we seek ways to maintain bonds across generations.

Some of us use sports to maintain a common bond, playing golf on a regular basis or attending our favorite team's home games. We may celebrate secular and spiritual holidays together and we break bread together, often in traditional ritualistic manners.

David Mueller and his dad Raymond shared a common love of flying. So rather than go fishing or go to a ballgame, they decided one afternoon to go off and start their own airline. They founded Comair in April 1977, both mortgaging their homes to raise enough money in order to finance their first twin engine Piper Navajo commuter plane. Ray served as Comair's first President while David acted as pilot, Executive Vice-President, luggage handler and all-purpose go-fer.

Comair's first scheduled flights operated between the Greater Cincinnati and Northern Kentucky Airport, and Cleveland, Detroit and Canton-Akron. The Muellers' goal for Comair was to provide a high frequency of flights between cities that lacked efficient quality air service. As the company grew, larger nine-passenger Piper-Chieftain aircraft were added to their fleet.

By 1981, Comair embarked on a major program to re-equip the airline with more modern turbo-prop planes and began flying Brazilian Embraer Bandeirante aircraft. In order to obtain the capital requirements needed to upgrade their fleet, Comair went public. In July 1981, Comair Holdings, Inc. common stock began trading under the symbol COMR in the NASDAQ National Market System.

Comair commenced a mutually beneficial business partnership with Delta Air Lines in December of 1981, when it became a part of the Deltamatic computerized reservation system (CRS). In the beginning, Delta simply handled the reservations system for Comair. However, it soon became apparent that Comair could feed customers from the smaller airports they serviced into longer haul flights handled by Delta out of the Greater Cincinnati and Northern Kentucky Airport, one of Delta's rapidly developing hub airports. In September 1984, Comair became a Delta Connection Carrier.

In July of 1986, Delta Air Lines purchased approximately 20 percent of Comair's common stock. A marketing agreement with Delta Air Lines allowed Comair to operate flights under the DL code and coordinate schedules for more efficient connections. In November of the following year, Comair joined Delta Air Lines in developing their Orlando hub in Florida. The company's two hubs at the Greater Cincinnati/Northern Kentucky International Airport (CVG) and the Orlando International Airport (MCO) enabled Comair to offer convenient connections to other Comair flights, as well as Delta flights to destinations throughout the world.

Air Transport World magazine voted Comair as the 1991 Regional Airline of the Year, an award given in recognition of Comair's outstanding growth and maturation from a small commuter airline into one of the industry's leaders. By 1993, Comair had grown to serve over sixty-eight locations in twenty-three states and three countries, employing over 2,200 aviation professionals.

During 1994, Comair and Delta Air completed terminal expansion projects totaling over $400 million at the Greater Cincinnati/Northern Kentucky International Airport, including Comair's Concourse "C." The innovative fifty-three-gate facility is the largest dedicated concourse in the world for a regional airline. The concourse has the offerings of any major airline hub facility including a food court, specialty stores and duty-free shopping.

Throughout 1995 and 1996, Comair continued to grow in new directions, including the May 1995 expansion of their Canadair jet service, which introduced new routes from the Orlando hub and further opened the market to Florida travelers. In addition, in late 1995 and through 1996, Comair instituted daily nonstop service from Boston to Montreal on behalf of Delta Airlines and added service to other new destinations.

Comair celebrated twenty years in flight in 1997 and completed a transition to a two-aircraft fleet, which currently consists of over sixty-five Canadair Regional Jets and twenty-nine Embraer Brasilias. It accomplished its best fiscal year ever, reaching record high passenger boardings of more than 5.4 million people.

Comair had grown to more than 3,500 aviation professionals and served eighty cities in twenty-eight states and three countries by 1998. The Company announced

▼▼▼▼▼▼▼▼▼▼▼▼▼▼▼▼▼▼▼▼▼▼▼▼

a $25 million expansion of its facilities at the Greater Cincinnati/Northern Kentucky International Airport. Comair estimated a steady growth over the next ten years, creating 900 new jobs to support the expansion.

June of 1998 marked the highest monthly boardings in history for Comair: 543,547 passengers boarded its flights. Charles Curran, Senior Vice President of Marketing, said with regard to Comair's record number of passengers, "Passengers clearly prefer to fly our jets through our Cincinnati and Orlando hubs. Now that Cincinnati is the first US hub with jet service in every market, we are reaping the benefits of stronger traffic and yields which should continue throughout the summer months."

It is not only the number of passengers served that reflect Comair's success. On July 22, 1998, Comair Holdings, Inc., the parent corporation of Comair, Inc., reported a first quarter net income of $34.3 million, or $.51 per diluted share on revenues of $187.9 million. This represented a 38 percent increase in earnings per diluted share from the previous year's first quarter.

During 1999, the Greater Cincinnati/Northern Kentucky International Airport became the first hub in North America to offer jet service to every destination it serves. Comair, Delta's hub in Cincinnati and the first regional carrier to provide jet service on all its routes, now eclipses all other major hubs in North America as the premier provider of jet service. The International Air Transport Association (IATA) rated the airport the most convenient hub in the US for the second consecutive year.

In the fall of 1999, Delta Air Lines elected to purchase Comair and tendered an offer of $26.5 per share. David Mueller, CEO of Comair Holdings, Inc. and Chairman of the Board of Comair, Inc., was retained by Delta with an exclusive consulting agreement. The other member of his senior leadership team, David A. Siebenburgen, President, Chief Executive Officer and Chief Operating Officer of Comair, Inc., accepted a position as Director of Regional Airlines for Delta Airlines. Raymond Mueller had retired earlier in the decade.

In the course of just over twenty years, Comair grew from one Piper Navajo, acquired through Ray and David mortgaging their homes, to a capitalized value well in excess of $2,000,000,000 (two billion US dollars). Not too bad for a father and son team who decided to make a living at what they liked to do.

Despite acquiring great wealth and recognition based on Comair's incredible success, David and Ray Mueller remain the open, friendly, easy-to-know best buddies they have always been. It is not unusual to find these two symbols of the American dream sipping on a cup of coffee in a local restaurant. However, doing so is becoming more difficult as neighbors, distant relatives, former employees and colleagues — along with local stock brokers, investment bankers and business students — want to inquire as to what the two of them have in mind for their next start-up company.

THE UNITED STATES OF AMERICA

The United States of America (USA) is the foremost nation in the Western Hemisphere in population and economic development. It has fifty states, forty-eight of which are coterminous and occupy the central one-third (3,615,122 square miles) of the North American continent. The two remaining states, Hawaii and Alaska, lie in the mid-Pacific Ocean and the northwestern extremity of the continent, respectively.

The most intriguing characteristic of the USA is its variety. The physical environment ranges from subtropical to arctic, high mountain ranges to flat, expansive prairies, moist rain forests and arid deserts. The 275 million citizens comprise a wide range of racial, ethnic and cultural backgrounds and reside in urban, suburban and rural areas. Not only is the population diverse in character, it is also mobile by nature. Twenty percent of Americans move every year, often in search of greater economic opportunity.

The sheer size of the American Gross National Product (GNP) leads to USs' great influence in global trade. This is not surprising as a central cultural goal, and a deeply held value by many Americans is the creation of economic wealth.

In support of the creation of economic prosperity, the central government plays a limited role in economic activity. The private sector is given wide latitude to create wealth. The greatest impact the government has on the economy is through fiscal and monetary policy. Indeed, second in influence only to the President of the United States is the Director of the Federal Reserve System. Thus, when we explore the topic of leadership in the United States, we tend to focus on economic leadership.

THE MBTI IN THE UNITED STATES

The MBTI was first introduced for commercial distribution in the United States in 1975. Since then, the Indicator has become the most widely accepted psychological instrument in the world. The success of the MBTI can be traced to the great attention devoted to its psychometric properties and its many applications.

In the United States there exist three main organizations devoted to the dissemination and application of the MBTI. Consulting Psychologist Press (CPP), based in Palo Alto, California, is the distributor of the MBTI. CPP licenses various organizations to conduct MBTI qualification training, publishes MBTI training materials, books and videos, and protects the copyright of the instrument from infringement. CPP also publishes a number of other psychological instruments that complement the MBTI and provide the organizational development specialist with a number of tools for organizational assessment and training.

The second organization focused on the MBTI is the Center for Applications of Psychological Type (CAPT), based in Gainesville, Florida. CAPT, founded by Isabel Myers and Mary McCaulley in 1975, is a research center, a leading provider of training on the MBTI and a publisher of books and training materials for use with the MBTI. CAPT houses the Isabel Myers Memorial Library, the foremost collection of dissertations, journal articles and unpublished research efforts related to the MBTI and psychological type. CAPT also conducts biennial conferences on the MBTI and leadership, education and multicultural applications of the MBTI.

The Association of Psychological Type (APT), based in Chicago, Illinois, is a membership organization founded by CAPT in 1979. APT conducts a biennial international conference and biennial regional conferences. APT publishes the *Journal of Psychological Type* and the *Bulletin of Psychological Type*, and conducts various MBTI training courses and workshops.

TYPE AND LEADERSHIP IN THE USA

We will explore the topic of leadership from a number of theoretical perspectives. For example, rather than focus solely on universal traits, we will examine what is known as the contingency approach to leadership effectiveness.

Pioneered by Fiedler (1964), the contingency approach goes beyond traits and looks at how favorable the overall situation is to the leader. At one extreme is the situation in which the leader has much authority, positive relations with the group and a well-defined task; at the other extreme is a situation in which there is little advantage to the leader, the leader has little authority, the group members do not get along and there is a poorly defined task. Fiedler has found that at both ends of the dimension, task-focused leaders do best while, in the intermediate circumstances, leaders who are concerned with interpersonal relations are judged to be more effective (Fiedler 1964; Strube & Garcia 1981; Peters, Hartke & Pohlmann 1985).

Task-focused leaders, who, according to Fiedler, are the most effective at both ends of the dimension, are found in both the Sensing, Thinking (ST) and Intuitive, Thinking (NT) columns of the MBTI table. Their leadership behavior is described as being task focused, project oriented, goal oriented or technically oriented. Leaders with a preference for Judging (J) enjoy setting goals, organizing resources, establishing priorities within described time frames and completing tasks or projects. Leaders with a preference for Perceiving (P) enjoy keeping their options open and not rushing too quickly to complete a project. They may be more excited by starting a project than by finishing it. At the completion of a goal, Js are likely to celebrate, while Ps are likely to wonder what's next.

Leaders who are concerned with interpersonal relations engage in supportive communication (listening, encouraging and clarifying). They are associated with SF and NF preferences. It is common to find their leadership behavior characterized by researchers as cooperative, service oriented and people oriented, with special emphasis on valuing harmony.

STYLES OF LEADERSHIP

Various leadership styles have also been noted in the past. Early approaches to stylistic variables have examined the impact of various dimensions on leadership style. First is the autocratic-democratic dimension (Lewin, Lippett & White 1939). Those leaders favoring the autocratic end of the spectrum prefer to make decisions alone; those at the democratic end prefer input from others. Of the MBTI scales, the most pertinent to this scale seems to be the J-P dichotomy; the autocratic end of the dimension appears to favor Judging, while more democratic processes are suited to Perceiving.

The second dimension, the directive-permissive dimension, is closely related to the first (Muczyk & Reimann 1987). Though in this case, leaders who are more directive tend to be labeled "micromanagers"; those who are more permissive have an employee-centered orientation and a tendency to delegate tasks to specified employees. Leaders who tend to be labeled "micromanagers" are associated with the Sensing preference for their desire to tend to the details, and Thinking for their task orientation. The employee-centered leader is projecting behavior associated with the Feeling preference. Micromanaging can also be related to a Judging type's need to come to closure and their need to feel they have control over situations and tasks.

The third dimension is task orientation-person orientation in nature (Bass 1990). Specifically, this dimension addresses whether leaders emphasize tasks over employee relations or employee relations over specific tasks. MBTI influences on this dimension and the directive-permissive dimension would likely be strongest for the T-F scale. However, research provides little evidence that certain types prefer one leadership style to another, although it does suggest that some preferences are associated with certain leader behaviors. Type theory suggests that leaders with a preference for Feeling would be more permissive and person oriented, whereas leaders with a preference for Thinking would be more directive and task oriented.

Hersey and Blanchard's situational leadership model indicates that leadership style should vary with the characteristics of the tasks and subordinates. Leaders with good type development will be able to apply the style that is appropriate to the situation, even though their natural style may be different.

Following from the description of the dimensions above, it is likely that type may have some influence on Comair's leadership styles. In the CAPT data bank (Macdaid 1986), NT and TJ types dominate the type tables of executive managers. It has been espoused that entrepreneurial leaders will reflect somewhat similar type distributions (see Table 1). Psychological types of *Inc. 500* founders clearly reflect an over-representation of NT at 51 percent and TJ at 49 percent (see Table 2) (Ginn 1989). This may reflect the attraction of an entrepreneur to problem solving situations in which they feel the freedom to explore multiple options. When they see or perceive a problem, the motivation is in the challenge to solve it.

TABLE 1

Managers: High Level Corporate Executives

N = 136

	SENSING		INTUTION						
	THINKING	FEELING	FEELING	THINKING			E	73	53.68
							I	63	46.32

ISTJ	ISFJ	INFJ	INTJ		
N = 33	N = 0	N = 1	N = 15		
% = 24.26	% = 0.00	% = .74	% = 11.03		
■■■■■■■■■■ ■■■■■■■■■■ ■■■■		■	■■■■■■■■■■ ■		
ISTP	**ISFP**	**INFP**	**INTP**		
N = 6	N = 1	N = 3	N = 4		
% = 4.41	% = .74	% = 2.21	% = 2.94		
■■■■	■	■■	■■■		
ESTP	**ESFP**	**ENFP**	**ENTP**		
N = 4	N = 4	N = 1	N = 11		
% = 2.94	% = 2.94	% = .74	% = 8.09		
■■■	■■■	■	■■■■■■■■		
ESTJ	**ESFJ**	**ENFJ**	**ENTJ**		
N = 27	N = 3	N = 1	N = 22		
% = 19.85	% = 2.21	% = .74	% = 16.18		
■■■■■■■■■■ ■■■■■■■■■■	■■	■	■■■■■■■■■■ ■■■■■■■		

JUDGMENT / INTROVERSION / PERCEPTION / EXTRAVERSION / PERCEPTION / JUDGMENT

E	73	53.68
I	63	46.32
S	78	57.35
N	58	42.65
T	122	89.71
F	14	10.29
J	102	75.00
P	14	25.00
IJ	49	36.03
IP	14	10.29
EP	20	14.71
EJ	53	38.97
ST	70	51.47
SF	8	5.88
NF	6	4.41
NT	52	38.24
SJ	63	46.32
SP	15	11.03
NP	19	13.97
NJ	39	28.68
TJ	97	71.32
TP	25	18.38
FP	9	6.62
FJ	5	3.68
IN	23	16.91
EN	35	25.74
IS	40	29.41
ES	38	27.94
ET	64	47.06
EF	9	6.62
IF	5	3.68
IT	58	42.65
S dom	41	30.15
N dom	28	20.59
T dom	59	43.38
F dom	8	5.88

Note: ■ = 1% of sample   8623114

Data collected by Ellen Van Velsor and David Campbell at the Center for Creative Leadership in Greensboro, North Carolina from January 1979 to October 1983. Subjects were comprised of vice presidents, presidents and chief executive officers in business and industrial organizations of more than 10 employees. Executives were approximately 5% female and 95% male. Subjects were attending a leadership development program at the center during this period. These data are used with permission and have not been published elsewhere to date.

Source: CAPT Atlas of Type Tables 1985

▼▼▼▼▼▼▼▼▼▼▼▼▼▼▼▼▼▼▼▼▼▼▼

TABLE 2

Type Distribution of Total Sample of Inc. 500 Founders

N = 159

	SENSING		INTUTION	
	THINKING	FEELING	FEELING	THINKING
	ISTJ N = 23 (14.5%) ■■■■■■■■■■ ■■■■	ISFJ N = 1 (0.6%) ■	INFJ N = 1 (0.6%) ■	INTJ N = 18 (11.3%) ■■■■■■■■■■ ■
	ISTP N = 10 (6.3%) ■■■■■■	ISFP N = 3 (1.9%) ■■	INFP N = 6 (3.8%) ■■■■	INTP N = 23 (14.5%) ■■■■■■■■■■ ■■■■
	ESTP N = 9 (5.7%) ■■■■■■	ESFP N = 2 (1.3%) ■	ENFP N = 2 (1.3%) ■	ENTP N = 18 (11.3%) ■■■■■■■■■■ ■
	ESTJ N = 15 (9.4%) ■■■■■■■■■	ESFJ N = 1 (0.6%) ■	ENFJ N = 5 (3.1%) ■■■	ENTJ N = 22 (13.8%) ■■■■■■■■■■ ■■■■

INTROVERSION JUDGMENT / INTROVERSION PERCEPTION / EXTRAVERSION PERCEPTION / EXTRAVERSION JUDGMENT

E	47%
I	53%
S	40%
N	60%
T	87%
F	13%
J	54%
P	46%
IJ	27%
IP	26%
EP	20%
EJ	27%
ST	36%
SF	4%
NF	9%
NT	51%
SJ	25%
SP	15%
NP	31%
NJ	29%
TJ	49%
TP	38%
FP	8%
FJ	5%
IN	48%
EN	47%
IS	23%
ES	17%
ET	40%
EF	6%
IF	7%
IT	47%

Note: ■ = 1% of N

Source: Journal of Psychological Type 1988

At Comair it appears that the springboard for the development of the company came more from a values-centered (F) mission. While it is true that the founder was solving a problem i.e., he was "a pilot who couldn't get a job," the creation of the company came more from the desire to offer a service to a community. Not only did the values encompass the serving of others, but it was further manifested by the importance of gaining support from his family before launching into an unknown territory. Some might compare this to Isabel Myers' explanation of the difference between an Extravert and an Introvert. An Extravert will jump right into the water without a great deal of contemplation, whereas an Introvert will stick a toe in, testing the water first before easing in. The belief in one's own ideas was foremost in the mind of Comair's founder. He had a vision (N) of how he could offer flights between cities that lacked efficient quality air service (T), thus displaying behaviors associated with descriptions of INT preferences.

As the company grew, senior management made a concerted effort to ensure their personal values for positive relations were extended not only to customers, suppliers and employees but also to colleagues in other airlines. The founders believed that company growth would be enhanced through a positive relationship with their competitors in the industry. Comair's ties with Delta Airlines began in 1981. By 1987, Comair and Delta were collaborating on the development of a system-wide hub airport in Orlando, Florida. This was tangible support for the founders' focus on a participative environment for all those involved with serving the traveling professional.

The vision orientation of the founder also led to the massive expansion of the company, not only in the product offered, but also in the financial market itself. Growing to the point of offering public shares through NASDAQ is a remarkable accomplishment. The growth pattern of reaching out to other companies, expanding to a public offering and seeking outside alternatives for their growing fleet are behaviors that come naturally to an Extravert. Introverts obviously can do these things, but it may be draining for them. Introverted growth of an organization may look more vertically integrated than horizontal.

The organization continues to function like one big family. The passion shown by the original founder for the concerns of his employees remains. One of the most salient points is that the employees share the values of the founder through their support of one another. A spirit of harmony would characterize the attitude of the organization. The organization as a whole appears to be NF.

Hersey-Blanchard Approach. One criticism of the trait approach to leadership style is that it is merely descriptive and does not address the ever-changing nature of the business world: the Comair of 1988 and the Comair of 1998 existed in two very different worlds. Building upon this notion that leadership is not static, but exists in a dynamic environment, it is apparent that one thing missing from the previous discussion is the role of the institutional environment and other external factors in leadership effectiveness. Addressing the notion of leadership effectiveness in different situations, Paul Hersey and Ken Blanchard (1977) note that three factors should be considered in leadership: the extent to which the leader is concerned with promoting good interpersonal relationships and communication among members; the concern of the leader with structuring the task for the group; and the maturity of the group members in terms of being able to work independently, taking initiative and responsibility.

The factor with the most impact is maturity, which indicates whether the leader should focus on tasks or relationships. Maturity does not address age-related concerns or the like; rather, it refers to the amount of experience the group has in a given setting. Depending on the maturity of the group, the leader may adopt one of the four following styles.

Telling. With an immature group of people, a leader will be most effective if he or she is task oriented. The leader will tell people what to do and how to do it. Task orientation is generally attributed to leaders whose preferences are ST or NT. A leader with a preference for Sensing will probably be very specific in describing the task, will allow hands-on experience to take place and will do this very methodically in a step-by-step way. The Intuitive leader will allow the people to figure out in their own way how they would like to approach the task.

Selling. With a slightly more mature group of people, a leader will be perceived as being effective if he or she is both task and relationship oriented. Group members will need some structure, and they will still need some guidance from the leader. With this type of group of people, a leader will find that the group cannot simply be told what to do; they expect their ideas to be heard. Therefore, a leader will have to "sell" the group on ideas. The leader who engages in spelling out the duties and responsibilities of an individual or group (who, what, when, where and how) and engages in supportive communications (why) has learned to exercise preferences for T and F, even though one of these preferences is more natural to the leader than the other. A leader who has good type development can demonstrate task behavior and relationship behavior intermittently, appropriate to the situation. Selling the idea behind the task is important when working with Introverts. The use of both Sensing and Intuition is important when selling the group on ideas. If the group consists of Sensing types and the leader presents an abstract, theoretical possibility, some Sensing types may disengage because of the lack of concrete data. On the other hand, an Intuitive type could become easily bored and distracted if the leader presented only factual data that appeared to have little consequence to the situation.

Participating. A group that is just above average in maturity will find an effective leader in a person who can tell them what to do, but has an interest in interpersonal relationships. The members of the group can set task goals and accept responsibility, but need a leader with whom they can volley ideas. There is some evidence that Ss and Fs are more participative decision makers than Ns and Ts. An Introverted leader is more likely to be a good listener when members of a group need an ear for their ideas. An Extraverted leader is more likely to want to brainstorm the ideas aloud with the group.

Members of a participative group need to be aware of the Judging type's need to come to closure on the goals defined by the group, and yet also allow Perceiving types to explore different options. A delicate balance must be maintained to meet the needs of each individual without undermining or disregarding one for the other. This is further evidence that an effective leader must be able to accurately evaluate each situation and make decisions that are sensitive to a variety of needs.

Delegating. A highly mature group will perceive a leader as being effective if he or she can delegate assignments and responsibilities. If the group has the skills to handle tasks and relationship issues, they will resent a leader who tries to tell them what to do and how to do it. Extraversion and Intuition are associated with "leading by delegating," while Introversion and Sensing are associated with "leading by example" (Hammer and Kummerow 1996). Judging types might run the risk of being too controlling while delegating, which can cause resentment especially with a Perceiving type. Perceiving types may run the risk of failing to follow up on what has been delegated or recognizing when it is appropriate to do so.

In the early developmental stages of Comair, Raymond and David Mueller had to focus on task behaviors associated with telling. The members of their group were new to the company and possibly to the industry. As the company grew and matured, so did the employees. The company now has many employees in leadership roles who take the initiative and responsibility for their decisions concerning the employees and the company. The cycle of telling, selling, participating and delegating repeats itself as new employees with little or no experience join the company.

TRANSFORMATIONAL LEADERSHIP: LEADERSHIP THROUGH VISION AND CHARISMA

Another view of leadership may explain the Comair phenomenon, namely, transformational leadership. Transformational leaders exert profound influence over followers by proposing an inspiring vision as well as inducing high levels of loyalty, respect and admiration among their followers. It is clear that during the founding years of Comair the leaders paid close attention to internal and external relationships and were careful to tend to the needs of their employees.

Going beyond descriptive traits of leaders and followers, views of transformational leadership focus on the leader-follower relationship itself (House 1977). By focusing on the relationship, several characteristic reactions to transformational leadership have been identified. Among these reactions are high levels of devotion, loyalty and reverence towards the as well as enthusiasm for the leader and his or her ideas (Conger 1991). A charismatic leader has a strong belief in his or her own ideas and is able to convey this belief in a way that creates the feeling that the follower is also a partner.

Not only did Ray and David Mueller have a dream, they believed in it so strongly that they invested their own money and resources to make the dream come true. Many entrepreneurs use other people's money to reduce their personal risk. Not the Muellers. They risked the possibility of disillusioning those they valued the most — their families.

The willingness for individuals to sacrifice their own needs for the needs of the group (Conger 1991) is another component to the leader-follower relationship. The dedication of the Muellers to this component created an environment of loyalty among Comair employees. Transformational leadership encourages levels of performance beyond those that would normally be expected. The tendency to motivate ordinary persons to do out-of-the-ordinary things when faced with adversity is yet another of its hallmarks (Conger 1991).

Leaders define the purpose of the organization in a way that gives meaning and purpose to actions requested from followers. Other behaviors seen in transformational leaders are high levels of self-confidence, confidence in their followers' abilities, concern for their followers' needs, excellent communication skills, and personal style (House, Spangler & Woycke 1991).

CONCLUSION

Our review of leadership, both general models of leadership and leadership within the context of Comair, would not be complete without taking a look at some potential blind spots for an organization in which the two key leaders share the same type, regardless of the type. At Comair, both leaders are ENTPs. Potential blind spots could be the possibility of overlooking relevant details, overextending themselves and taking on more than they can handle, or it could be that new ideas are so attractive that they may move on them without completing those already started.

Because of the enormous success Comair has enjoyed, one would conclude that both leaders have progressed in their type development and can clearly predict and examine potential pitfalls. Through the experience of building the business, they developed their less preferred functions.

Such a growth process allows leaders to be circumspect about their own shortcomings and learn new ways to deal with or overcome them. Leaders often surround themselves with people who possess skills and behaviors opposite their own, or they may reach inside for the strength and wisdom to nurture those preferences that are not as natural, comfortable or tested. Type development is a wonderful way to look at both strengths and blind spots as part of a journey to wholeness, or, as Maslow would say, self-actualization. A successful, effective leader knows himself or herself well, which is a giant step toward understanding others.

▼▼▼▼▼▼▼▼▼▼▼▼▼▼▼▼▼▼▼▼▼▼

The ability to size up a situation despite a lack of data (N) and the willingness to make a decision based on partial data (J) are fast becoming two of the most prominent characteristics of successful leaders. In the age of technology, things are moving so swiftly that a leader who cannot do this will give way to a leader who can. The luxury of having time to digest, analyze and dissect data before coming to a rational decision is diminishing daily. Quick decisions based largely on intuition may become the rule rather than the exception. Some decisions may be wrong, but to keep up with the pace of a globally changing economy and marketplace, it is a necessary risk to run, and a rather small one in light of the consequences of not being able to decide until all of the facts are in.

REFERENCES

Bass, B.M. (1990). *Bass and Stodgill's handbook of leadership* (3rd ed.). New York: Free Press.

Clark, K.E., Clark, M.B. & Campbell, D.P. (Eds). (1992). *Impact of leadership.* Greensboro, NC: Center for Creative Leadership.

Conger, J.A. (1991). Inspiring others: The language of leadership. *Academy of Management Executives,* 5 (1), 31–45.

Demarest. L. (1997). *Looking at type in the workplace.* Gainesville, FL: Center for Applications of Psychological Type, Inc.

Fiedler, F.E. (1964). A contingency model of leadership effectiveness. In L. Berkowitz (Ed.). *Advances in experimental social psychology: Vol. 1* (pp. 149-190). New York: Academic Press.

Fitzgerald, C. & Kirby, L. K. (Eds.). Developing leaders: *Research and applications in psychological type and leadership development.* Palo Alto, CA: Davies-Black Publishing.

Gardner, J. W. (1990). *On leadership.* New York, NY: The Free Press

Geier, J.G. (1969). A trait approach to the study of leadership in small groups. *Journal of Communication,* 17, 316–323.

Ginn, C.W., & Sexton, D.L. (1988). Psychological types of Inc. 500 founders and their spouses. Journal of Psychological Type, 16, 3–12.

Hammer, A. L., & Kummerow, J. K. (1996). *Strong and MBTI career development guide.* Palo Alto, CA: Consulting Psychologists Press.

Hammer, A. (1996). *MBTI applications: A decade of research on the Myers-Briggs Type Indicator.* Palo Alto, CA: Consulting Psychologists Press.

Hersey, P. (1984). *The situational leader.* New York, NY: Warner Books.

Hersey, P. & Blanchard, K.H. (1977). *Management of organizational behavior: Utilizing human resources.* Englewood Cliffs, NJ: Prentice-Hall.

Hersey, P. & Blanchard, K.H. & Johnson, D. E. (1996). *Management of organizational behavior utilizing human resources* (7th ed.). Englewood Cliffs, NJ: Prentice- Hall.

House, R.J. (1977). A theory of charismatic leadership. In J.G. Hunt & L.L. Larson (Eds.), *Leadership: The cutting edge* (pp. 189–207). Carbondale, IL: Southern Illinois University Press.

House, R.J. , Spangler, W.D., & Woycke, J. (1991). Personality and charisma in the US presidency: A psychological theory of leadership effectiveness. *Administrative Science Quarterly*, 36, 364–396.

Howell, J.M & Frost, P.J. (1989). A laboratory study of charismatic leadership. *Organizational Behavior and Human Decision Processes*, 43, 243–269.

Kirkpatrick, S.A. & Locke, E.A.(1991). Leadership: Do traits matter? *Academy of Management Executives*, 5 (2), 48–60.

Lewin, K., Lippett, R., & White, R.K. (1939). Patterns of aggressive behavior in experimentally created "social climates." *Journal of Social Psychology*, 10, 271–299.

McCaulley, M. H. (1990). The Myers-Briggs Type Indicator and leadership. In K. E. Clark & M. B. Clark (Eds.), *Measures of leadership* (pp. 381–418). West Orange, NJ: Leadership Library of America.

Muczyk, J.P. & Reimann, B.C. (1987). The case for directive leadership. *Academy of Management Review*, 12, 647–687.

Myers, I. & McCaulley, M. (1985). *Manual: A guide to the development and use of the Myers-Briggs Type Indicator*. Palo Alto, CA: Consulting Psychologists Press.

Peters, L.H., Hartke, D.D. & Pohlmann, J.T. (1985). Fiedler's contingency theory of leadership: An application of the meta-analysis procedures of Schmidt and Hunter. *Psychological Bulletin*, 97, 274–285.

Shewchuk, R. M. & O'Connor, S. J. (1995). Health care executives: Subjective well-being as a function of psychological type. *Journal of Psychological Type*, 32, 23–29.

Strube, M.J. & Garcia, J.E. (1981). A meta-analytic investigation of Fielder's contingency model of leadership effectiveness. *Psychological Bulletin*, 90, 307–321.

Van Velsor, E. & Fleenor, J. W. (1994). Leadership skills and perspectives, gender and the MBTI. In C. Fitzgerald (Ed.), Proceedings from the Myers-Briggs *Type Indicator and Leadership: An International Research Conference* (pp. 49–59). College Park, MD: University of Maryland University College National Leadership Institute.

Walck, C. L. (1992). Psychological type and management research: A review. *Journal of Psychological Type*, 24, 13–23.

Yukl, G. (1981). *Leadership in organizations*. Englewood Cliffs, NJ: Prentice-Hall.

Zaccaro, S.J., Foti, R.J., & Kenny, D.A. (1991). Self-monitoring and trait-based variance in leadership: An investigation of leader flexibility across multiple group situations. *Journal of Applied Psychology*, 76, 308–315.